SULEIMAN THE MAGNIFICENT

London : Humphrey Milford
Oxford University Press

Suleiman the Magnificent in 1559
From an engraving made in Constantinople
by Melchior Lorichs
(cf. p. 294)

SULEIMAN
The Magnificent
1520–1566

By Roger Bigelow Merriman

Gurney Professor of History
and Political Science in
Harvard University

CAMBRIDGE, MASSACHUSETTS
HARVARD UNIVERSITY PRESS
1944

PREFACE

I MUST BEGIN by telling my readers that this book is only partially my own. The inspiration to undertake it and a portion of the material it contains were derived from an unfinished life of Suleiman the Magnificent which was written by my beloved friend, the late Archibald Cary Coolidge in 1901–02. He and I discussed it constantly during the next five years, and I frequently urged him to complete and publish it; but other things intervened, and when he died in 1928 the manuscript was deposited in the Harvard Archives just as he had left it twenty-six years before. There, some twenty months ago, I found it, with the words "For R. B. Merriman" written in his secretary's hand on the fly leaf; and this I took as a summons to put it in shape for publication. My first intention was to leave as much as possible of his work untouched, write the three chapters which had been left undone, and edit the book under his name; but this plan did not prove practicable. So instead I have rewritten it *ab initio*, and made a number of changes in the original form. I hasten, however, to add that a considerable portion of Chapter I and scattering paragraphs and sentences in Chapters II–VI and IX–XI have been taken, with some revision, from Professor Coolidge's manuscript. Chapters VII, VIII, and XII are wholly my own.

No apology is offered for the fact that the following pages are chiefly a story of diplomacy and campaigns. Military considerations invariably came first in the Ottoman mind, and Suleiman was primarily a conqueror. Professor Coolidge's unfinished manuscript is even more of what has been called a "drum and trumpet history" than is this book, but I am glad to take this opportunity to testify to my unshaken belief in the doctrine which he constantly preached —namely that a knowledge of the narrative is the indispensable foundation for everything else. Constitutional, economic, social, psychological, and all the other various "aspects" of history which have been successively labelled with capital letters, and have temporarily, each in turn, held the center of the stage in recent years, are perfectly meaningless without it. Moreover they are none of them really new, as their chief proponents would have us believe; they have all been studied—without their modern titles— ever since the time of Herodotus.

I trust that the publication of this life of one of the greatest yet least known sovereigns of the sixteenth century will serve among other things to remind Harvard men all over the world of the immense debt which the University owes to Professor Coolidge. To one who, like myself, has studied and taught here for over half a century, that debt looms larger and larger as the years go by. Others have already written of his unfailing kindness, humor, and tact, of his boundless generosity and unselfishness. Here, however, I want especially to emphasize the greatness of his achievement in broadening the University's horizon. The Widener Library and the collections which he gave or obtained for it are perhaps the most conspicuous monument to his success in this respect; but the Corporation records and the University Catalogues of the last fifty years tell a no less notable tale for the curriculum. When Professor Coolidge came back to Harvard in 1893, the only undergraduate instruction given in modern history outside of the United States consisted of two general courses on Western Europe in the seventeenth, eighteenth, and nineteenth centuries; the Scandinavian, Slavic, Ottoman, and Iberian worlds were left practically untouched; the African, Asiatic, and

Latin-American ones wholly so. Two years later we find
Professor Coolidge himself offering two half courses, to
be given in alternate years, on the history of the Scandinavian lands and on the Eastern Question, and in 1904–
05 another on the Expansion of Europe since 1815. In
1896 he persuaded the Corporation to embark on an even
more daring adventure, and invite "Mr." (later Professor)
Leo Wiener to give instruction in Slavic Languages and
Literature, with the understanding that he was also to as-
sist at the Library in cataloguing Slavic and Sanskrit books;
and in 1907–08 Professor Coolidge himself offered a full
course on the history of Russia. All this was the entering
wedge for greater things to come, not only at Harvard but
elsewhere; it deserves, in fact, to be regarded as the origin
of the scientific study of Slavic history, languages, and lit-
eratures in America. A half course in Spanish history was
first given in 1903, and a professorship of Latin-American
history and economics was endowed a decade later. Instruction in the history of Asia and of the African colonies was
to follow in the succeeding years. For every one of these
and for many other advances, Professor Coolidge was directly or indirectly responsible. Invariably he foresaw and
pointed out the need. Often he gave generously to meet it,
and his judgment of men was sound and keen. It has been
well said of him that he was far more interested in the pro-
duction of scholars than in the products of scholarship itself. To him more than to any other man is due what the
Harvard History Department was able to accomplish in
the days of its greatness. To us who have been brought to
open our eyes to wider horizons by the tragic events of
the past five years, his visions of a half-century ago seem
prophetic.

When one leaves the familiar shores of Western Europe
and ventures out into the Levant, one needs the safest and

wisest of pilots, and I have been fortunate in finding them. The names of two friends—Professor A. H. Lybyer of the University of Illinois, and Professor R. P. Blake of Harvard—stand at the head of the list. The one has gone through my galleys and the other my manuscript with the most assiduous care, and both have saved me from countless errors and told me much I did not know. Rev. J. K. Birge, Chairman of the Publication Department of the Near East Mission of the American Board, has generously placed his intimate knowledge of Turkish and modern Turkey at my disposal. Dr. Erwin Raicz, of the Harvard Institute of Geographical Exploration, has drawn the map, and incidentally taught me much about the Danube campaigns. Such accuracy as the note on the portraits of Suleiman may be found to possess is chiefly due to the liberal help of Dr. A. Weinberger of the Houghton Library at Harvard, of Mr. W. G. Constable of the Boston Museum of Fine Arts, and of Miss Agnes Mongan and Miss Margaret Gilman of the Fogg Art Museum; and the officials of the Harvard and Yale University Libraries have facilitated my researches in many different ways. Mr. G. W. Robinson has given me all sorts of precious aid—as he has with other volumes, during the past thirty years and more. My wife has been my sympathetic critic, collaborator, and companion from first to last; without her constant encouragement this book would never have been finished.

R. B. M.

Cambridge, Massachusetts
September, 1944

CONTENTS

ILLUSTRATIONS

Early History of the Ottoman Turks

Few periods in history possess such fascination as the first half of the sixteenth century. All over Western Europe the spirit of the Renaissance had triumphed, and was wakening the human mind to ever greater activity. It was a golden age of art, of letters, and of science: an age of daring exploration and adventure, of passionate religious emotion and controversy. The discoveries of da Gama and Columbus had opened up new worlds to European enterprise; the teachings of Luther and his successors rent hopelessly in twain the Western Church of the Middle Ages. It was also an epoch of decisive moment in the growth of nations. Italy became at once the intellectual guide and the political prey of ruder and stronger powers. The Holy Roman Empire of the German people, though internally more disrupted than ever, was officially headed by the mighty House of Hapsburg, the marvellous success of whose marriage policy had already won it the lordship of the Netherlands and the kingship of the Iberian realms, and promised the speedy realization of its traditional aim: *Austriae est imperare orbi universo.* France and England, consolidated under the strong rule of the Valois and the Tudors, were full of youthful life and energy and eager to expand, while Spain in a few short years acquired the largest empire on the globe. In this age of intense activity the leading figures stand out with unprecedented clearness. The spirit of the Renaissance was above all individualistic, and at no time in the annals of mankind do we find a greater number of outstanding personalities in the political as well as in the religious and artistic world. The Spain, the France, and the England of that day at once recall the names of Charles V, Francis I, and Henry VIII: all men of mark, who played no small part in making history, and well deserve the study and scholarship that have been lavished on them.

Modern historians, however, have devoted singularly little attention to one meriting it equally well, the fourth great sovereign of the time, Suleiman "the Magnificent," "the Great," "the Lawgiver"—the ruler of the Ottoman Empire at the height of its glory and strength, a conqueror of many lands, whose fleets dominated the Mediterranean and whose armies laid siege to Vienna, whom Francis I of France addressed as a suppliant, and to whom Charles V's younger brother Ferdinand paid tribute. A great English historian has justly observed that "the thrones of Europe were now filled by the strongest men who ever contemporaneously occupied them. There may have been greater sovereigns than Charles, Henry, Francis, and Solyman, but there were never so many great ones together, of so well-consolidated dominion, so great ability, or so long tenure of power." [1] Of that remarkable quartet the Turkish Sultan was assuredly not the least. In the politics of Western Europe his influence was profound, for he played a more decisive part in the struggle between Charles V and Francis I than did Henry VIII of England, and the danger of a Turkish invasion of Germany continually affected the course of the Protestant Reformation. The history and character of Suleiman are also of lively interest in themselves. He was the last and perhaps the greatest of that extraordinary series of able rulers who built up the Ottoman state from a little vassal principality into a mighty empire, and made it the terror of Christendom. He was equally noteworthy as a warrior and a statesman, and his private

[1] William Stubbs, *Lectures on European History* (London, 1904), p. 122.

character, though stained by a few acts that even his inherited surroundings and traditions cannot excuse, was yet
such as to command the admiration of his enemies. But,
before attempting to portray him, we must devote the rest
of this chapter to a hasty sketch of his predecessors, who
made his reign possible. No other line in all history can
show such a long and almost uninterrupted succession of
really remarkable men.

In the middle of the thirteenth century events of high
importance were taking place both in the Christian and in
the Mohammedan worlds. The death of the Emperor Frederick II ("Stupor Mundi") on December 13, 1250, marked
the end of the greatness of the mediaeval Empire. The
Latin Empire of the East, the chance foundation (1204) of
misdirected crusaders, was nearing the close of its short
and inglorious span of life; in 1261 Constantinople was
recaptured by the Greeks. Russia had just fallen under the
terrible yoke of the Mongols, who delayed for centuries
her participation in the affairs of Western Europe. England was becoming increasingly restless under the misgov-
ernment of Henry III. In the Mediterranean lands the
conflict between Cross and Crescent still continued with
varying fortunes. In the Iberian Peninsula the tide had
definitely turned in favor of the former, and the Moors
had lost all their possessions save the little realm of Granada.
But farther east the Christian kingdom of Jerusalem had
been almost obliterated, and St. Louis had been defeated
and made prisoner at Mansurah in Egypt, where internal
troubles led shortly afterward to the establishment of the
first Mameluke dynasty. It was at this juncture, when
Western Asia was already threatened by the Mongol attack soon destined to overwhelm Baghdad and put an end
to the Abbasside Caliphate, that, according to a more or
less credible tale, a wandering adventurer from the east-

ward, at the head of a small following, plunged into a battle that was being fought on the Anatolian plateau.

This unexpected combatant was a warrior named Ertoghrul, and he belonged to another tribe of the same race as the Seljuk Turks, who had defeated the East Roman Emperor at the battle of Manzikert in 1071, and subsequently overran the whole interior of Asia Minor. Broadly speaking, the name Turk (*Turcae*), which we find in the classical writers of the early Christian era, may be used to designate that section of the Finno-Ugric inhabitants of the great steppes of Asia which was the more Western and Caucasian in its affiliations; while the other, which looked towards China, is called Mongol. These tribesmen had no race prejudices: they had mingled freely from the earliest times with their white neighbors on the West, and their yellow ones to the eastward; "the Turkish peoples (for the Western world) are then in general those Tatars who have had the greatest admixture of Caucasian blood." [2] They were divided into many tribes, of which few save the Seljuks had yet reached a stage much more advanced than the nomadic; the small band led by Ertoghrul formed the remnants of one of the lesser of them. [3] It would appear that he did not even know the names of the combatants in the battle which he had joined, but he was chivalrous enough to take the weaker side. It was only after victory had been won by his aid that he learned that he had assisted Kay-Kubad, the Seljuk Turkish Sultan of Rum (or Iconium), against a Mongol army. The Sultan, in gratitude, took

[2] A. H. Lybyer, *The Government of the Ottoman Empire in the Time of Suleiman the Magnificent,* Harvard Historical Studies, 18 (Cambridge, Mass., 1913), p. 12.

[3] Further information about the origin of the Turk may be found in an article by J. Marquart entitled "Über das Volkstum der Komanen" (Anhang 2. "Über die Herkunft der Osmanen"). It is published in the *Abhandlungen der königlichen Gesellschaft der Wissenschaften zu Göttingen,* Philologisch-Historische Klasse, Neue Folge, Band XIII, Nro. 1. (Berlin, 1914), pp. 187–194.

his preserver into his employ; and subsequently, in return for further service, rewarded him with a grant of land around the present town of Sugut. This territory is situated in Western Asia Minor, not far from the cities of Isnik and Ismid, formerly Nicaea and Nicomedia.[4]

We know but little of Ertoghrul, although legend has been very busy with his name. At his death in 1288 he was succeeded by his son Osman, about whom we have more definite information. At first the new ruler continued to play the role of the faithful vassal of the Sultan of Rum; he aided his master against further Mongol attacks, and obtained fresh favors in return for his devotion. But he was also constantly occupied in warfare with the semi-independent commanders of the Greek frontier posts—a warfare of foragings and skirmishes for plunder as much as for conquest, which gradually increased his territory and his prestige. In the course of this warfare Osman, the future greatness of whose empire is supposed to have been foretold him by a marvellous dream, is said to have become a Mohammedan.[5] If the tale be true, he could thenceforth regard himself, not as a mere freebooter and ambitious chief, striving only to add to his own territories, but as a champion of Islam, whose cause was sacred in the eyes of all true Moslems.

Meanwhile many changes were taking place among the great powers of the East. The Mongols had at last met their match in the Egyptian Mamelukes; their progress had been

---

[4] H. A. Gibbons, *The Foundation of the Ottoman Empire* (Oxford, 1916), pp. 21–22; W. L. Langer and R. P. Blake, "The Rise of the Ottoman Turks and Its Historical Background," in *American Historical Review* XXXVII, no. 3 (April 1932), 489 f.

[5] The story of this dream, accepted by Gibbons (pp. 23 ff.), is regarded by Langer and Blake (p. 495) as "utterly unconvincing." They feel it to be "almost a certainty that the Ottoman Turks . . . were Moslems even before they left Central Asia." They do believe, however, that "religion played some part, perhaps an important part, in the story of Ottoman expansion" pp. 496–497.

checked, and their dominion was breaking up; but they still remained formidable to the Turks. By the close of the thirteenth century they had put an end to the Seljuk empire. Out of its fragments were formed upwards of a score of small independent Turkish principalities,[6] which for the most part took their names from their rulers. That of Osman (or "the Ottoman" as we call it) was neither the largest nor the most powerful, but it was so close to Christian territory as to offer all the temporal and spiritual advantages of a war for the faith, and Moslem recruits from all Asia Minor were speedily attracted thither. In the following years Osman's attacks on his enemies redoubled. It is true that his force, chiefly composed of light cavalry, could at first do little against the walls of the Greek cities, but the fact that those cities were left to fend for themselves by the government of Constantinople was ominous for the future. After the reconquest of its capital in 1261, the energy of the Byzantine Empire seemed to slacken. What remained was used up in internal disputes, in conflicts with Venetians and Catalans, with Servians and Bulgarians, and with Turkish pirates in the Mediterranean. The cities of Asia Minor were given no help; year after year their power of resistance weakened, as the Ottoman bands laid waste the open country, and cut off supplies and communication with the outside world. Ten years of this sort of blockading brought the city of Brusa into Osman's hands in 1326; but the news of the triumph only reached him on his deathbed. He died as he had lived, in the simplicity of a nomad chief, leaving as his sole personal possessions, besides his horses and sheep, one embroidered gown, one turban, one saltcellar, one spoon, and a few pieces of red muslin.

He had designated as his successor, not his studious and peaceable elder son, but his younger one, Orkhan, who

[6] Gibbons, Appendix B.

took the title of "Emir." [7] Already distinguished as a
warrior on more than one occasion, Orkhan now continued in the same path. Before long Nicaea and Nicomedia had fallen into his hands; he also increased his territories at the expense of Karasi, one of the other Turkish
principalities. Then followed a peace of twenty years, during which he governed wisely and well, and consolidated
the institutions he had already established; indeed, it is
rather as an administrator than as a conqueror that Orkhan
is famous in Turkish history. Aided by his older brother
and vizir, Ala-ed-Din, and by other counsellors, he introduced the first Ottoman coinage, regulated the costume of
his subjects, divided up his territory into provinces, and
above all reorganized his army. Hitherto the Turkish
troops had consisted of the ordinary levies of feudal cavalry, who served in return for land and plunder. By the
creation of the famous corps of the Janissaries, Orkhan
obtained at little cost a body of highly disciplined regular
infantry, thus strengthening his army in precisely the element in which Asiatics have almost always been weakest
in comparison with Europeans. He also instituted a force
of regular cavalry; in fact, he may be justly said to have
established the nucleus of a national standing army at least
a century earlier than any of the Christian sovereigns of
the West.

In 1346 Orkhan had taken to wife a daughter of the
Byzantine emperor, John Cantacuzenus, with whom he
henceforth remained on friendly terms. This, however,
did not prevent him from continually attempting, by one
means or another, to get a foothold in the European dominions of his father-in-law. At last, in 1357, his oldest
son Suleiman crossed the Hellespont by night with a few

[7] Edward Gibbon, *Decline and Fall of the Roman Empire*, ed. J. B. Bury,
7 vols. (London, 1900), VII, 26. But "Emir," an Arabic word meaning
"Commander," does not really connote "Commander of the Faithful" until
the time of Selim I.

companions on two rafts, and seized the ruined castle of Tzympe. Reënforcements soon followed, in spite of the remonstrances of the Emperor; and an earthquake, which threw down the walls of the city of Gallipoli, gave the newcomers an invaluable base for further operations. Even the death of Suleiman, which was followed shortly afterwards by that of his father, only served to clear the way for a new leader.

The next Emir, Murad I, was forty-one years old at the time of his accession in 1359, and a truly remarkable man. Primarily a soldier of Islam, stern, severe, and recklessly brave, with a tremendous voice which thundered over the battlefield, he was also a great builder of mosques, of almshouses, and of schools. And yet he could neither read nor write. When his signature was needed, he dipped his thumb and three fingers in the ink, and applied them —well separated—to the paper; a popular legend tells us that this mark was used to form the basic pattern of the "tughras" or calligraphic emblems of subsequent Ottoman rulers.[8] Murad came to the throne at a most fortunate moment. Not only did he inherit a reorganized army—full of religious and warlike ardor and led by brilliant officers; the political situation in southeastern Europe was also highly favorable to his designs. The death in 1355 of Stephen Dushan, the greatest of the Servian princes, had deprived the petty Balkan states of the one leader who might have been able permanently to check the Turkish advance. Only two enemies were really to be feared. The warlike kingdom of Hungary—then nearing the height of its power under Louis the Great of the House of Anjou—was, on

---

[8] On the reliability of this legend cf. *The Encyclopedia of Islam, s.v.* "tughra," vol. IV, especially p. 824; also H. A. Gibbons, p. 127, n. 2. If the story is to be believed at all, the large oval space at the left probably represents the mark of the thumb, while the three wavy lines at the top show that of the fingers. The tughra of Suleiman the Magnificent is reproduced on the title page of this book.

paper at least, a formidable antagonist; but Louis was too much occupied with the affairs of the West, and especially of Poland, to devote due attention to the danger to the Balkans from Asia Minor; and the religious differences between his Roman Catholic Hungarian and Orthodox Slavic subjects made it wellnigh impossible for them effectively to combine. In the republic of Venice the Turks had another even more dangerous potential foe. The wealth and resources of the city of the lagoons, her daring commanders and her skilful diplomats, her splendid fleet and her many strategic possessions in the Levant made her a power not lightly to be reckoned with; but for the time being she was much more concerned with her struggle against her commercial rivals the Genoese than with the protection of her territories in the Balkans. Her fleets might harass the Turkish seacoasts and cut off communications, but they could not check the advance of the Ottoman armies.

Murad did not long leave the world in doubt about his intentions. His forces marched suddenly to the northwest and captured Adrianople, which from 1366 till 1453 remained the European capital of the Turks, corresponding to Brusa in Asia Minor. The fall of Philippopolis soon followed. Thus the Turks had, almost at a stroke, separated Constantinople from nearly all contact by land with the rest of Christendom, at the same time that they directly menaced Bulgaria and Servia. The Balkan states were terrified, and a league was formed between Hungary, Servia, Wallachia, Bulgaria, and Bosnia to oppose the Ottoman advance; but in 1371 a great Christian army was surprised at night near Chirmen on the Maritza and dispersed by a few thousand Ottoman cavalry, and Servia and Bulgaria were soon reduced to the position of tributary states. Fresh hostilities led to fresh conquests; in 1383 Sofia was taken by storm. At the same time Murad was equally suc-

cessful in his contests with the other Turkish princes of
Asia Minor. Here too he added steadily to his dominions,
and finally in a decisive battle crushed an army that had
been gathered against him by his most dangerous rival, the
Emir of Karaman. Scarcely was this accomplished when
he was recalled to Europe to meet a new coalition of his
Christian enemies, who had just routed one of his generals
at Toplitza in Bosnia. In 1389 the plain of Kossovo ("black-
birds") witnessed the first of a series of really great victories of the Ottoman Turks over their Christian opponents, a series unbroken by a single important defeat on
land by Europeans for over two hundred years. Murad had
often prayed, before the fight, that he might die a martyr
to the faith: and on the battlefield that prayer was answered.[9]

With Bayezid I (Yilderim, "the Thunderbolt") we have
a new type of ruler, equal and in some respects superior in
ability to his predecessors, but in character a proud and
lustful Eastern despot, whose magnificence was only
matched by his cruelty. It seems probable that he was the
first Ottoman ruler formally to assume the title of Sultan.[10]
His first act was to put his younger brother to death in
order to render himself secure against any possible rivalry

[9] Conflicting stories and legends have come down as to the manner of his
death. Busbecq (*Life and Letters,* ed. Forster and Daniell, I, 153, and note)
says he was assassinated by a Croatian. The Ottoman historians believed that
Murad was killed by a wounded Servian soldier while walking across the
field of battle. The Servian songs and the Byzantine historians say that he
was killed by Milosh Obravitch, son-in-law of the Servian chief Lazar, who
gained an audience with Murad during or after the battle in the guise of a
deserter. Hammer, *Histoire de l'Empire Ottoman* (Paris, 1835–43), I, 284–
290; H. A. Gibbons, pp. 176–177, with references.

[10] Gibbon, *Decline and Fall,* VII, 34–35, says "Bajazet condescended to
accept a patent of Sultan from the caliphs who served in Egypt under the
yoke of the Mamelukes; a last and frivolous homage that was yielded by force
to opinion, by the Turkish conquerors to the house of Abbas and the successors of the Arabian prophet." Gibbon rests his statement on Joseph de
Guignes, *Histoire générale des Huns,* 4 vols. (Paris, 1756–58), IV, 336; de
Guignes, in turn, on Benschounah (ibn Shihna), a contemporaneous Syrian

for the throne. The deed was done on the field of Kossovo
in the presence of his father's unburied corpse. It was a
precedent imitated by his successors, with but few exceptions, for many generations to come, and the theologians
justified it by the verse in the Koran which declares that
"revolution is worse than executions."

As a soldier Bayezid was worthy of his surname. The
victory of Kossovo was actively followed up. Bulgaria was
incorporated in the Sultan's dominions; Servia was reduced
to vassalage and Hungary threatened, while in Asia Minor
the remaining Turkish princes were driven out of their
possessions, which were annexed by the conqueror. Sigismund of Hungary, too weak to maintain the struggle alone,
had turned to Western Europe for assistance. Aided by the
Pope, he succeeded in organizing a belated crusade, led
by a body of French nobles left unoccupied by a lull in
the Hundred Years' War. The expedition, however, ended
in 1396 with the fatal battle of Nicopolis, where the army
of the crusaders and Hungarians was overwhelmingly defeated by Bayezid, owing largely to its incredible lack of
discipline. Constantinople seemed inevitably doomed by
this disaster. Already it had been threatened and it was now
rigorously blockaded; but, though deserted by the West,
it was to be saved for another half-century by an unexpected diversion. Bayezid had come into conflict with another and even greater Asiatic conqueror than himself, the
terrible Tatar prince Tamerlane, who had built up a
mighty empire in Turkestan, overrun Persia, and invaded
Russia and India; shortly afterwards he was even to estab-

---

historian. A. Rambaud in Ernest Lavisse and Alfred Rambaud, *Histoire
générale* (Paris, 1893–1901), IV (1894), 748, likewise reckons Bayezid the first
Ottoman Sultan. Yet there is good evidence that his father had been generally known by that title; while, on the other hand, Teodoro Spandugino,
Commentari dell'origine de Principi Turchi (Florence, 1551), says expressly
that Mohammed "the Restorer," who ruled from 1413 to 1421, was the
first of the Ottoman house to assume it.

lish relations with the distant king of Castile. At first his dealings with Bayezid were friendly, since both were warriors of the Faith; but as their boundaries approached and the victims of each fled to the court of the other, inevitable disputes soon turned into open hostility. To avenge a first attack Bayezid collected his forces and hastened to meet his adversary, who had disdainfully turned aside to wage war on the Mamelukes and devastate Syria. It was at Ankara, the scene of Ertoghrul's exploit, that the Turks of the East and the West finally faced each other, on the twentieth of July, 1402. Bayezid fought with all his old fury. But, despising his enemy, he allowed himself to be outgeneralled; his army was outnumbered, and there was treachery among his troops, some of whom saw their former princes serving in the ranks of the enemy. By the end of the day the Ottoman army was annihilated, and the Sultan, who had fallen from his horse in an attempt to escape, was left an honorable prisoner in the hands of his rival.

If the defeated state had crumbled to pieces after this fearful disaster, it would have gone down in history merely as one of the many Eastern empires whose rapid rise had been followed by an equally sudden fall. It had suffered indeed a stunning blow. Its military prestige was temporarily shattered. Asia Minor had become the prey of plundering hordes of victorious Tatars. Bayezid died in captivity in 1403, and his sons, barely escaped from the field of battle, plunged at once into furious civil war. No better proof can be given of the permanence of the work of their earlier rulers than the fact that, instead of yielding to the many difficulties by which they were beset, the Turks emerged at the end of ten years, weakened indeed and exhausted, but with their fundamental vitality still unimpaired. When Mohammed I, "the Restorer," the ablest of the sons of Bayezid, had finally triumphed over his brothers, all that was needed was a few years of rest to enable the Turks to set forth again on the career of conquest and greatness which the Christian world had fondly imagined to be a thing of the past. Mohammed was exactly the sovereign demanded by the situation. In his earlier years he had shown himself a fearless warrior; now that at last he was firmly seated on the throne, he did his utmost to give his subjects peace, and his honorable character commanded the respect of all men. Even his reign, however, was not entirely free from war. His attempts to build a navy brought him into conflict with Venice, but the Turks were as yet not quite prepared to meet the first maritime power of the day. In 1416, outside the port of Gallipoli, the Venetian commander Loredano destroyed the Ottoman fleet, and the Sultan, unable to avenge himself, wisely made peace. It was reserved to his successors to demonstrate how completely the Turks had recuperated under his rule.

Murad II (1421–51), a stern soldier, was also a patron of art and a builder, pious, just, and honorable, but he was destined to spend the thirty years of his reign in almost unbroken warfare. Angered by various provocations on the part of the Greeks, he made a determined attempt to capture Constantinople, but, for the last of many times, the "New Rome," thought but a shadow of her former self, beat back all the efforts of her assailants. Foiled in this direction, Murad made a lasting peace with the Byzantine Emperor, and turned his attention to other regions, where he met with more success. In Asia he easily drove from their thrones most of the Seljuk princes who had been restored by the grace of Tamerlane, and reduced the strongest of them, the ruler of Karaman, to a position of vassalage. In Europe he began by checking the growth of Venice, which had just bought from the Greeks the city of Saloniki. The Sultan could not possibly permit the ambitious republic, already too powerful in Eastern waters, to retain the most valuable port on the Aegean Sea. In 1430 a short siege delivered it into Murad's hands, from which there was no taking it away. In the next few years he was mainly engaged in a series of vigorous and generally profitable campains against Albania, Servia, Wallachia, and Hungary, during which he gradually extended his dominions at their expense. But the Turkish advance into the Balkans was destined to be strongly opposed by two worthy champions of Christendom: the Albanian chief, George Castriota or Skanderbeg, who kept the Ottomans out of his native land until his death in 1467; and the Hungarian national hero John Hunyadi, who fought the Moslems on a far larger scale though for a shorter time. Under his leadership the Hungarians, supported by the Poles, took the offensive against the invaders and drove them out of Servia. So completely, in fact, did the tables seem to be turned, that Murad, who appears to have had a vein of mysticism in his nature, consented to a humiliating peace, and shortly after abdicated in favor of his son Mohammed, with the idea of spending the rest of his days in seclusion at the peaceful Anatolian town of Manissa (Magnesia). But he did not remain long in retirement. The shameful violation by his Christian foes of the peace to which they had pledged their word was enough to cause him to reassume his authority, march against them, and overwhelm them at Varna on the Black Sea in 1444.[11] The king of Hungary was slain on the battlefield; the sight of his head on a pike struck terror among his troops. The papal legate

[11] Richard Knolles, in his *Generall Historie of the Turkes* (London, 1603, p. 297), tells us that in the early stages of the battle, when the Christians were apparently winning, Murad "pluckt the writing out of his bosom, wherein the late league was comprised, and holding it up in his hand with his eies cast up to Heaven, said:

"*Behold, thou crucified Christ, this is the league thy Christians in thy name made with me: which they have without cause violated. Now, if thou bee a God, as they say thou art, and as we dreame, revenge the wrong now done*

Cesarini, who had urged on his Crusaders by assuring them that no promises made to the Moslems were binding, was also killed in the ensuing flight. Hunyadi with great difficulty made his escape to his native land. Once more the Sultan insisted on going into retirement, this time because he felt that he had accomplished the work that God had given him to perform; but a revolt of the Janissaries, which gave Hunyadi the opportunity to launch a fresh offensive, convinced him that it was his duty again to resume office. The Janissaries were brought to order. Hunyadi was once more utterly defeated in a second battle of Kossovo in 1448. Three years later (February 5, 1451), the Sultan Murad died.

Christian Europe, by a strange delusion which we shall see repeated later, imagined Murad's successor, Mohammed II, to be a weakling, because he had twice permitted his father to depose him. In reality, now that at the age of twenty-one he at last had the power firmly in his grasp, he was to show the world that he was greater than any of his predecessors, and far more dangerous. According to descriptions by defeated Greeks and Westerners, he was fierce, unscrupulous, and determined, passionate and debauched, faithless and cruel after a fashion unequalled even in Ottoman annals; he was also as ominously reticent in regard to his own plans as he was absolutely tireless in their execution. "If a hair of my beard knew my schemes, I should pluck it out," he once told an indiscrete official who had ventured to question him. In war he was an indefatigable and skilful leader; as a statesman he showed

---

unto thy name, and me, and shew thy power upon thy perjurious people, who in their deeds denie thee their God."

And Cotton Mather (*Magnalia*, edition of 1702, book vii, p. 117), who obviously derived the story from Knolles, adds that "immediately the Course of the Battel turn'd; the Perjurious King was kill'd; and the Turks won a most unexpected Victory."

himself sagacious and far-seeing; as a lawgiver and organizer of his empire he displayed real genius. He quoted Persian poetry as he rode into the deserted palace of the Caesars after the storming of Constantinople, and he gazed with deep appreciation on the glorious ruins of Athens. He sent to the Signory at Venice to ask for a good artist to paint his picture, and the Signory replied by despatching Gentile Bellini to the Porte, where he arrived in September 1479, and remained till the end of 1480. It seems probable that he did several portraits of the Sultan, and although the authenticity of the best known of them, which is now in the National Gallery in London, has been contested, it gives, despite its lamentable condition, an excellent idea of Mohammed's character and personality.[12] Such was the man who, like his father, was to rule for thirty years of ceaseless effort to extend his empire, and who, though he also was to suffer two significant defeats, was destined to accomplish more than any of his predecessors. Like his father, also, he directed his first enterprise against the imperial city which had defied so many attacks, and which the Ottomans ardently desired to make their capital; and Mohammed was to succeed where Murad had failed.

The siege of Constantinople, which began on April 6, 1453, and lasted fifty-three days, is perhaps the most famous and dramatic in all history. It is brilliantly described by Edward Gibbon. The Sultan had concealed his preparations with masterly cunning. He had gathered overwhelming forces and he urged them on with passionate energy. Huge mortars hurled great balls of stone against the city's ramparts; mines were exploded; desperate attacks were launched at the gate of St. Romanus and repulsed by "Greek fire." But Mohammed soon saw that

---

[12] On Bellini's visit to Constantinople and what he did there, cf. L. Thuasne, *Gentile Bellini et Sultan Mohammed II* (Paris, 1888).

all his efforts would be unavailing without command of
the inner harbor of the Golden Horn to the northeast of
the city; and the mouth of the Golden Horn was blocked
by a boom of iron chains which all the power of the Turkish navy had been unable to break. What could not be
achieved by sea must of necessity be accomplished by land.
On the night of May 19, some seventy Turkish ships were
hauled, with sails unfurled, on greased ways which had
been prepared during the preceding four weeks, across the
tip of the promontory of Pera and launched where the
Christians were unable to oppose them. From that moment
onward, the result was a foregone conclusion. On May 29,
five Turkish columns simultaneously launched furious attacks; the Genoese John Giustiniani, "whose arms and
counsel were the firmest ramparts of the city," was
wounded and fled; Constantine Palaeologus, the last of the
Greek Emperors, was slain in the ensuing confusion by
an unknown hand, and after his death the defence col-
lapsed. Shortly after midday the Sultan made his formal
entry into St. Sophia, and gazed with wonder and delight
at what he saw. We are told that as he walked up the central aisle, he found one of his soldiers digging out the pol-
ished stones from the flooring; but Mohammed promptly
cut him down with his scimitar. "I have given the captives
and the movables to my followers," he declared, "but the
buildings are mine." A moment later an imam ascended
the pulpit and made the declaration of Islam. Justinian's
Holy Temple of the Incarnate Word had become a
mosque. The Eastern Empire had come to an unhonored
end.

The real greatness of the new "Kaisar-i-Rum" (Emperor of Rome) was proved quite as much by the use which
he made of his victory as by the ways in which he won it.
A few days of merciless pillaging followed the surrender.
Such was the custom of the time, and it was inevitable that

it should be officially sanctioned. There were sacrilege, murder, and rape. All sorts of precious relics of classical and Byzantine art were destroyed. Bronze columns and imperial tombs were smashed and made over into cannon, cannon balls, bullets, and coins. "One hundred and twenty thousand manuscripts are said to have disappeared; ten volumes might be purchased for a single ducat." [13] But Mohammed seized the earliest possible opportunity to put an end to these desecrations. He was determined to convert his prize, the historic metropolis of Christian Orthodoxy, into the capital of Islam (Istambul) and of the Ottoman Empire. Most of the basilicas and monasteries were made over into mosques, like St. Sophia; and the Sultan set a seal on what he had already done there by the erection of the first of the four minarets by which it is flanked today. As the buildings thus made available proved inadequate for the accommodation of the Faithful, the succeeding age witnessed the construction of an enormous number of Moslem almshouses, schools, and places of worship. Constantinople began to renew its architectural youth under the inspiration of its first Turkish master. But though Mohammed was determined to leave no doubt that he regarded himself as the champion of Islam, his attitude towards his Christian subjects was almost unbelievably tolerant, if measured by the standards of contemporaneous Europe. The Patriarchate was vacant at the time the city was taken, but three days later Mohammed ordered that a new incumbent be elected and consecrated according to the ancient rites. A few days afterwards he received him in solemn audience, and formally presented him with the jewelled cross, the emblem of his dignity, after the manner of his Byzantine predecessors. "Be Patriarch," he de-

[13] Gibbon, *Decline and Fall*, VII, 198. These estimates are unquestionably much exaggerated. Most of the best manuscripts had been taken to Italy long before. Much greater damage had been done to the city when the crusaders took it in 1204.

clared, "and may Heaven protect thee: count on the continuance of my good will, and enjoy all the rights and privileges of thine office." As long as good order was maintained, the Christian worship was freely permitted in those churches which had not been converted into mosques; and Easter continued to be celebrated, with traditional magnificence, in the Christian quarter of the city. And there are plenty of other evidences that Mohammed had no fears of the presence of a large element of Christian Europeans in his new capital. Many of the inhabitants of the Balkan states which he subsequently conquered were deliberately transported to Constantinople and established there, and the city's population soon exceeded the figure of its late Byzantine days. Particularly characteristic was his policy towards the Genoese, who had maintained themselves for centuries in the suburb of Galata as a semi-independent colony, with laws and franchises of their own, and had not seldom made serious difficulties for the Palaeologi. When he learned of the troubles they had caused, the Sultan threatened them with wholesale slaughter. However, on their payment of an enormous bribe he relented, and solemnly swore that all their ancient privileges should be maintained, provided they continued to behave themselves. To make assurance doubly sure, he gave orders that all their fortifications be demolished.

Europe fondly hoped that Mohammed would rest content with the organization of his first conquest, but was doomed to disappointment. Constantinople, in the new Sultan's eyes, was not an end but a beginning. It has been well said that for many a minor dynasty in Southeastern Europe and Asia Minor his reign was like the Day of the Last Judgment. In one place only did he meet serious defeat on land, when the heroic Hunyadi, in the last weeks of his life, rolled the Ottoman armies back before Belgrade in the summer of 1456; and the memory of that disaster continued to rankle till it was terribly avenged, just sixty-five years later, by Mohammed's great-grandson. Everywhere else on land the Turkish forces proved irresistible. Between 1462 and 1464 Bosnia was subdued and its last sovereign executed; in 1467 Herzegovina was annexed. During these same years Wallachia had been made a tributary state; Moldavia had been attacked, and the last vestiges of independent Christian rule had been effaced from the mainland of Greece. Albania remained unconquered until Skanderbeg's death in 1467. In the succeeding years it became the battleground of local chieftains, Venetian captains, and the Turks; but after Ottoman cavalry had gone around the head of the Adriatic and attacked the Venetian mainland, it was evident that the Moslems were destined to dominate it. In the meantime Mohammed exterminated the Greek Empire of Trebizond; he conquered the Genoese settlements in the Crimea, and finally reduced to vassalage the powerful Khan of the Crimean Tatars. On the Asiatic mainland he extended his boundaries by extinguishing the last embers of the rival Seljuk state of Karaman; and he blasted the hopes of his enemies that a new Tamerlane would arise to defeat him by shattering the hosts of the Turcoman sovereign of the dynasty of the White Sheep, near Terjan, in 1473. He was now the undisputed master of the whole of Anatolia.

But Mohammed was not satisfied with land conquests alone. The Turks hitherto had been pitiably weak on the sea. Now, with an Empire situated on two continents and one of the most splendid ports in the world, the Sultan set himself to the task of creating a navy. He began by closing and fortifying the Dardanelles, thereby excluding all strangers from the Black Sea. In 1455 a Turkish fleet entered the Aegean and conquered several of the smaller Greek islands. Venice alone made feeble efforts to resist him; in 1463, war was declared between the republic and the Porte, and dragged out its course for sixteen weary years. There were no great naval battles, because Venice was careful to avoid them; but in 1470 she was ousted from the island of Euboea, and thereafter lost all claim to the mastery of the Eastern Mediterranean. So greatly was she impressed by the power of the new foe, so deeply discouraged by the failure of Western Europe to support her, that in 1479 she decided to make her peace with the Sultan, and pocket her territorial losses in return for the maintenance of her commercial privileges. Relieved of all anxiety of attack from the republic, Mohammed launched two new naval expeditions in 1480. The first landed an army at Otranto in the kingdom of Naples. The town was stormed, and the surrounding country laid waste. The whole of Southern Italy was in abject terror. There was no prospect whatsoever of aid from the North. But the second and greater of Mohammed's maritime ventures proved unfortunate. It was composed of a fleet of 160 ships, carrying a powerful army, and it was commanded to capture Rhodes, the island fortress of the Knights of St. John of Jerusalem. But it was met by an unexpectedly heroic defence; almost it accomplished its purpose, but not quite, and the unsuccessful commander of the Turks was relieved and disgraced. Mohammed was planning personally to take command of a fresh expedition in the ensuing year, when death suddenly overtook him, on May 3, 1481. Rhodes on the sea, with Belgrade on land, remained bitter remembrances, which the Turks felt in honor bound to wipe out; and it was to be the happy fortune of Suleiman the Magnificent, in the years 1521 and 1522, to succeed in obliterating them both.

After such a brilliant reign, it was almost inevitable that there should be a reaction. The Turkish troops in Italy, left unsupported, were obliged to withdraw; while at home a war for the throne broke out between the two sons of the late Sultan. But when the elder of them, Bayezid II, had triumphed over his brother Jem, he showed little inclination to continue his father's conquests. Indeed he spent most of the first fourteen years of his reign in planning and plotting to prevent his Christian enemies from utilizing Jem against him. The tale of the latter's adventures at the courts of Innocent VIII and Alexander VI, of his transference to the guardianship of Charles VIII of France, and death at Naples in the spring of 1495, is full of dramatic incidents wholly typical of the Italian Renaissance.[14] Throughout his reign Bayezid waged desultory war on sea and on land, in Europe, Asia, and Africa, but never with decisive results. The Turks, who had become accustomed to the dramatic victories of Mohammed, grew increasingly restless and discontented. Less and less was the Sultan able to control his subjects, his soldiery, and his turbulent children, and in 1512 a series of revolts ended in his abdication in favor of his youngest son Selim, who had won the support of the Janissaries. Bayezid was permitted to retire from Constantinople to his birthplace; but on the way thither he died, poisoned—so it was popularly believed —by his Jewish doctor at the behest of his successor.

The brief reign of Selim "the Terrible" (1512–20) witnessed a speedy and ominous resumption of his grandfather's conquests. Indeed the new Sultan, in the first five years of his rule, added more territory to his dominions than had any of his predecessors; all of it, be it noted, was won from his own coreligionists. His Christian neighbors to the westward thanked God that he elected to leave them alone, and sent embassy after embassy to his court to beg on bended knees for the renewal of truces and capitulations. They had good reason to fear, for though the new Sultan took delight in the society of scholars and theologians, wrote poetry himself in three languages, and even

[14] Cf. L. Thuasne, *Djem Sultan* (Paris, 1892).

sought refuge from the cares of state by occasional indul-
gence in opium, he was first and foremost a savage warrior and a bloodthirsty despot. He began, in orthodox fashion, by ridding himself of all possible rivals for the throne.
His two elder brothers and eight nephews were disposed
of in rapid succession. He also made it clear from the outset that he proposed to tolerate no independence on the part
of any of his subordinates, many of whom throughout his
reign were handed over without warning to the executioner; hence the curse which became proverbial among
the Turks, "May you be the vizir of the Sultan Selim!"
Having regulated matters to his satisfaction at Constantinople and gathered all the reins of power into his own
hands, he surveyed the state of his neighbors to the East
and the South.

At Selim's accession the Ottoman dominions included
practically all of Asia Minor, but Persia, which for the
preceding century and a half had been split up into a number of minor principalities, had now at last begun to gather
itself together under a new dynasty, ably represented by
Ismaïl I, who in 1499 had been proclaimed Shah. The
presence on his flank of what now threatened to become a
powerful state was enough to rouse all the fighting spirit of
Selim. The fact that Ismaïl belonged to the Sufi sect of the
Shiite form of Islam was sufficient to fire his burning zeal
for the maintenance of Sunnite orthodoxy. Sufi doctrines
had of late begun to spread among the Sultan's own subjects, and Selim gave orders that all who were tainted with
this heresy should be exterminated on a given day. It is said
that 40,000 persons were massacred in the ensuing purge.
Having thus shown the strength of his own sentiments,
and obtained from the head of his clergy a declaration that
there was more merit in killing one heretic Persian than
seventy Christians, Selim led a great force across Asia
Minor to the eastward. Shah Ismaïl, who had no infantry

and not a single cannon, retreated, laying waste the country behind him as he went; but Selim was not the man to be deterred by any "scorched earth" policy. The sufferings of his army were terrible; even the Janissaries murmured, and on one occasion the Sultan's own tent was riddled with bullets; but Selim never wavered; and his persistence was at last rewarded, when Ismaïl was forced to accept battle at Chaldiran (August 24, 1514), in order to save his capital, Tabriz. The Turkish troops were exhausted, and most of their horses were gone; but their infantry and artillery sufficed to win the day. Shah Ismaïl was wounded; his baggage and harem fell into the hands of the enemy. Fresh outbreaks of the Janissaries prevented the Sultan from following up his victory to the extent that he wished; nevertheless in the course of the next two years he incorporated into his possessions the Jezirat or northern part of Mesopotamia and the mountainous region of Kurdistan, where, however, he left the tribal government of the turbulent inhabitants practically undisturbed. He returned to Constantinople in triumph; and after punishing the instigators of the recent mutinies, he reorganized his Janissaries in such fashion as to relieve him of all fear of disobedience in the future.

Even before the end of his Persian campaigns, Selim had turned his attention to another rival. Ever since the middle of the thirteenth century, Egypt, with its dependencies in Syria and on the Red Sea, including the holy cities of Mecca and Medina, had been ruled by the famous Mamelukes. Originally a body of slaves, they had finally become masters of the land; and they had kept up their numbers by the old method of purchase, first of Turkish, later of Circassian, children. This military aristocracy of a few thousand cavalrymen, whose Soldan was merely their chief, were intensely proud of their past, and promised to be a formidable foe. But, aided by treachery, Selim defeated them near Aleppo on August 24, 1516, their leader perishing in the ensuing flight. As Damascus surrendered without resistance and the inhabitants of Lebanon also submitted, this victory made Selim master of Syria and Palestine, whose administration he proceeded to reorganize before pushing on into Egypt itself. On January 23, 1517, at Ridania, the Mameluke cavalry, fighting with desperate bravery, were mowed down by his cannon. Twenty thousand men are said to have been left dead on the field. Cairo was now taken, and Tuman Beg, the last Mameluke Soldan, was pursued until he was betrayed by an Arab chief and hanged at the gates of the town. The Mamelukes as a body, however, were not exterminated or even deprived of all power. Selim left the administration of Egypt as it was, with a Mameluke bey at the head of each of its twenty-four provinces; but over them all, in place of a Soldan of their own, he placed a Turkish governor.[15]

Selim reaped other rewards from the conquest of Egypt besides increase of territory and military fame. He also won the proud title of "Protector of the Holy Cities," with the overlordship of Mecca and Medina, a dignity to which both he and his successors attributed great importance. The story—generally accepted until very recently—that he took the title of Caliph from the last Abbasside, whom he found in Cairo, is of more doubtful authenticity. It now seems clear that some of his predecessors had occasionally been addressed as Caliph (though in a somewhat limited sense) by other Moslems, but that Selim and Suleiman took pains to avoid the use of the title. The "Ottoman legists of their time inclined to the view that the Caliphate had [really] lasted only thirty years—until the death of

---

[15] The most recent account of the Turkish conquest of the Mameluke Empire is that by G. W. F. Stripling, "The Ottoman Turks and the Arabs, 1511–1574," in *Illinois Studies in the Social Sciences*, XXVI, no. 4 (1942), 38–55.

Ali," [16] the last of the four successors of the Prophet; and the first diplomatic document known to have called the Turkish Sultan Caliph is the treaty of Kuchuk Kainarji with Russia in 1774. Of course the title died with the establishment of the Turkish Republic in 1922–24.—But even if we eliminate his claims to the Caliphate, we must admit that Selim had rendered notable service to the Turks and to Islam. The last three years of his life were spent in peace; but while officially absorbed in problems of internal government, he was also getting ready, with characteristic secrecy and thoroughness, another great expedition, presumably intended to wipe out the disgrace of Rhodes. The Christian West, which he had hitherto spared, was in an agony of suspense. But death interrupted him in the midst of his preparations, on September 22, 1520, in his fifty-fourth year. [17]

[16] Cf. A. H. Lybyer's article on the Caliphate in the *Encyclopedia of the Social Sciences*, III, 145–194, and references there.

[17] So at least Hammer, IV, 137, 358. He quotes the Venetian reports giving Selim's age at his accession as thirty-eight or thirty-six, and dismisses them with the remark that "he then looked ten years younger than he was." It is to be noted, however, that Jovius says that he died in his forty-sixth year (*Turcicarum Rerum Commentarius* (Paris, 1539), p. 59), and Iorga (*Geschichte des Osmanischen Reiches*, 4 vols. (Gotha, 1908–13), II, 342) accepts the same figure.

Youth and Accession of Suleiman
Contemporaneous Europe

Selim the Terrible left behind him only one son, the Sultan Suleiman, surnamed by Christian writers "the Great" or "the Magnificent," and by his own people "El Kanuni" or "the Legislator." We know almost nothing of his early years; but it seems clear that he was born in the latter part of the year 1494 or possibly in the early months of 1495, and that his mother, whose name was Hafssa Khatoun, was a woman of rare charm and intelligence. Some writers have maintained that she was a Circassian or a Georgian; but there is much to support the statement of Jovius that she was the daughter of the Khan of the Crimean Tatars.[1] The power and popularity which both her husband and her offspring subsequently enjoyed at Kaffa (Feodosia) lend added weight to this conclusion. Indeed, there is good reason to believe that Suleiman spent at least a portion of his boyhood there among his mother's kinsmen.[2] But as his father was only the youngest of the eight sons of Bayezid II, the infant's chances of ever coming to the throne can hardly, at the outset, have appeared promising.

Sixteen years later, however, the situation had entirely changed. Suleiman was thrust prominently into the fore-

---

[1] Cf. Busbecq, I, 112, note; Lybyer, p. 58, note 2; Bragadino in Alberi, *Relazioni degli ambasciatori veneti al Senato . . . edite da Eugenio Alberi*, 15 vols. (Florence, 1839–63), 3rd ser., III, 101. She died in 1533 at the age of fifty-five, and was buried in a tomb near that of Selim (Hammer, V, 181).

[2] Cf. Iorga, II, 310, note 2, 342–343.

ground, and his prospects were much enhanced by the family troubles which convulsed the last years of his grandfather's life and finally cost him his throne. The number of Bayezid's surviving sons had by this time been reduced to three; and one of them, Korkud, had little ambition to rule. It speedily became evident that the only serious rivals for the succession would be Bayezid's oldest and favorite son, Achmed, and his youngest, the "Terrible" Selim. Both were governors of provinces; and since it would be essential to gain control of the capital, the treasury, and the household troops as soon as the old Sultan should die, the relative proximity of these provinces to Constantinople was a matter of primary importance. Achmed had been given Amasia, in North Central Asia Minor, while Selim had been stationed at Trebizond, farther eastward; but Achmed's advantage was almost nullified by the fact that Bayezid unexpectedly appointed Selim's sixteen-year-old son, Suleiman, to the governorship of the district of Boli, which intervenes between Amasia and Constantinople, and thus blocked Achmed's way in the future race for the throne.[3] The appointment of young princes of the blood to rule regions more or less remote from the capital was a practice too common in Ottoman statecraft to merit special attention, though the selection of Suleiman is, under the circumstances, very difficult to explain. In any case we know that Achmed complained so loudly that Bayezid transferred his grandson from Boli to Kaffa in the Crimea. Thither he was speedily followed by his father Selim, who, being convinced that as long as he remained at Trebizond his chances of the succession were slight, was determined to get nearer to the main theatre of operations. At Kaffa he appears immediately to have taken matters into his own hands, practically superseding his son and acting like an independent ruler, and the mass of the Crimean Tatars ral-

[3] Hammer, IV, 103 ff.

lied to his standard. When Bayezid ordered him to return to Trebizond, he replied by begging for a governorship in the Balkans, so that he might have a chance to fight against the Christians, and, above all, to be near enough to his imperial sire to kiss his hand. It was the custom, so he pointed out, "for governors of provinces to do so every year." [4] Thrice was the request repeated, and thrice refused. Nevertheless, the insubordinate prince started westward at the head of some 25,000 men, and soon was joined by reënforcements. We need not follow the details of the ensuing confusion. At Chorlu, near Constantinople, Selim's forces were met and routed by his father's trained Janissaries, who charged to the cry of "Death to the bastard!", but the victory had no lasting results. Selim made his escape to the Crimea. His father tried in vain to pacify him by offering him the governorship of the great province of Semendria, on the Danube; but Selim was in no mood for compromise. His reckless bravery had won him the admiration and loyalty of the Janissaries with whom he had just fought, and without the Janissaries the cause of Bayezid was lost. Early in 1512 Selim reappeared at Constantinople, and forced his father to abdicate.[5]

During all these troubles we hear little or nothing of Suleiman; but after his father had obtained the throne, he was summoned to his presence at Constantinople and left in charge there while Selim went off to end the fratricidal strife in Asia. When at length the "Terrible" Sultan had disposed of his brothers and nephews, he turned his attention to the conquest of Persia. Suleiman did not accompany him on the ensuing campaigns, but remained behind, this time as governor of Adrianople. There are occasional mentions of communication between the two; as when, writing from Tabriz, Selim announced his great victory

[4] Iorga, II, 310, n. 7.
[5] Hammer, IV, 121–123.

over the Persians to his son as well as to the Khan of the
Tatars, the Soldan of Egypt, and the Doge of Venice.[6] At
the close of the Persian and Egyptian wars the Sultan returned in triumph to his capital, and then proceeded to
Adrianople, whence, eight days later, Suleiman departed
with much pomp for Manissa, the chief town of the province of Sarukhan on the coast of Asia Minor, to which he
was now assigned. We have no means of knowing what
the relations between father and son at this period really
were. Even if it does not seem probable that they were
affectionate, we have no sure proof of the rumors which
have come down to us that the Sultan really hated his offspring, or thought to put him to death. The tale that he
once sent the prince a poisoned garment, which was prudently tried on a page who died from its effects, is undoubtedly an absurd fable. But it seems not improbable that Suleiman's prompt departure from Adrianople
was all that availed to save him from hostile intent on the
part of his terrible sire; for even though the Sultan had
no other heir, rebellions of princes against their parents
had been all too common in Oriental history. Selim's
own conduct toward his father had been the most recent
instance of it, and his suspicious and ruthless nature was
ever on the lookout for danger. Four years earlier, when
the Janissaries had mutinied during the Persian campaign, they are said to have threatened to replace their sovereign with his son. However all this may be, Suleiman himself was now established in comparative safety at Manissa,
and the period during which he was doomed to remain in
obscurity was destined to be unexpectedly brief.[7]

The death of Sultan Selim, according to custom, was
kept concealed until his successor should be notified in time
to arrive and prevent any disorder among the soldiery. In

[6] Hammer, IV, 203.
[7] Hammer, V, 6–7.

the present case it was not found necessary to preserve the secret to the very end, for the interval was short. On Sunday, September 30, 1520, only eight days after his father's decease, the new Sultan reached Constantinople, where he was welcomed by the Janissaries, who clamored for the usual gifts on the accession of a new master. At dawn on the following day, Suleiman issued forth from the inner rooms of the palace to receive the homage of the high officials. That afternoon he went to the gate of the city to meet the funeral procession with his father's corpse, which he then escorted to the mosque where the burial service took place. His first official decree was an order for the erection of a mortuary chapel with a mosque and a school in honor of the departed—the mighty conqueror of Persian and Mameluke.[8] Two days later there was distributed the bakshish or donation, not only to the Janissaries, who had demanded and received more than had been given them at the accession of Selim, but also to the other household troops and to various civil officials. Then followed acts of mercy and justice. Six hundred Egyptian captives were set free, and a number of merchants, whose goods had been confiscated for trading with Persia, received an indemnity; on the other hand, a few salutary executions of evil-doers showed that the new ruler intended to be respected as well as beloved.[9]

The reign certainly opened under most favorable auspices. According to an Oriental superstition, there arises at the beginning of each century a great man who is destined to dominate it, or, in Turkish phrase, "to take it by the horns." Suleiman also profited from the Moslem belief that the number ten, that of the fingers and toes, of the Commandments in the Pentateuch, of the disciples of Mohammed, of the parts and variants of the Koran, and of

[8] Hammer, V, 8.
[9] Hammer, V, 8–10.

the "astronomical Heavens" of Islam, is the most perfect and fortunate of all numbers.[10] Suleiman was born in the year 900 of the Hegira, that is to say, by Oriental reckoning, in the first year of the tenth century; he was also the tenth Sultan of the Ottoman line, and had been given the imposing name of Suleiman or Solomon, which is especially venerated in the East. He was, in fact, the first acknowledged Ottoman sovereign to bear that name; for the Suleiman who conquered Gallipoli in 1356 had died before his father Orkhan and was therefore never a real Sultan, while the Suleiman who disputed the throne with Mohammed I has always been regarded as a pretender by Turkish historians. When the latter speak of "El Kanuni" as "Suleiman II," it is in the sense of the second Solomon of the world.[11] It is noteworthy to what extent the destinies of the Europe of that time had been delivered into the hands of young men. Suleiman at his accession was twenty-six, the same age as Francis I; Henry VIII of England was three years older; Charles V, Emperor and king of Spain, was but twenty, and Louis, king of Hungary and Bohemia, only fourteen. Even the Pope, Leo X, was not quite forty-five. The new Sultan had already had some ten years of experience in the art of government; and the terrible severity of his father's reign, while it had maintained the bonds of despotic discipline, offered an easy popularity to a more gracious successor. Never had the empire been more tranquil at home or more respected abroad.

The reports of the Venetian ambassadors shed precious light on the character and appearance of the new Sultan throughout his reign, and it is significant that Titian should have painted him in his "Ecce Homo" in 1543 and Veronese in his "Marriage at Cana" some fifteen years later.[12]

---

[10] Hammer, V, 4–6.
[11] Hammer, V, 4.
[12] Cf. note on portraits at the end of this volume.

Our earliest description of him is from the pen of Bartolomeo Contarini, and is dated October 15, 1520, less than a month after his accession. It tells us that "he is twenty-five years of age, tall, but wiry, and of a delicate complexion. His neck is a little too long, his face thin, and his nose aquiline. He has a shadow of a mustache and a small beard; nevertheless he has a pleasant mien, though his skin tends to pallor. He is said to be a wise Lord, fond of study, and all men hope for good from his rule." [13] Yet despite the apparent slightness of his frame, his early training and experiences at Boli and Kaffa had sufficed to furnish him with a body able to endure the strain of thirteen hard campaigns, and one authority tells us that, like other Turkish children of noble birth, he was taught to labor at a trade, so that, if necessary, he should be able to earn his bread by the sweat of his brow.[14] On the other hand, he had spent at least one-third of his life previous to his accession at Constantinople, where he had acquired the ways and manners of the Turkish *gentilhomme par excellence*. Indeed, his popularity in the capital was an asset of enormous importance to him till the end of his days. Unlike his father, his interests and attention were directed rather to the West than to the East, to Europe rather than to Asia. He took no pleasure in Persian philosophy or poetry, though he delighted in stories of conquerors like Alexander the Great. Especially did he pride himself on his ability to converse with his officers—the great majority of whom had been born in the Balkans—in their native dialects. He had no enthusiasm for the persecution of Moslem heretics, nor did he believe that it was his sacred duty to extirpate Christians. Certainly he was no religious fanatic. On the other hand, no one of his predecessors had ever had any-

[13] Marino Sanuto, *Diarii*, 59 vols. (Venice, 1879–1903), vol. XXIX, col. 391.
[14] Lybyer, p. 76, note 5; Spandugino, *Petit traicté de l'origine des Turcqz*, tr. and ed. by Charles Schéfer (Paris, 1896), p. 179; Iorga, II, 343, and references there.

thing like such a lofty conception of the dignities and responsibilities of his office as "Commander of the Faithful." Every important event of his long reign furnishes fresh evidence of this fundamental fact, and many who had not fully grasped it were destined to suffer cruelly for their mistake. The new Sultan looked out on the world around him with a calm, cold, perhaps slightly whimsical gaze, as if wondering where the demands of his own position, and the insolence of its prospective challengers, would first compel him to strike.[15]

As Suleiman was Selim's only son, and as Selim had made such a clean sweep of all his relatives at the time of his own accession, there was no danger that the new Sultan's right to the throne would be disputed by any scion of the house of Osman. In only one corner of the broad extent of his dominions did the change of sovereigns produce a serious revolt. A certain Ghazali, a bey, apparently of Slavonic birth, had deserted his Mameluke master at the time of the conquest of Egypt, and had been rewarded for his treachery by Selim with the governorship of Syria. He now deluded himself into thinking that the time had come for him to win complete independence. He easily made himself master of Damascus, Beirut, and Tripoli, with most of the adjacent seacoast; but Aleppo defended itself stoutly till Ferhad Pasha, the merciless third vizir, arrived with an army to relieve it. Ghazali retreated on Damascus, where he was speedily and completely defeated; he was caught, moreover, while attempting to escape, and was killed by one of his own adherents.[16] The affair had certain ominously significant aftermaths. When the head of the defeated rebel was brought back to Constantinople, the Sultan proposed to send it, as a token of friendly sentiment,

---

[15] Iorga, II, 342–347 and references on 346–347; Hammer, V, 10–11.
[16] Cf. G. W. F. Stripling, "The Ottoman Turks and the Arabs, 1511–1574," *Illinois Studies in the Social Sciences*, XXVI, no. 4 (1942), 64–65.

to the republic of Venice; and the Venetian resident at
the capital had no little difficulty in dissuading him from
so doing.[17] Even the victorious Ferhad Pasha was ultimately
rewarded with death. On his way back from Damascus, he
had invited the Turkish ruler of an adjacent sanjak to his
camp. When the latter appeared with his four sons, Ferhad Pasha reproached them for their failure adequately to
support him, and finally handed all of them over to the
executioner. Suleiman was not the man to tolerate such
high-handed conduct. On the other hand, Ferhad Pasha
had married the Sultan's sister, and the latter pleaded her
husband's cause so eloquently that Ferhad Pasha was finally
transferred to the governorship of the Balkan province of
Semendria,[18] with a large salary, in the hope that this mark
of imperial favor and proximity to Constantinople would
make him see reason. But it was all in vain. Ferhad Pasha
was as ruthless and insubordinate as ever in his new domain.
When summoned by Suleiman to explain his conduct, he
was so insolent in his replies that the executioners were sent
for at once. It would appear that he gave them a fight
for their lives before he was finally overpowered and
killed (November 1, 1524). We are also told that his
widow made haste to present herself, clad in deep mourning,
before the Sultan, and dared to express the wish that she
would soon have the privilege of wearing mourning for
her brother as well.[19]—But the real significance of Ferhad
Pasha's end, as well as of many other contemporaneous
episodes, was that it proved that the new Sultan proposed
to be master in his own house, and Suleiman's Eastern neighbors were prompt to read the signs of the times. Long before Ferhad Pasha had been finally disposed of, the Persian
Shah Ismaïl, who had been watching and waiting on the

[17] Hammer, V, 14.
[18] Hammer, V, 61. He had been governor of Tripoli in Syria since 1521;
Stripling, *op. cit.*, p. 61.
[19] Iorga, II, 357-358 and references.

course of events, took pains to send the friendliest messages of congratulation to Suleiman.

The powers of Christian Europe were less wise. It will be worth while to devote a couple of paragraphs at this point to their attitude towards the recent progress of the Turks. During the weak reign of Bayezid II, King Louis XII of France, "the eldest son of the Church," and heir to inspiring memories of the mediaeval struggles of the Cross against the Crescent, had despatched two expeditions, in 1499 and 1501, to dislodge the Moslems from their island strongholds in the Levant. Both, however, had disastrously failed, owing chiefly to the refusal of the Venetians to fulfil their promises of coöperation; and now the memory of them was revived, with acid clarity, after the accession of the "Terrible" Selim in 1512. If the Christians had been defeated when the Turkish Sultan was so notoriously inefficient, what could they possibly hope to accomplish against an enemy now led by an able ruler who literally thirsted for war? No wonder that Western Europe trembled. There was, of course, much talk of new crusading. Pope Leo X kept constantly harping on the necessity for it. During Selim's Persian and Egyptian campaigns, he had repeatedly pointed out the opportunity thereby offered. If the Sultan should be victorious, he declared, he would be much more dangerous and therefore should be attacked at once; if, on the other hand, he should be defeated, there would be the best of all chances to render him harmless forever. In principle no one seemed to disagree with the Pope. King Francis I of France was especially zealous for a crusade. When he was striving to win the imperial crown, in 1519, his agents were instructed to emphasize his fitness to lead an army against the Moslems. He himself declared, in typically grandiloquent fashion, that if elected he would engage within three years either to reach Constantinople, or else to perish on the way. The

Emperor Maximilian and the other sovereigns of Western Europe all promised their loyal support for the great cause; but when it came to translating their words into deeds every one of them drew back. They were far too anxious to get the better of one another to unite for a common cause. The smaller states to the east of them were in terror of their lives.

Under all the circumstances it is no wonder that the powers of Western Europe hailed the news of the death of Selim with feelings of profound relief. Most of them had been convinced that the "Terrible" Sultan, after finishing off his own coreligionists, intended to launch devastating attacks against the Christians. Rumors that he was preparing to assault Rhodes had already reached them. Moreover, it was well known that the savage corsair Khaireddin Barbarossa, whose elder brother Aruj had made life miserable for the Spaniards in the western basin of the Mediterranean for many years before his death in 1518, had sent an envoy to Constantinople to declare himself the vassal of the Sultan. It looked as if Selim was planning to add North Africa to his empire, and possibly even to attempt the reconquest of Spain.[20] And then came the happy and unexpected news of Selim's early death. The West knew nothing of Suleiman. "It seemed to all men," as Jovius puts it, "that a gentle lamb had succeeded a fierce lion, . . . since Suleiman himself was but young and of no experience . . . and altogether given to rest and quietness." When Pope Leo had "heard for a surety that Selimus was dead, he commanded that the Litany and common prayers be sung throughout all Rome, in which men should go barefoot." [21]

Christian Europe was soon to discover that it was sadly

[20] R. B. Merriman, *Rise of the Spanish Empire*, 4 vols. (New York, 1918–34), II, 255 ff.; III, 288 ff.

[21] Paolo Giovio, *A Shorte Treatise upon the Turkes Chronicles*, tr. Peter Ashton (London, 1546), folio C.

mistaken in the estimate thus hastily made. On the strength
of it men ceased, for five most crucial months, to trouble
themselves about the affairs of the Levant. The Pope, indeed, continued to dwell upon the opportunities for a
great crusade, but the sovereigns of Western Europe still
hung back. All of them knew that for many years past
contributions which had been made for the fight against
the Moslems had been diverted to other uses less holy and
far nearer home; moreover, whereas in Selim's day they
had felt that the sacred cause was wellnigh hopeless any-
way, they now were convinced that everything was so
serene that there was no reason that they should bestir
themselves. It is really extraordinary how completely they
failed to comprehend the character and abilities of the
new Sultan. They thought that he had no knowledge of
the duties of his office; whereas, as a matter of fact, he had
had more experience of the art of government previous
to his accession than had any one of his predecessors. It
is true that Suleiman was not of a bloodthirsty disposition,
nor did he delight in war as a mere pleasure. On the other
hand, as we have already pointed out, he was thoroughly
imbued with a sense of his own position and of the duties
as well as the dignities that it implied. We must not forget
that the Ottoman state regarded all its members, from the
sovereign to the humblest soldier, primarily as warriors
for the Faith, and that it was chiefly through combats
against the Christians that its rulers had risen from nomad
chiefs to become lords of a mighty empire. Even the wars
of Selim against other states of his own creed were, as he
conceived of them, in the nature of a pan-Islamic move-
ment. Their ultimate object was to group under one head
all the powers of the Moslem world, so as to render them
more terrible than ever to their Western enemies. The
guardianship of the Holy Cities had further emphasized
this idea; and the extent of its influence is strikingly dem-

onstrated in the subsequent history of the Ottoman Empire
by the fact that from the day that it ceased to be a conquer-
ing power it began to decline. Suleiman, a thoroughly pious
and zealous Mussulman, showed throughout his whole
reign that he regarded it as his first duty to be a soldier
of Islam. In this duty as Commander of the Faithful he
never faltered to the end of his days. In order, however,
to understand the wars and the diplomacy of the next
forty-six years we must begin by taking a glance, from
the Turkish standpoint, at the contemporaneous situation
in Western Europe.

Ever since the first battle of Kossovo in 1389 had
crushed the powers of resistance of the Slavs of the
Balkan Peninsula, two states had done more than all the
rest of Christendom to check and to hamper, though they
had been unable completely to prevent, the progress of
the victorious Turk. The republic of Venice on the seas,
and the kingdom of Hungary on land, had been the bul-
warks of Western Europe. In spite of many reverses, and
in spite of the fact that the disproportion between the
resources of the combatants grew greater and greater as
time went on, both Venice and Hungary had managed to
hold their own; and both could look back with pride on
what they had already accomplished. Venice, it is true,
had lost more than one outpost, and no longer commanded
the seas; nevertheless she still remained the great commercial power of the Levant; her fleet was still a factor to be
reckoned with; and her fortunate acquisition in 1489 of
the island of Cyprus—though it not improbably was accomplished by shady means—obliterated the memory of the
loss of Euboea in the reign of Mohammed II. The Hungarians too, in spite of their defeats at Nicopolis and Varna,
and at the second battle of Kossovo in 1448, had succeeded
in keeping their own frontiers intact. In the bloody border

warfare which raged there even in times of nominal peace, the successes were at least evenly divided. With all their efforts, the Turks had not been able to overcome these two barriers to their further progress.

During the past two or three decades, however, the relative positions of the three states had been profoundly modified to the advantage of the Turks. Even before Selim's conquests in Persia and Egypt had enhanced the power and prestige of the Ottoman Empire, its two nearest Christian rivals had begun to show ominous signs of disintegration and decay.

Contemporaneous historians are wellnigh unanimous in dating the beginning of the decline of Venice from her defeat at Agnadello (May 14, 1509) at the hands of her Christian enemies, banded together in the League of Cambray. "In this battle," says one of them, "there was conquered a rich, wise, and powerful people, who had never been subjugated since the days of Attila, king of the Huns." [22] But if we look at the picture from the vantage point of the twentieth century, we shall not be at a loss to find many earlier portents of ultimate disaster. In the first place the power of the republic rested on too small a foundation. No one city-state, however rich, well situated, public spirited and well governed, could possibly hope permanently to hold her own against the great modern consolidated monarchies of the West which had begun to replace the loose feudal aggregations of the Middle Ages. The wealth of the republic, primarily dependent on her commerce, was exhausted by the expense of the wars which she was obliged to wage, both to the east and to the westward, in order to maintain her ancient prestige. Her trade, moreover, was still further menaced by two other recent events. The conquest of Egypt by Selim had put her Eastern commerce almost wholly at the

[22] Jean de Saint-Gelais, *Histoire de Louys XII* (Paris, 1622), p. 217.

mercy of the victorious Turks. The most valuable part
of that commerce, moreover, was also threatened by the
Portuguese discovery in 1486 of a new way to the East
around the Cape of Good Hope. Not only did the Portuguese begin to trade at once in all those Oriental products
which since the days of the crusades had come up the
Red Sea and the Persian Gulf and had been distributed
through Europe almost exclusively by Venetian merchants
and vessels; they went further, and soon set to work to
block the ancient routes in order to divert this precious
commerce into the new channels so profitable to themselves. Against all this Venice alone could do nothing;
and now she had no friends to help her. After the disaster
at Agnadello, she was no longer regarded as a power of
the first rank. When we add to all this the degeneration
in the character of her citizens, due chiefly, perhaps, to
the ever increasing narrowness of her jealous oligarchical
government, the atmosphere of suspicion that pervaded
everything, and the timidity that was increasingly evident
in all her counsels, we cease to wonder why she could
no longer play her old role in the world. The most clear-
sighted of her statesmen already realized that she was
henceforth incapable of meeting her ancient rivals on
equal terms alone; and ever since Selim's conquest of
Egypt they had bent all their energies towards maintaining good relations, at the least possible sacrifice, with those
in authority at Constantinople. Hitherto they had on the
whole been successful in these attempts; but there was
grave danger lest when they ceased to be feared, they
would begin to be despised.[23]

The kingdom of Hungary was in even worse case. It
had not gradually declined; it had fallen with appalling
suddenness from the highest pinnacle of its glory to the

[23] W. R. Thayer, *A Short History of Venice* (New York, 1905), pp. 254–
263.

depths of degradation and despair. Under the great Matthias Corvinus (1458–90), the younger son and successor of John Hunyadi, it had not only held back the Turks; it had even contemplated the organization of a crusade which should drive them from the Balkans. To the westward it had annexed Moravia, Silesia, and Lusatia, and driven the ridiculous Hapsburg Emperor Frederick III a fugitive from his capital at Vienna. Matthias' court gave brilliant welcome to the most outstanding figures of the Italian Renaissance. His entertainments were worthy rivals of the most magnificent of Western Europe. Commerce and industry flourished; internal order and security were complete. And then, in the twinkling of an eye, the entire situation had changed. Matthias had been suddenly cut off, in the midst of his triumphs, at the early age of forty-seven. The Hungarian nobility desired a king who should be their servant rather than their master; and their desires were gratified by the choice of Ladislaus Jagello as the successor of the great Corvinus. The new sovereign had been king of Bohemia since 1469; he was also the son of Casimir IV of Poland; outwardly it seemed as if his inheritance of itself would be enough to insure the maintenance of the power of the crown. But Jagello proved pitiably weak. The royal authority lapsed. The feuds of the nobility grew fiercer. Every year saw the confusion increase; and the effective military strength of the kingdom, equally essential to its continued existence and dependent on the power of the monarchy, ebbed away to the vanishing point. A single example will suffice. In 1514 an attempt to launch a crusade served to collect some 40,000 peasants, who promptly turned their arms against the nobles who had oppressed them, and the country was devastated by a horrible social war. When the aristocracy had put down the revolt, at the cost of 50,000 lives, they refused to be satisfied with the usual punishments, and at the next meeting of the Diet they solemnly condemned the whole body of the peasantry to perpetual servitude. After Louis II had succeeded to his father's throne in 1516, the selfish struggles of the various party leaders became more violent than ever. The new sovereign, "born too soon, married too soon, king too soon, and dead too soon," was but ten years old and utterly unable to check them.[24]

Venice and Hungary were thus no longer competent to act as the defenders of Europe against the Turk. They had rendered Christendom the inestimable service of holding back the Moslems until successors were ready to take their places, but it was evident by this time that the main burden must henceforth be borne by others. And the recent emergence in Western Europe of powerful national states, ably led by absolute kings, foreshadowed the way in which the need was to be met. As yet these states had had few direct dealings with the East, and were absorbed in their own jealous rivalries; but circumstances were soon to broaden their horizons and force them to take account of the advance of the Ottoman Empire. The entrance of the Turks into close continuous relations, sometimes hostile and sometimes friendly, with the great nations of the west, is enough in itself to shed lustre on the reign of Suleiman the Magnificent.

The dominant fact of the European political situation at the time of the Sultan's accession was of course the preponderance of the power of the House of Hapsburg, now headed by the recently elected Holy Roman Emperor, Charles V. This prince, the grandson on his father's side of the Emperor Maximilian and of Mary the daughter of Charles the Bold of Burgundy, and on his mother's of Ferdinand and Isabella of Spain, was born in 1500 at

[24] Armin Vámbéry, *The Story of Hungary* (New York, 1886), pp. 267–283; Lavisse and Rambaud, IV, 617–622.

Ghent in the Netherlands, and during the first seventeen and a half years of his life never left his native land. As a young man he was unimpressive and unattractive; neither in aspect nor in conversation did he give any promise of the ability, ambition, or independence which he was afterwards shown to possess. But kingdoms and principalities seemed literally to fall, unsought for and undreamed of, into his lap. The early demise of his father Philip in 1506 made him the heir of the Hapsburg domains in the Low Countries, Burgundy, Switzerland, and Austria, as soon as his grandfather Maximilian should die. The deaths of Queen Isabella in 1504, of her two eldest children, and of their offspring, made it probable that he would inherit the Spanish kingdoms, with their dependencies and colonies in Italy, the Mediterranean and North Africa, and the New World; and that probability became a certainty a little later, when his mother Joanna went hopelessly insane, and his grandfather Ferdinand abandoned all efforts to oust him from the succession. Charles had left the Netherlands in September, 1517, to get official recognition in his Iberian realms; and though he had cut a sorry figure there, he had succeeded for the most part in accomplishing his object, only to be recalled, three years later, to the north, by the news that he had been chosen Roman Emperor-Elect on June 28, 1519, in succession to his paternal grandfather, Maximilian, who had died in the previous January.[25] A truly portentous inheritance, the greatest that Europe had seen since the days of Charlemagne; moreover, Charles's position was still further strengthened by the fact that his aunt Catharine of Aragon was the wife of Henry VIII of England, and by the introduction of Hapsburg influence into the affairs of the Scandinavian North through the marriage of his sister Isabella to Christian II of Denmark. Only one important

[25] R. B. M., II, 319, 335; III, 1–52.

part of Western Europe had escaped him: the France of Francis I, his unsuccessful opponent in the recent imperial election; the France which divided his Spanish from his German inheritance; the France with which he inherited bitter rivalries, in Italy, in Burgundy, and in Navarre; the France which was to fight him, with intermissions, for the next thirty-five years.

For the moment, however, we are principally concerned with the reaction of this immense extension of Hapsburg territory and power on the progress of the Ottoman Turk. Obviously, if the Moslem advance was to be stemmed, the task would devolve on Charles. He fell heir in his Austrian domains to the work that Hungary had hitherto performed on the Danube; in his Spanish, Italian, and Mediterranean lands he must take up the naval side of the struggle where Venice had laid it down. At the outset, like almost everybody else in Western Europe, he underestimated the seriousness of the "Turkish peril"; on the other hand, he was clear-sighted enough to realize its existence. Moreover, it was evident that he could not be at both danger-points at once, to say nothing of his innumerable and far-scattered responsibilities in Western Europe. And it can be no matter of surprise, under the existing circumstances, that he chose Spain, and the naval role which the possession of his Spanish dominions implied, for the part that he preferred to play. In the first place, he had been there, whereas he had never been in Austria. He had had an inhospitable reception, it is true; nevertheless he had been keen enough to see that Spain was destined to be the main source of his power; the Mexican silver mines had already begun to yield him revenue. Spain was also far nearer to the theatre of future operations in the West; and for the time being Charles's impending struggle with Francis I took precedence over everything else. Finally, there was the all-powerful argument of ancient Spanish tradition. For nearly eight centuries past, the national task of Christian Spain had been the expulsion of the Moslems from the peninsula; it was not till 1492 that the last Mohammedan sovereign had been driven out. And the fall of Granada was not the end of hostilities. There followed furious, if intermittent, struggles for the possession of outposts in North Africa. Cardinal Ximenes, who represented the royal authority in Spain between the death of King Ferdinand, and the arrival, eighteen months later, of his grandson, was most ardent, though for the most part unsuccessful in the Spanish cause.[26] On the other side, as we have already seen, the corsair Khaireddin Barbarossa had been taken over in 1518 into the service of Selim, and had begun that series of terrifying raids on Charles's Mediterranean possessions which were to continue, practically unchecked, until his death in 1546. The cause of the Turks and that of their coreligionists from Spain and in North Africa were now, to all intents and purposes, the same. We cannot wonder that Charles elected to meet the foe in that portion of his dominions which not only possessed the largest resources, but which also continued to be animated by a spirit which had wellnigh disappeared from the rest of Western Europe: the fierce devoted zeal of the warrior for the faith, who fights for the next world as well as for this; the same spirit, indeed, as that of its Moslem opponents.

Charles, then, had chosen the Spanish, Mediterranean, naval end of the conflict for himself. There remained the problem of the Danube. He already knew enough of Germany to realize that it could give him no effective support. The selfishness of its individual princes and the cumbersomeness of its constitutional machinery served to paralyze it in such fashion that it could accomplish nothing against

[26] R. B. M., II, 240–260; Ernest Mercier, *Histoire de l'Afrique Septentrionale* (Paris, 1888–91), III, 15–27.

a foreign foe. The Holy Roman Empire was but a ghost of its former self; in the future it was by nations and dynasties that results were to be achieved. Somehow the tottering kingdom of Hungary must be bolstered up, and if possible annexed by the traditional Hapsburg method of marriage. The Emperor Maximilian had foreseen the need of this and had planned for it. There must be a double union, between Charles's younger brother Ferdinand and Anna the sister of Louis Jagello, and between Louis and Mary, the sister of Ferdinand and Charles. All the details were arranged before the end of 1520, and both weddings were celebrated in the summer of 1521.[27] If, as seemed not improbable and ultimately occurred, Louis should die childless, there was an excellent chance that Ferdinand might become king of Hungary and Bohemia. Obviously from every point of view it was essential that he be further strengthened by the addition of Austria to his domains. There would thus be created a really powerful buffer state against the Turk, and Charles would be relieved of further anxiety in that quarter. At the Diet of Worms in 1521 the young Emperor announced his intention of handing over his Austrian dominions and their dependencies to Ferdinand. On February 7, 1522, the transaction was completed by a convention signed at Brussels.[28] The Turk was now confronted by the power of the House of Hapsburg on land as well as on the sea.

A few details remain to be added, to complete the picture of Western Europe as it presented itself to the gaze of the "Magnificent" Sultan in the early months of 1521. Despite all Charles's inherited territorial and political preponderance, the outlook for the House of Hapsburg was

[27] Karl Brandi, *The Emperor Charles V*, tr. C. V. Wedgwood (London, 1939), pp. 54, 99, 136, 140.
[28] Cf. H. Pirenne, *Histoire de Belgique* (Bruxelles, 1902-1932), III, 89 ff.; H. Baumgarten, *Geschichte Karls V.*, 3 vols. (Stuttgart, 1885-1892), II, 112-113.

by no means wholly bright. The inevitable war against
Francis I had indeed begun favorably, and the young
Emperor had the advantage, for the time being, of the
cordial friendship of his uncle Henry VIII. On the other
hand, almost all his own dominions were honeycombed
with discontent. In Castile the resentment aroused by his
Flemish advisers and his own inability to speak Spanish
resulted in the famous revolt of the Comuneros. It was by
far the most serious outbreak by which the power of the
crown had been challenged since the accession of Ferdinand and Isabella; and though the rebels were decisively
defeated (April 23, 1521) on the field of Villalar, the
royal authority was not effectively reëstablished for many
months to come. There also occurred almost simultaneously an ominous rebellion in Valencia, the only one of
Charles's Spanish realms which he had left unvisited. It
had its repercussions in the Balearics, and led to many
cruel outrages against the Moorish portion of the population. Indeed, the ultimate result of it was to extend, in
1525, to the realms of the Crown of Aragon the edict of
expulsion of the Moors which had been put forth in 1502
for Castile. The natural consequence of this was a series
of desperate raids on the Valencian coasts by Khaireddin
Barbarossa—fresh proof of the identity of the cause of the
Spanish Moslems with that of the Ottoman Turks.[29] And
finally, and vastly most important of all, the authority of
Charles V as the lay head of Western Christendom had
been solemnly challenged (April 18, 1521) by a heretic
Saxon monk named Martin Luther at the Imperial Diet
at Worms.[30] Four years earlier, when he first heard that
religious trouble was brewing in the Empire, Pope Leo X
had hazarded the contemptuous guess that "it was but a
monkish quarrel"; but his legate Aleander, who was on the

[29] R. B. M., III, 67-116, *passim.*
[30] *Deutsche Reichstagsakten unter Kaiser Karl V.,* II, 551-555.

ground, came far nearer the truth when he reported from the Diet that "Nine-tenths of Germany shout "Hurrah for Luther,' while the other tenth cries 'Down with the Pope.' " [31] The Protestant Reformation had in fact begun.

It was at this critical moment in the political and religious history of the world that Sultan Suleiman set forth on his first campaign against Christian Europe.

[31] Lavisse and Rambaud, IV, 407.

Belgrade and Rhodes

It would be interesting to know just how accurately the Sultan was informed of the great events that had occurred in Western Europe during the last two or three years of his father's reign and the first few months of his own.[1] There were of course nothing like resident Turkish representatives, either diplomatic or consular, in any of the European states except Venice; but the Venetians were already famous for the accuracy and extent of their knowledge about what was occurring all over the world. Their local representative, or bailo, was almost always present in Constantinople, and it seems inconceivable that Suleiman and his agents should not have learned much from him. There can be no doubt that he desired to know of everything that was taking place beyond his own borders as

[1] There is no question that the Turks were exceedingly well acquainted with the recent progress of geographical exploration in the West. The map drawn by the Turkish admiral Piri Reis in Gallipoli in 1513, and presented by him to Selim the Terrible in 1517, was discovered in Constantinople in 1929, and was published there in 1935, with the Turkish *lemmata* translated into English, French, and German. It gives the appearance of having been torn out of what was originally a map of the world, and represents the western shores of France, Spain and Africa, the Atlantic Ocean, and the eastern coast of South and Central America. There seems little doubt that Piri Reis had in his possession a copy of the chart which Columbus is known to have been compiling as he sailed along, and which is now lost; if so, the Turkish admiral's map may lay claim to be one of the very first to show the two continents in something like their proper relationship. The *lemmata* are masterpieces of laconic information and are always interesting if not invariably correct. Many of the names of the islands in the Caribbean are also misplaced, but it is evident that Piri Reis was well acquainted with the delimitations established by the Tordesillas Line.—The inference from all this seems to be that the Turks knew a great many other things as well.

well as within them, and he had plenty of secret emissaries and spies. We may be sure that he was fully and promptly informed of the extent of Charles V's vast inheritance, of his election as Emperor, and of his German coronation (October 23, 1520) at Aix-la-Chapelle. The young Christian sovereign threatened, in fact, to overshadow him, and that was not to be tolerated. Suleiman longed to measure swords with the head of the House of Hapsburg. Indeed he frequently expressed his disappointment, in the course of the next thirty-five years, that the Holy Roman Emperor insisted on keeping under cover in such fashion that it was impossible to find him, and delegated the task of fighting the House of Osman to vicars and subordinates.

Under all the circumstances it was evident that the new Sultan must give speedy proof that he proposed to play a part in European politics. The fact that his father Selim had busied himself exclusively with conquests in Asia and Africa was but an added reason why he should do so. There were two obvious places for him to begin operations: all the more obvious because both recalled bitter memories of past Turkish defeats which he was in honor bound to avenge. Belgrade blocked his route up the Danube, and made contact with the Hapsburgs impossible. Until Rhodes should be wrested from the Knights of St. John of Jerusalem, his fleets could not venture into the Western Mediterranean, nor were his ships safe outside the Dardanelles.

Belgrade, the White City, the ancient Singidunum, is situated on the southern side of the Danube at its junction with the Save, which, coming from the westward, flows at this point nearly north, with Belgrade on its right bank. The town is on a tongue of high land, protected on two sides by water, and its highest part, the citadel, is at its tip.

Immediately below it is a large island in the Danube; opposite it, to the northwest, above the confluence with the Save, is the town of Semlin. Few places have been besieged and captured as often as Belgrade. In 1343 it was fortified by the Servian king Stephen Dushan; some years later it was taken by the Hungarians; in course of time it returned again to Servia, only to be ceded by George Brankovic, the last independent prince of that country, to Sigismund of Hungary, who strengthened its defences. This was a wise precaution, for in 1440 it was again besieged, though in vain, by Murad II. In 1456 Mohammed II, fresh from his capture of Constantinople, assailed it in his turn, but was repulsed, as we have already seen, with the loss of his artillery, by Hunyadi and a crusading army under John of Capistrano. Since then the town had been left undisturbed, though it was destined to be the scene of many a bloody conflict in the succeeding centuries.

Even in times of nominal peace between Hungary and the Ottoman Empire there was almost uninterrupted warfare on their borders. This warfare was waged by pashas and governors, and for the most part through irregular incursions, though the forces engaged were often large enough to fight pitched battles with heavy loss of life. In 1515 John Zápolya, the voivode or governor of Transylvania, whom we shall encounter again, had led ten thousand men, in spite of an existing truce, in a raid on Servia. Here he was defeated by the pasha of Semendria, with the loss of the cannon of Belgrade, which he had taken with him on the expedition, so that the city was short of artillery when next attacked by the Turks. But officially the truce continued. The Hungarians, unaided, were far too weak to undertake serious offensive operations, and Sultan Selim was busy in other directions. When Suleiman came to the throne, one of his first acts was to despatch to the Hungarians a chaush (messenger), named Bahram, to offer them peace on condition that they should pay him tribute. At the same time fresh attacks were made along the frontier. The Sultan can hardly have had any expectation that his terms would be accepted. Probably he was merely summoning his enemy to submit before making a formal declaration of war. In any case the Hungarians were so enraged at the insult implied by Suleiman's demand that they answered by casting his envoy into prison. According to one account, the chaush was finally sent back to Suleiman with his nose and ears cut off. Others maintain that he was murdered, and yet others state that a false report that he had been murdered was sent back to Constantinople. In any case it is obvious that enough had been done to rouse the fury of the Sultan, while the arrival, at about the same time, of the severed head of the rebel Ghazali from Syria convinced him that he had nothing more to fear from his Asiatic possessions. He therefore determined to take immediate measures for revenge.

Hungary was near enough to Constantinople to be able to appreciate, more justly than most of Western Europe, the character and ability of the new Sultan. As reports of his preparations continued to pour in during the early months of 1521, the country was rent afresh with confusion and discord. The peril was obvious and imminent, and the more clear-sighted were convinced that it could not possibly be met without aid from the rest of Europe. Ambassadors were accordingly sent to the Pope, to the republic of Venice, to the king of Poland, and to the Emperor and the imperial Diet. Leo X was full of sympathy, but replied that unfortunately he had no money to spare. Venice declared that she could not possibly act alone, but would not fail to exhort all the princes of Christendom to give aid. Sigismund I, who had been king of Poland since 1506, although he was the uncle of Louis of Hungary, was far too cautious to expose his own realm

to the risk of war with the Turk. It was to the Empire
that the Hungarians felt they had most reason to look for
substantial assistance. On April 3, one of their envoys,
Hieronymus Balbus, addressed the Diet at Worms in a
lengthy speech, in which he dwelt on the horrors of Turkish invasion, the debt that Europe owed to Hungary for
defending it for so long, the perils of the present moment,
and the urgent need of immediate help from the Empire
in its own interest as well as in that of the entire Christian
world.

"For who prevented the unbridled madness of the
Turks from raging farther?" he asked;

The Hungarians. Who checked their fury that overwhelmed
like the swiftest torrent? The Hungarians. Who warded off
the Turkish darts from the throats of the commonwealth of
Christendom? The Hungarians. Who, finally, preferred to
turn against themselves the whole power and onslaught of
the barbarians, rather than lay open to them an entrance into
the lands of others? The Hungarians. Long, long ere now, a
terrible tempest would have burst into the vitals of Germany and Italy, were it not that, as if a wall had been set up
against it, it was dammed in and kept from spreading by the
Hungarians themselves, so that till recently it has only raged
within the bounds of Pannonia. But now the Hungarian kingdom is in such straits, and its people have been so continuously
slaughtered, that it is not only unable to subdue its foes, but
unless it be aided from without, it cannot any longer restrain
or resist them.[2]

Balbus had unquestionably been eloquent, but unfortunately his appeal could not possibly have been worse
timed. The month of April, in which he made it, saw

---

[2] *Oratio habita in Imperiali Conventu Die Tertia Aprilis MDXXI*. Sum-
mary in *Deutsche Reichstagsakten unter Kaiser Karl V.*, II, 758–759.
"Responsum Imperatoris et Statuum," *ibid.*, p. 759.

the young Emperor's multifarious cares and responsibilities in Western Europe pile up in such fashion as they were never destined to do again. Charles was involved in a bitter quarrel with the Diet over the constitution of the Imperial Council of Regency. He had just despatched a letter to Francis I which was almost equivalent to a declaration of war. The progress of the various revolts in his Spanish kingdoms was ominous. On April 18, Martin Luther had made his famous speech to the Diet: [3] on the nineteenth, the young Emperor had solemnly condemned him.[4] It was on that very evening, or the next day, that the imperial reply was handed to the Hungarian envoys. We cannot wonder that it was discouraging. Nothing could possibly be done to help Hungary at the present, though large hopes were held out for the future. If King Louis should prove unable to defend himself in the immediate crisis, the Empire would approve of his making a truce with the Turks for a year, "provided always, that it should be one not dishonorable nor injurious to himself, to the Catholic faith, or to the commonwealth of Christendom."

Hungary, then, could have no aid from without, and must count on her own resources. And her conduct, in the weeks that elapsed between the arrival of the ominous news from Worms and the approach of the Ottoman army, gave sadly conclusive proof of the indiscipline, insubordination, and disunion of her subjects. Her Council of State was convened on April 24. The defence of her two border fortresses of Belgrade and Sabač (on the south bank of the Save, some sixty miles to the westward) was obviously the first problem to be solved. But both were commanded by proud Hungarian noblemen, who stoutly refused to hand over their charges to any officer appointed

---

[3] *Deutsche Reichstagsakten unter Kaiser V.*, II, 551-555.
[4] *Deutsche Reichstagsakten*, II, 558.

by the crown. They declared that they were quite competent to perform their duties alone, provided only that they were furnished with money, provisions, ammunition, and cannon; and when the Council became importunate, they withdrew to their own estates. The sailors of the Danube flotilla, who had received no pay for three years, seized the opportunity to go to Buda-Pesth and complain; as they got nothing but indefinite promises, they also speedily dispersed. In June Hungarian society made haste to betake itself to Pressburg, to be present at the wedding of King Louis with his Hapsburg bride, and participate in the magnificent festivities which had been arranged to celebrate it.

Meanwhile Suleiman had left Constantinople on February 16. At Sofia, whence definite news of his advance first reached Hungary, he was joined by Ferhad Pasha with three thousand camels carrying ammunition; thirty thousand more camels which had been collected in Asia and were now laden with grain followed on, a day's journey behind; a requisition of ten thousand wagon loads, to be paid for from the treasury, was laid on the Christian population of the region. There were three hundred cannon, and forty ships were equipped on the Danube. At Nish the army was divided. One part, commanded by Ahmed Pasha, the beylerbey of Rumelia, and followed a few days later by Suleiman himself, moved against Sabač; the Grand Vizir Piri Pasha with another force marched on Belgrade. The akinji, or irregular cavalry, were also separated into two bodies, one to serve as scouts to the main army, the other to make a raid into Transylvania.

Sabač defended itself with fruitless heroism. Ahmed Pasha captured it before Suleiman arrived, and the western flank of Belgrade had been turned. We may follow the events of the next three weeks in excerpts from the diary of the Sultan;

On July 7, came news of the capture of Sabač; a hundred heads of the soldiers of the garrison, who had been unable like the rest to escape by the river, were brought to the Sultan's camp. July 8 these heads are placed on pikes along his route. Ahmed Pasha is admitted, with the Sanjak Beys, to kiss his hand. Suleiman visits the fort, and orders the construction of a bastion with a moat: he also commands that a bridge be built over the Save, so that his army may cross to the northern bank. Suleiman establishes his headquarters in a hut, so as to accelerate the construction of the bridge by his presence. The pashas, armed with sticks, spur on the efforts of the workmen. . . . July 18. Day of rest. The bridge is finished; but the Save is flooded. July 19. The water covers the bridge so that it can no longer be used. Orders to cross by boats. Provisions sent overland to Belgrade. . . . July 29. Suleiman sets forth for Belgrade along the Save. July 31. He arrives before the walls of Belgrade amid the cheers of his army.[5]

The Grand Vizir had already been there for a month, and had captured Semlin; the south side of the Danube was now completely blocked from the westward. Suleiman spent the first of August in surveying the situation; on the second a general assault was launched, but was repulsed with a loss of five or six hundred men. The next day heavy cannon were planted on the island in the Danube, and the city was bombarded from that point. "Five hundred Janissaries," so runs the Sultan's diary, "were ordered to go up the Danube in boats so as to intercept the succors which the Hungarians had promised to send." August 8—like August 8, 1918—was a "black day" for the besieged. A triple attack was delivered. "The enemy," continues the diary, "abandoned the defence of the town and set fire to it; they retired to the citadel." There they held out for three weeks more, but the Hungarians, now reduced to less than half their original num-

[5] Quoted in Hammer, V, 408–410.

ber, had begun to quarrel with the Servian mercenaries; finally, after one of the great towers had been blown up by a mine, the latter forced their masters to surrender on August 28. The Hungarians had been promised that they should have leave to depart unmolested, and the Sultan's diary would lead us to believe that the promise was kept; it seems more probable, however, that most of them were massacred. The Servians, on the other hand, were transplanted to the environs of Constantinople, where they founded a village, called Belgrade, which exists to the present day. In spite of the twenty different attacks which the Turks are said to have delivered, the siege does not seem to have cost them heavily. A number of smaller fortresses, deserted by their garrisons, also fell into the hands of the invaders, while the few troops which the Hungarians had sent to their rescue were forced to remain helpless observers of the disaster they were unable to prevent. Two days after the capitulation, the Sultan went to say his Friday prayers in the lower town, in a church which had been converted into a mosque. The troops were rewarded, an administration was installed, and three thousand Janissaries were left behind as a garrison.

On October 19, Suleiman reëntered Constantinople, where the inhabitants came out, rejoicing, to receive him. During his absence he had lost two infant children, and a third died of the smallpox ten days after his return; but these bereavements were not suffered to interfere with the celebrations of his triumph. His success had already been announced to all the magistrates and governors of his realms, and a special envoy was despatched to the Venetians, who received him on October 28 in solemn audience, and rewarded him with a present of five hundred ducats.[6] The Doge wrote the same day to his ambassador in England to tell him that the Sultan's messenger had also "de-

[6] Marino Sanuto, *Diarii*, vol. XXXII, coll. 68–70, 72–73.

clared that his master had left all his artillery in those parts [i.e., at Belgrade] for the purpose of returning in the spring to follow up the victory. This news is lamentable, and of importance to all Christians." [7]

Thus one of the two great outposts of Christendom had fallen into the hands of the Ottomans. Within a year of his accession the new Sultan had successfully carried through an enterprise in which two of his most distinguished predecessors had failed. The last important barrier had been removed from the Danube route into the northwest.

In 1522 Suleiman undertook and accomplished the corresponding, though far more difficult enterprise on the Mediterranean: the conquest of the island of Rhodes, just off the southwestern corner of Asia Minor. The island is an irregular narrow pointed ellipse, with its axis running from the southwest to the northeast. Forty-nine miles long and twenty-one across at its widest point, it has an area of 564 square miles. A mountain top near the centre rises to more than 4000 feet above the sea. Separated by a channel about seven miles wide from the mainland, it lies some eighty miles from Crete on the one side, and two hundred and fifty from Cyprus on the other. Its sole important town, and the key to the possession of the entire island, was the strongly fortified city of Rhodes, about two miles to the southeast of the extreme north tip, that nearest the mainland. Seventeen minor castles were perched at intervals on the cliffs along the shore; but there was not the remotest chance of their defending themselves if the city of Rhodes should be taken. [8]

[7] *Calendar of State Papers, Venice,* III, 185.

[8] On the topography and monuments of Rhodes see Fradin, Baron de Belabre, *Rhodes of the Knights* (Oxford, 1908), with plans and many unique illustrations from photographs taken by the author; and Albert Gabriel, *La Cité de Rhodes, MCCCX–MDXXII* (Paris, 1921).

During the thirteenth century the island had been a rendezvous of Italian adventurers and Turkish corsairs, but in 1309 it was conquered by the Knights Hospitallers of St. John of Jerusalem, who had been obliged to leave the Holy Land after the fall of Acre in 1291, and had spent the intervening eighteen years in Cyprus. On their arrival at Rhodes, they at once set to work to make it their permanent home. The fortifications of the city, already formidable, were vastly strengthened. Each one of the eight "langues" or companies, into which the Order, according to the languages spoken by its members, was divided, was charged with the duty of defending a portion, or bastion, of the walls. Frenchmen, Germans, Englishmen, Italians, Castilians, and Aragonese and the men of Auvergne and Provence vied with one another to render impregnable the sections committed to their safekeeping. But the Knights were not content with measures of passive defence. They regarded it as their sacred duty to continue the onslaughts of the crusaders, and to attack the Moslem wherever he could be found. During the two centuries after their arrival, they made themselves masters of eight of the adjacent islands and erected a fortress on each of them. They welcomed and aided Christian pirates. When Moslem prisoners were taken, they were usually butchered. In 1320, we are told, 6250 Turkish captives were slaughtered in cold blood; a fanatical Englishwoman on her way to the Holy Land is said to have killed a thousand of them with her own hand.[9] The story is hard to believe, though it is supported by contemporary evidence. In any case it is indicative of the spirit of the times, and we cannot wonder that the Turks regarded the Knights as professional pirates and cutthroats. In the fifteenth century milder counsels had prevailed. The Knights got a foothold on the mainland at Budrun, the ancient Halicarnassus; and it

[9] Belabre, pp. 17–18.

would appear that, despite the continuous clash of arms, there was a certain amount of traffic between them and the Moslems. But the official Ottoman attitude of bitter hostility to the Knights remained unchanged; indeed, in the reign of Selim the Terrible, it was greatly intensified. Their stronghold was directly on the line of communication between the capital of the Empire and its newly acquired province of Egypt.[10] They intercepted the ships from Constantinople to Suez, which carried pious pilgrims to Mecca. Their most recent offence was their support of the rebellion of Ghazali. It was enough to stir the wrath of any good Moslem.

Under all the circumstances Suleiman was in no need of justification for an assault on Rhodes. But it was not an enterprise to be lightly undertaken. The Belgrade campaign in the previous year had shown him, indeed, that effective aid to the garrison was unlikely to arrive from the West. On the other hand the bravery and military skill of the Knights were unquestionable, and their fortifications, already strong, had been strengthened still more since the attack of Mohammed II. In fact Rhodes was probably the strongest of all the fortresses of the early sixteenth century. Opinion in the Divan was sharply divided as to the wisdom of assaulting it again. Some of the older writers on Turkish history, among them the Elizabethan Oxonian Richard Knolles, strive to show that the Sultan sought at once to resolve these doubts and to test the mettle of the Knights by entering into a correspondence with the newly elected Grand Master, Philip Villiers de L'Isle Adam, in the winter of 1521-22. They give us the text of a series of letters which are said to have been exchanged between them, letters which begin on both sides with compliments, congratulations, and boastfulness, and finally terminate

---

[10] Jacobus Fontanus, *De Bello Rhodio Libri Tres* (Roma, 1524), fol. B recto.

with challenges and abuse. But it seems probable that this correspondence is apocryphal.[11] The Sultan fulfilled the obligation, prescribed by the Koran, of summoning his enemy to surrender before he attacked him;[12] but it is doubtful if he did anything more. The considerations which finally determined him to attack were, first, the demands of his favorite corsair, Kurtoglu, who had been roughly handled by the Knights and passionately called for revenge, and, secondly, the information conveyed to him by two spies, a Jewish doctor and the Grand Chancellor of the Order, that Rhodes had not enough provisions or powder, and that there were certain places where the fortifications were in bad repair.

The die was now cast, and both sides prepared with all their might for the impending struggle.

The Grand Master had by this time been considerably strengthened by the arrival of contingents from the different commanderies of his Order in Europe. A larger portion of its forces than ever before were now assembled at Rhodes. He could count on at least 700 Knights, and 4000 to 5000 men-at-arms, besides volunteer battalions of the inhabitants of the town, and a naval brigade of sailors from the fleet. Both of the latter contingents must have been able at least to render good service in defensive construction, and in mining and countermining, even if they could not fight. There was also a valuable body of some 500 archers who had been recently brought over from Crete. The statements of the older historians that the garrison counted only about 5000 men are doubtless an underestimate, though far less in degree than their exaggerations of the numbers of the Turkish forces who attacked them. Particularly useful to the besieged were the services of Martinengo, a Brescian engineer, who on his arrival was

[11] Hammer, V, 27, 415.
[12] *Négociations de la France dans le Levant*, ed. Ernest Charrière (Paris, 1848–60), I, 91–92.

so much impressed by the enthusiasm of the Order that at his request he was admitted to its ranks. All the houses outside the walls were razed to the ground, and their inhabitants with all available foodstuffs were brought into the city. The mouth of the harbor was blocked with massive chains. Two things alone were lacking for a successful defence; first, an adequate supply of powder and ammunition for a protracted siege; secondly, and vastly more important, effective aid from outside, which for six months had been awaited in vain. The moment of Rhodes's peril coincided with that phase of the contest between Charles and Francis in the west which ended in the defeat of the latter at Bicocca (April 27, 1522), but it was obvious that the struggle was soon bound to flare up again. While the Emperor repeatedly expressed his concern over the fate of the Knights he could do nothing for the moment to help them. Pope Adrian VI, the successor of Leo X, declared that the state of his finances made it impossible for him to contribute anything to the aid of the soldiers of Christendom, though he could not speak of the subject without tears. The Venetians, who had never been on very good terms with the Knights, equipped a strong squadron for purposes of observation; for in spite of their friendly relations with the Sultan, they were by no means convinced that the Turks had not designs on Cyprus. They feared that it was

> a pageant
> To keep us in false gaze. When we consider
> Th' importancy of Cyprus to the Turk;
> And let ourselves again but understand,
> That, as it more concerns the Turk than Rhodes,
> So may he with more facile question bear it,
> For that it stands not in such warlike brace,
> But altogether lacks th' abilities
> That Rhodes is drest in; . . . .[13]

[13] *Othello*, Act I, scene 3.

The Venetian fleet, however, had strict orders to avoid any act that might irritate the Turks. As soon as it should become evident that no attack was intended against Venetian territories, it was immediately to return home. Europe still clung to the comfortable belief that, since Rhodes had defended itself successfully before, it could unquestionably do so again.

On June 18 the Ottoman fleet set sail from Constantinople. It seems probable that it numbered about 300 sail, though the estimates vary; it carried 10,000 men, under the orders of the vizir Mustafa Pasha, who had been appointed seraskier, or commander-in-chief of the expedition. The wind was favorable, and five days later the Knights could watch the enemy approach; but, curiously enough they made no effort to prevent a landing; all the defence was concentrated within the city walls. On June 24—the feast of St. John, particularly sacred to the Hospitallers, who possessed precious relics of the Baptist—the Turks began to disembark their troops on the western side of the island,[14] and the Turkish engineers usefully employed the next four weeks in discovering the most advantageous sites for their batteries; not a shot was to be fired until Suleiman himself should arrive. The Sultan had left his capital, two days before the fleet, at the head of an enormous army which he led along the western shores of Asia Minor; it seems safe to estimate its total forces at 100,000 men, though the contemporaneous Christian authorities make it much larger. Its progress was comparatively slow, though Suleiman was encouraged by the receipt of all sorts of good news on the way. Not till July 26 did he reach the port of Marmarice, at the head of the bay opposite Rhodes. Two days later he landed on the island, where he was welcomed by salvos of artillery, and

---

[14] Jacques de Bourbon, *La grande et merveilleuse et très cruelle oppugnation de la noble cité de Rhodes* (Paris, 1527), fol. B ii recto.

established his headquarters on the high hill of San Stefano, overlooking the sea, a little more than a mile distant from the western bastions of the city.[15] The troops he brought with him promptly occupied the positions that had been prepared for them, encircling the fortress to the southward, from sea to sea. His fleet commanded the adjacent waters, and the investment was complete. On July 29, the siege began. It was to last one hundred and forty-five days.

The besieging forces were divided into five great groups or army corps, each under a commander of its own, though all were subject to the general direction of the seraskier, who always kept closely in touch with the Sultan. Beginning on the westward, these army corps were drawn up, respectively, opposite the bastions of France and Germany; of Auvergne, Castile, and Aragon; of England; of Provence; and of Italy. Contemporary authorities estimate them at 50,000 men apiece, which is probably an exaggeration. Moreover, it must always be remembered that the Turkish armies of this period were by no means exclusively composed of fighting men in the literal sense of the word. On this occasion, a very considerable portion of the Sultan's forces was made up of wretched peasants from Bosnia, Bulgaria, and Wallachia, most of them probably Christians, who had been conscripted to perform the thankless and dangerous task of digging trenches and parallels under fire. It was indeed on these unfortunates that the heaviest work devolved; for any hopes that Suleiman may have cherished that the fortress could be speedily taken by assault were rudely shattered in the first days of the siege. From the beginning of August it was plainly evident that persistent and furious bombardment of the walls was the indispensable preliminary to success, and that the cannon and the men to man them would have to be brought close, through ditches dug in the stony soil. The size and num-

[15] "Beyond danger of artillery," says Jacques de Bourbon, fol. B iv verso.

ber of the Turkish artillery were the wonder of all beholders. The "Bastard" Jacques de Bourbon, the best of the contemporaneous authorities, gives a number of interesting details.[16] There were apparently six brass cannon firing stone balls three and a half "palms" [17] in circumference; fifteen iron and bronze guns which threw stone projectiles half as large again; twelve "bombards" firing stones of nine to ten palms, and two others with balls of eleven. We also hear of twelve bronze mortars which threw hollow shot—apparently a sort of primitive shell [18]—over the tops of the walls into the city itself; and there were small guns and "sakers" innumerable. The cannon fired 1713 stone projectiles against the walls during the month of August alone, the mortars 1721. We read, however, in the Sanuto Diaries, that the Knights gave their opponents quite as good as they sent, and their fire must have been rendered terribly effective by the care with which the engineer Martinengo had measured the distances to all potential emplacements before the siege began. But the most important and effective of all the means used by the Turks against the fortress was their mining operations. These could not be employed on any extensive scale till the beginning of September, for it took the besiegers all the month of August to get men enough to the ramparts to burrow under them; the Knights, moreover, under the direction of Martinengo, proved unexpectedly skilful in detecting and foiling the efforts of their foes. Nevertheless, on September 4 and 10 two mines were successfully exploded under the English bastion and brought down considerable

[16] *Oppugnation de Rhodes*, fols. B iv verso—B v recto.

[17] The Roman palm of 8½ inches is doubtless meant, rather than the modern one of 3 or 4.

[18] Jacques de Bourbon, fol. C ii verso, etc. It is probable that these "shells," if they were used at all, were launched from some kind of catapult. The first explosive shells to have been fired from mortars seem to have been invented in 1543. Cf. C. W. C. Oman, *Art of War in the Sixteenth Century*, p. 351.

portions of the wall. On both occasions the Turks attempted to follow up the advantage they had won by launching strong infantry assaults. Though both were repulsed with heavy loss, the Turks were encouraged to continue. Between September 13 and 23, all infantry attacks were indeed countermanded, and the bombardment slackened; but the mining operations were continued with redoubled vigor.

On September 23, a number of the newly established mines were sprung. Those under the Spanish and Italian bastions proved particularly effective; and "from midday to midnight," as the Sultan's journal puts it, "the heralds announced an assault on the next day." The entry conveys no real idea of the extent and magnitude of the ensuing attack, probably because it was destined to be repulsed; but we know that it was delivered on all sides at once, and the Christians estimated the numbers who participated in it—doubtless with the usual exaggeration—at no less than 100,000 men. There were terrific hand-to-hand conflicts, perhaps the most desperate in all the annals of the warfare between Christians and Ottomans. The fighting was especially furious on the Spanish bastion, where the Agha of the Janissaries succeeded temporarily in planting his standard; but in the end the assailants were everywhere driven back. Their losses are said to have reached a total of 15,000 men.[19] A number of the Turkish leaders were demoted, either temporarily or permanently, in consequence of the defeat. Suleiman's diary mentions only one of them—"The Sultan in his anger ordered the arrest of Ayas Pasha" (who commanded the Turkish left), but on the following day there was a Divan, and "Ayas Pasha was reëstablished in his functions."[20] We know, however, that a few days later

[19] Jacobus Fontanus, *Ad Adrianum Pont. M. Epistola missa e Rhodo* (Tubingae, 1523), fol. a iii recto, says 10,000.
[20] Quoted in Hammer, V, 421.

the seraskier Mustapha Pasha was sent off to be governor of Egypt, and was replaced in the chief command by Ahmed Pasha. The admiral of the fleet was also disgraced for having failed to render due support, and we are told that the corsair Kurtoglu, who accompanied him, was bastinadoed and expelled from the forces.

The defeat had been so decisive that the Knights cherished hopes that the Sultan might abandon the siege, but they were doomed to disappointment. Suleiman knew that the eyes of all Europe were on him and that failure would be the worst possible blow to his prestige. To show that he intended to persevere he gave orders that his pavillion be replaced by a building of stone, and sent for the Janissary garrisons in Syria and Mesopotamia to fill his depleted ranks. On the other hand he risked no more general attacks for the time being; in October he resumed mining operations. Whenever these were successful and the walls were breached, he ordered local assaults—as on October 12 against the English bastion, and again on the twenty-ninth against the French one; but each time they were repulsed with heavy loss. On the last day of November another and far greater assault, a veritable storming operation, in fact, was launched in a drenching rain against the Spanish and Italian bastions. It was by far the most serious attack since the great onslaught of September 24; but, like its predecessor, it failed, and cost the Turks upwards of 3000 men. The morale of their soldiers was rapidly deteriorating; they often had to be beaten forward with sticks to the attack. Winter was coming on; their sappers could do nothing with frostbitten fingers; there was always the chance, however remote, that the West might be able to send reenforcements. Of course the Sultan could not think of giving up the great enterprise on which he had staked so much, but he was beginning to hope that he might possibly be able to accomplish his object without further shedding of blood.—Word came to him, also, that the Knights were deeply discouraged. They too had lost heavily; their powder was running ominously short. Information kept reaching the Sultan, sometimes by blunted arrows with messages attached, discharged from the city into the Ottoman camp, sometimes from deserters who dropped from the walls, that the Knights would be willing to consider a surrender on terms satisfactory to themselves. On December 10, the defenders were delighted and amazed to see a white flag, indicative of a desire for parley, hoisted aloft over the Sultan's headquarters. They made haste to respond with another. Shortly afterwards two Turkish emissaries appeared with an official letter from Suleiman, requesting an interview with the Grand Master. The latter replied by despatching a Knight and a burgess of Rhodes to the Sultan's camp to learn what he had to propose.

Suleiman's terms were indeed generous. In return for the surrender and evacuation of Rhodes and the adjacent islands by the Knights, they were to be permitted to depart unmolested, taking with them all their transportable property, and such of the Greek population as desired to accompany them, while those who wished to remain were to be guaranteed undisturbed possession of their houses and property, complete religious liberty, and five years' exemption from tribute. When the Christian envoys returned, with the Sultan's proposals, to the city, the opinion in favor of their acceptance was almost unanimous.[21] Much weight was laid on Martinengo's professional verdict that the fortress was no longer defensible. A three-days' truce was accordingly arranged to settle details, but unfortunately it only served to bring about a reopening of hostilities. The most probable story is that the Grand Master, thinking that it might still be possible to persuade Suleiman to depart with his object

[21] Fontanus, *Ad Adrianum Pont. M. Epistola*, fol. a iii verso.

unachieved, sent two Knights out to the seraskier, bearing
a letter written a half-century earlier by Bayezid II to one
of Villiers de L'Isle Adam's predecessors, in which the
Knights were guaranteed the free possession of Rhodes as
long as the House of Osman should rule over the Turks;
that the seraskier promptly tore the letter in two and
trampled it under foot, cut off the noses and ears of two
soldiers whom he had newly captured, and sent them back
to the Grand Master with a missive of insult and abuse.
In any case, we know that Suleiman at once ordered the
bombardment to be resumed. On December 18 the Turks
broke through the Spanish bastion and established themselves for the first time inside the walls. The garrison had
now reached the limits of its endurance. The prospect of
long continued street-fighting was horrifying, and the
Grand Master finally yielded to the clamor of the citi-
zenry, who dreaded the fate of a town taken by storm.
On December 21, he dispatched a Knight and two bur-
gesses to the Sultan to arrange terms of surrender. The
following is a free translation of the Latin document in
which the ambassador of the Order announced the event
to the government of France:

In the year 1522 from the Virgin birth, and in the papacy
of Adrian VI, Suleiman the Emperor of the Turks, with a
fleet of three hundred ships, and two hundred thousand soldiers, landed at Rhodes on the feast of St. John the Baptist.
He blockaded the city until Christmas day by land and sea,
pushing up to it mines to the number of 52, and throwing in
all day and all night more than 85,000 balls of brass and stone
of stupendous size. He had also assaulted it twenty times, when
P. Villiers de L'Isle Adam, who, though he had received
no supplies or reënforcements, had defended it with a few
Knights with the utmost constancy and courage, and had
killed a hundred and twenty thousand of the enemy, was at
length overcome by time. Suleiman had overthrown the walls;

during forty days he had held the ground of the city for the space of a hundred and fifty paces in depth and width, and though obstinately eager for victory, he nevertheless proposed peace. The Grand Master acted towards him with the utmost prudence and magnanimity, and came to terms of surrender as follows:

"Suleiman stipulates that the Latin and Military Order shall leave the city and island of Rhodes within ten days: they shall withdraw their garrisons everywhere; he agrees that their departure shall be free and safe.

"P. Villiers de L'Isle Adam stipulates, in accordance with the opinion of the Common Council of the Latin Knights and soldiers and of the citizens of Rhodes, that any postponement of their departure shall be in the hands of the Latin and Military Order. On the departure of the Latin and Military Order, they shall have the right to carry away with them arms, weapons, engines of war, and all material of war from the fortresses. Those who remain in Rhodes shall be free from all payment of tribute for five years. They shall have the perpetual right to offer service to Christ; they may build new churches if they please or repair old ones; they shall always be permitted to have the care of their children.

"No one shall be forced to leave Rhodes against his will; and every one, both Latin and Greek, who does not at this time follow the Order, shall have the free and safe right to depart at any time within three years with all his property and household. Ships and supplies are to be furnished as far as Crete for the Order and its followers.

"Suleiman shall solemnly swear, in accordance with the ancestral customs and laws of his country, that these agreements shall forever be maintained, free from treachery or guile." [22]

The account of the siege was biassed and inaccurate, and the terms of the surrender as given were self-contradictory at points; but the Order had certainly put up a

[22] Charrière, I, 92–93.

masterly bit of "face-saving" for the benefit of Western Christendom.

Hostages were exchanged, and the bulk of the Ottoman army was withdrawn from the vicinity of the town; only a small body of the Janissaries was permitted to enter it to take possession. Unfortunately some freshly arrived troops got out of hand, forced their way into the city, profaned the churches and maltreated the inhabitants before order could be restored; but there is no evidence that Suleiman was in any way responsible for these outrages. On Christmas Day he made his own triumphal entry into Rhodes, and thereafter expressed a wish to see the Grand Master, who accordingly waited on him, but was kept for hours in attendance before he was invested with a robe of honor and admitted to the Sultan's presence. When at last the foes were face to face, they gazed at one another for a time in a silence which Suleiman was the first to break. He condoled with his adversary; he assured him that it was the lot of all princes to lose cities and realms, and praised his gallant defence.[23] A week later, on the eve of his departure, when the Grand Master came to kiss the Sultan's hand and offer him a present of four golden vessels, Suleiman assured his favorite, Ibrahim, that "it caused him great sorrow to be obliged to force this Christian in his old age to abandon his home and his belongings." [24]

On January 1, 1523, the Grand Master left Rhodes forever, with the last detachment of the Knights. Only 180 of them in all, and 1500 mercenaries and armed citizens, had survived to make their departure. Before they could reach Crete, a hurricane destroyed several of their smaller vessels, and forced many of the fugitives on the others to throw overboard their few remaining possessions. The governor of Crete received them kindly, and enabled them

[23] Fontanus, *De Bello Rhodio*, fols. K i verso–K ii recto.
[24] Hammer, V, 41.

to continue their journey to Sicily and Rome, where the Order acted as the guard at the conclave which elected Pope Clement VII. For five years more they remained homeless; in 1528, a subsidiary branch of them was established in Tripoli; finally, in 1530, the Emperor granted them the islands of Malta and Gozzo, where we shall hear of them again.[25] Villiers de L'Isle Adam died at Malta in 1534.

Suleiman installed garrisons on Rhodes and the adjacent islands, and also at the continental outpost of the Order at Budrun. On January 6, 1523, he started back to Constantinople. In addition to his conquest of the great fortress, he had succeeded before his departure in getting hold of a son of the celebrated Prince Jem, the brother of Bayezid II, who had become a Christian and lived with the Knights. In accordance with the inexorable custom of the House of Osman, he and his children were promptly put to death. As no mention is made of the prince in the terms of the capitulation, and as it must have been evident that the Sultan would be most anxious to get possession of him, it would appear that the Grand Master had tacitly consented to give him up. If so, it is the only stain on his otherwise noble and heroic conduct. In the meantime formal notification of the great victory had been duly despatched to the chief officers and judges of the Empire, and also to its principal neighbors to the east and the west. Prominent among the congratulations which Suleiman received when he reached his capital at the end of the month were those sent him by the Shah of Persia and the government of Venice. Certainly the Sultan had done enough to shatter the delusions which Europe had fondly cherished two years before. He was not the "gentle lamb" which the Western powers had supposed him to be, but rather a mighty conqueror, who had brilliantly succeeded in two difficult and conspicuous

[25] Cf. R. B. M., III, 295, 343 n.

undertakings which had defied all the efforts of his predecessors.

Rhodes had indeed been won at a frightful cost. Even
if we accept the lowest Christian estimate of the Turkish
losses, we find that they numbered ten times that of the
defenders. Yet there are certain considerations which
should constantly be borne in mind in connection with
this and all the other Turkish military operations, and
especially the Turkish sieges, of the period. They go far
to explain what otherwise would be impossible to account
for. In the first place, the bulk of the Ottoman armies still
consisted of feudal Timariot cavalry, wellnigh useless in
capturing fortresses. Moreover, this cavalry was really
only available during the warmer months of the year. If
they were kept in service till November, their horses died,
and they either mutinied or melted away. In fact, it may
be truthfully said that the entire Turkish army was essentially a summer force. The Sultan usually accompanied
it on its campaigns; and the Sultan, who dominated every
department of the Ottoman state, was obliged to go back,
with his chief ministers, to Constantinople during the
winter months, to deal with the problems of internal government. There appear to have been only three, or at most
four, occasions, during his entire reign, when Suleiman
was absent from the Porte at the Christian New Year.
And when the Sultan returned to his capital, it was cus-
tomary that his household troops should return with him.
Of these the Janissaries were by far the most important,
but the Janissaries, at Suleiman's accession, numbered a
bare 12,000 men. Only a portion of them, moreover, can
have been present at Rhodes. Three thousand, as we have
already seen, had been left to garrison Belgrade; there were
500 more at Cairo; there must also have been small detachments at Constantinople, and in outposts recently con-

quered. What, then, was the Sultan's army composed of, when he landed at Rhodes, in the summer of 1522? A lot of feudal cavalry, whose usefulness steadily diminished; a nucleus of perhaps 8,000 Janissaries; some 30,000 topji, or regularly trained artillerymen; an enormous number of azabs, or lightly armed irregulars, who were only employed in time of war or for such duties as garrison work; and finally the hordes of Christian peasant captives who, as we have already seen, had been conveyed to the scene of action to dig trenches and parallels under fire. These last, and the azabs, were hurled forward in repeated attacks till the trenches were filled with their dead bodies—like the Germans at the Albert Canal in 1940—so that at the right moment the Janissaries might be brought forward to launch the decisive attack. The system was callous and wasteful; but it is difficult to see how Suleiman, in view of the resources at his disposal, could have adopted any other. In any case there can be no doubt that, in the eyes of the Sultan and his people, the glory and profit of the conquest of the "Stronghold of the Hellhounds" far outweighed any sacrifices it may have cost.

❧ IV ❧

Mohács

During the three years that followed the capture of Rhodes, Suleiman was content to rest on his laurels, and we hear little or nothing of the clash of arms. In the annals of the court and administration the most noteworthy incident of this period was the unprecedented rise of Ibrahim Pasha. He was by birth a Christian Greek, the son of a sailor from the town of Parga on the Ionian Sea. As a child he was carried off by pirates and sold to a widow at Magnesia, who had him carefully educated. From her he passed into the hands of Suleiman at the time of the latter's residence there as prince governor, and when his master came to the throne, Ibrahim was at once promoted to the post of grand falconer and chief of the corps of pages. As time went on, the Sultan became more and more attached to him, and heaped on him one mark of distinction after another. The favorite, who was one year older than his master, was handsome, very intelligent, and quick-witted. Besides Turkish, he knew Persian, Greek, and Italian; he played on the viol, and he delighted in the reading of history and romances. In 1523 Piri Pasha, the old Grand Vizir, who had already lost influence because he had opposed the expedition against Rhodes, was dismissed with a pension. The vacant dignity was conferred not, as men had expected, on the next vizir, Ahmed Pasha, who had been seraskier during the latter part of the siege, but on Ibrahim, who was also made beylerbey of Rumelia, that is, the chief governor of European Turkey. He lived

Suleiman Imperator
Silver-point drawing by Albrecht Dürer,
dated 1526
(cf. pp. 295–296)

on terms of the closest intimacy with his sovereign, often eating at the same table, and sleeping in the same tent. On June 22, 1524, he married a sister of the Sultan, and the wedding was celebrated with the utmost magnificence.[1] Too much importance, however, should not be attached to this particular mark of honor, of which there are many instances in Turkish history. Direct connection with the House of Osman was no insurance against danger and disgrace. Indeed, it was only four months later that Suleiman, as we have already seen, commanded the execution of his brother-in-law, the vizir Ferhad Pasha. Another distinction which Ibrahim received at the same time was far more impressive to the Oriental mind. The horse-tail, or old nomad standard (called the bunchuk), was the recognized emblem of dignity in office, and four horse-tails were ordinarily conferred with the rank of Grand Vizir; but Ibrahim, alone of those who filled the post in Ottoman annals, was granted no less than six, only one less than the Sultan himself. Ahmed Pasha could not bear to witness the success of his rival, and obtained for himself the post of governor of Egypt. There he soon rose in vengeful revolt, in the hope of making himself independent sovereign of the land. As Egypt had only recently been conquered, and the Mamelukes had been permitted to retain much power, the danger was serious; but Ahmed's efforts were foiled by a conspiracy among his own followers, and his severed head was sent back to Constantinople. Ibrahim was despatched to Egypt in the autumn of 1524 to restore order, and made his state entry into Cairo in the following March amid celebrations of unprecedented splendor.

[1] The most recent authority on Ibrahim is Hester D. Jenkins, *Ibrahim Pasha* (New York: Columbia University, 1911). The arguments advanced therein (pp. 24–25) to prove that he was a eunuch seem to me wholly unconvincing; on the other hand it must be admitted that marriages of sultanas to eunuchs were not uncommon. Miss Jenkins thinks that "Ibrahim probably married the sister of Suleiman . . ." because "it had never been deemed advisable that the daughters of sultans should have male children."

Meanwhile the Sultan busied himself with the government of his dominions and with the pleasures of the chase, to which at this period of his life he devoted almost as much time as did some of his Christian contemporaries. There is little to note in his relations with foreign powers. In 1521 Venice had obtained from him a valuable treaty, by which all her commercial privileges were maintained, and her bailo or representative at Constantinople was accorded a large measure of jurisdiction over his compatriots and permitted to hold office for three years. The republic, in return, was forced to pay an annual tribute of 10,000 ducats for the island of Cyprus, in recognition of an ancient Egyptian claim, and 500 for Zante. In December, 1523, an embassy arrived at Constantinople from Vassili Ivanovich, the Grand Prince of Moscow. Its object was to renew previous attempts to promote direct trade relations and particularly to induce the Sultan to forbid his vassals the Crimean Tatars from harrying the Muscovite territories; but the ambassador was able only to obtain meaningless expressions of general good will from the Turks, who saw no profit to themselves in granting anything more. In 1525 the truce with Poland was renewed for another seven years. Evidently the vast majority of Suleiman's European neighbors were most anxious to keep the peace. With Persia, on the other hand, it was evident that the wars of Selim's day would sooner or later break forth afresh. When Shah Ismaïl died in 1524, Suleiman sent his successor Tahmasp a letter not of congratulation but of menace, couched in abusive terms of truly Oriental arrogance.[2] Many, in fact, believed that the military preparations which the Sultan had begun to order in the spring of 1525 were intended for a campaign to the eastward.

One of the chief causes that roused Suleiman to fresh military activity was the fractiousness of the Janissaries,

[2] Hammer, V, 63–65.

who rather expected a campaign every three years. It
had taken some time for them to recover from their
losses at Rhodes, but it would seem that Suleiman had
already resolved to increase their numbers. We are told
that the 12,000 whom he had inherited from his father
had been raised to 20,000 by 1530. In any case it is clear
that the entire body, both the veterans and the new recruits, became increasingly restless from inaction, and disgusted by their master's absorption in the pleasures of the
chase. Finally, in March, 1525, they rose in revolt and
plundered the houses of several of the chief officials. Suleiman dauntlessly faced the storm. When some of the muti-
neers forced their way into his presence, he slew three
of them with his own hand; but he was finally forced to
retreat when their comrades aimed their bows at him.[3]
The disturbances were eventually quelled by a mixture
of severity and largesse. The Agha of the Janissaries was
put to death, as were also a number of his subordinates;
others had their pay diminished; but 200,000 ducats were
distributed to appease the soldiery. It was evidently essential that they be given employment as soon as possible.
Ibrahim was recalled from Egypt, and preparations were
made for another great campaign. The direction this new
campaign was to take was probably partly due to French
instigation. This, however, is a story by itself, which it
will be more convenient to postpone till a later page. The
immediately decisive factor was the state of Suleiman's
relations with the kingdom of Hungary and the conditions
that prevailed within it.

Hostilities between Hungary and the Turks had not
ceased after the capture of Belgrade. While the Sultan
was busy in other directions, his border governors continued to harass their enemies and succeeded in taking a
number of fortresses. The victories, it is true, were not

[3] Hammer, V, 62.

all on one side. In 1524 a force of some 15,000 akinji was completely defeated by Paul Tömöri, the warlike archbishop of Kalocsa, who had been given the task of defending the frontiers of his country with the scantiest means. On this occasion the head of the Turkish commander was sent to Buda, where it was received with jubilation. In the following year Christopher Frangipani, a Hungarian noble descended from a well known Italian family which had immigrated thither many generations earlier, contrived to relieve the fortress of Jajce in Northern Bosnia, which had been besieged for some time and was in great straits. Suleiman needed no excuse for any declaration of war when he should choose to reopen the campaign. We can scarcely believe that the envoy whom he despatched to Buda in 1525 really expressed any earnest desire for peace. At any rate the Hungarians regarded him rather as a spy than as an ambassador and speedily sent him back; indeed, in the previous year, if we can trust one report that has come down to us, it would seem that the Sultan had already given them warning that he soon intended to make a fresh invasion. He was well informed of the hopeless confusion that reigned within their borders, and of the unlikelihood of their being rescued in their extremity by the West. Not only was there adequate excuse for an attack on Hungary; there was every probability that it would prove successful.

A great surge of patriotic enthusiasm had swept over the Hungarian kingdom when the loss of Belgrade was made known. At the next meeting of the Diet stern measures were taken to punish the cowards and the negligent, and enormous taxes were voted to pay for large forces of foreign mercenaries, whose aid was now recognized to be indispensable to the defence of the realm. It was one thing, however, to vote taxes, and quite another to collect them. The wave of Christian fervor which had been evoked by the fall of Belgrade proved as evanescent as it had been intense, and almost no money came in. Hungary was divided between two factions: the "Court party," of the king and most of the magnates, and the "national party," supported by the mass of the lesser nobility, and led by John Zápolya, the almost independent voivode of Transylvania. King Louis, when he grew old enough to exercise royal authority, showed himself good natured, weak, and pleasure-loving, but in no way the man for such a crisis. On the eve of the Turkish invasion he was in the habit of rising at noon and spending the rest of the day in hunting. His wife Maria, the sister of Charles V and Ferdinand, was more energetic, but over-fond of the festivities to which all the money that could be had was devoted; moreover she and her German favorites were generally disliked as foreigners. Tömöri was thus left to defend the frontiers as best he could. His few soldiers were continually on the verge of mutiny for lack of pay. Indeed, had it not been for timely contributions from the Pope, he could hardly have held his ground at all. As it was, he repeatedly asked to be relieved of his office. Obviously the Hungarians would be unable to defend themselves alone, and those who realized it clung blindly to the hope of foreign aid.

Long and bitter experience should have taught them the futility of this. Everyone recognized their need and expressed his sympathy, but all had their own interests to look after first. Poland and Venice were quite unwilling to run any risk of turning the Turkish arms against themselves; they were too near. Henry VIII of England, on the other hand, was too far off. He appears to have promised funds, though it is doubtful if he ever sent them. Francis I, since the battle of Pavia, had completely reversed the traditional policy of his country, and was justly suspected of being in alliance with the Sultan. Pope Clement VII alone bestirred himself actively. He had already aided the Hungarians with money, and now he sent them 50,000 ducats, the distribution of which was superintended by a zealous papal legate; but even Clement at this juncture was much more anxious to curb the Hapsburg power in the West than to defend the Danube lands against the Turk. There remained the two Hapsburg brothers, Charles and Ferdinand, whose interest in aiding Hungary was more immediate than that of any one else. Charles V had always recognized that one of the first of his many duties as the temporal head of Christendom was that of protecting it against the onslaught of Islam. At the time of the siege of Rhodes, when Pope Adrian VI had urged him to make peace with Francis in order that they might march together against the Moslems, he had always replied that before he could devote his energies to the protection of Christendom, which he constantly maintained to be his chief desire, it was essential for him to gain the victory over his Western rival. Since then fortune had favored him. In Spain, where he was now residing, all opposition had been crushed. In the Empire his brother Ferdinand was acting as his vicar. In Italy, his generals had won for him at Pavia (February 25, 1525) the most brilliant victory of the age. His defeated adversary, Francis I, had been sent a prisoner to Madrid, and had been obliged, before he was set free, to consent to a humiliating treaty (January 14, 1526) in which he conceded virtually everything which his victorious rival demanded. Yet Charles's path was still beset with difficulties. In spite of his continually increasing revenues from Mexico, he was always in financial straits. Francis had hardly got back to his own country before he broke the treaty which had been extorted from him in his captivity, and the next result of the Emperor's successes was the formation of the powerful League of Cognac between France, the Papacy, and the Italian states, to liberate Italy from his tutelage and reëstablish the balance of power. In view of all these circumstances, and of the fact that he himself could not venture to depart from Spain, Charles felt that he must leave the question of helping the Hungarians to his brother Ferdinand and to the Empire, which was directly menaced.

In Germany, as was usual at that time, much was said and little done. The Emperor had offered to devote a grant of 20,000 infantry and 4,000 horse, which had been voted him at Worms, to a war against the Turks; but the ensuing Diets at Nuremberg (1522 and 1524) had reduced this quota to 6,000 men; and these, since the Turks did not then seem to be threatening, were never raised. Ferdinand was zealous in the good cause, and as active as circumstances would permit. Not content with continually urging others to bestir themselves, he asked leave to garrison the Hungarian province of Croatia with his own troops. As the Hungarian Diet refused to listen to this request, he negotiated directly with the Croatian nobles, and in February, 1526, the Estates of the province formally put themselves under his protection. As they had given up the hope of being defended by the kingdom to which they belonged, they decided at the critical moment to contribute nothing to its defence. The Empire was in no position to come to the rescue. Charles was absent; the Council of Regency commanded little respect; and the country was fiercely agitated by the religious question. So far the decrees of the Diet of Worms against Luther had not been, and as yet could not be, enforced; but neither side felt confident of the future, and both Romanists and Lutherans were forming leagues to strengthen themselves. Worse still was the fact that many of the new faith looked askance at a crusade against the Turks, because it had been instigated by, and promised to redound to the advantage of, the Papacy. Some years before, Luther had declared that "to fight against the Turks is to resist the Lord, who visits our sins with such rods." These words, already condemned in a bull of Leo X, had been widely repeated; and, taken literally by some, had damaged the Reformer's cause.[4] In 1522–23 the western part of the Empire had been shaken by the struggle between Sickingen and his knights with the archbishop of Treves and his allies. In the following two years the terrible Peasants' War devastated Swabia and Franconia. When, therefore, the Diet of Spires met in 1526, it had many problems to consider. Among them was the report that the Ottoman armies were actually on the march. If help were to be given, there was not a moment to lose; and so the Diet after due deliberation voted to send an embassy to Buda, to inquire into the state of affairs and to report thereon. The vote was proclaimed on the day before the battle of Mohács, which sealed the fate of the Hungarian nation.

During the autumn of 1525 Suleiman had discussed with his counsellors the possibilities of a second invasion up the Danube. False rumors reached Ferdinand that the Sultan had decided on a campaign against the capital city of Buda-Pesth. There was also talk of an expedition through Transylvania, with the aid of Wallachian vassal troops, but it was rejected on account of the difficulty of crossing the Carpathians. Instead it was thought wiser to follow the line of the Danube, along which supplies could be carried on boats. Most of the country to be traversed was flat, and though bridges over two large rivers, the Save and the Drave, would have to be built, it was probable that the first and larger of these could be constructed beforehand under the protection of the garrison of Belgrade. On December 1, a call to arms was issued, and the winter was spent in military preparations.

[4] The sixteenth and seventeenth centuries have a considerable literature of theological speculation on the relation between the Turkish Empire and the Book of Revelation. Cf. e.g. Joseph Mede, *Opera* (London, 1672), pp. 472–476; also Massachusetts Historical Society, *Collections;* Fourth Series, VIII (1868), 48–49, 371–372, 675.

On Monday (reckoned a lucky day) the twenty-third of April, 1526, Suleiman, accompanied by Ibrahim and two other vizirs, left Constantinople at the head of more than 100,000 men with 300 cannon. The Sultan's diary gives many details of the advance, which continued for more than eighty days before contact was established with the enemy. There were torrential rains and swollen streams; the current in the Danube was so strong that the Turkish river fleet of some eight hundred boats found it almost impossible to keep abreast of the army. Nevertheless the strictest discipline was maintained. Soldiers were executed for treading down the young crops, or even letting their horses graze on them; and the Sultan was encouraged by the constant arrival of reënforcements. But the thing that stands out above everything else in this portion of Suleiman's own record is the prominence and implicit approval accorded to the Grand Vizir. The egotism which is elsewhere so prominent is here overshadowed by the Sultan's affection for and confidence in his new favorite. Certainly Ibrahim was a tower of strength. At every difficult point he was sent ahead to prepare the way. When the army reached Belgrade it found a bridge already constructed for it across the Save. Tömöri, who had already withdrawn the greater part of his few troops from the river, finally retired to the north bank of the Danube. A garrison of about 1,000 men, however, had been left in the town and fortress of Peterwardein, which lies on the south bank of the Danube, about midway between the mouths of the Save and the Drave. This garrison offered the Turkish army the first serious opposition it encountered. But it was all in vain. On July 12 Ibrahim reached the outskirts of Peterwardein; three days later he took the town by storm. The citadel proved a more difficult problem, and had to be bombarded for several days before it was attacked; but on the 27th, so runs the Sultan's diary, "two mines open a breach in the walls of the citadel; it is taken by assault; only twenty-five (of our) men killed. The Grand Vizir has 500 soldiers of the garrison decapitated; 300 others are sent off to slavery." [5] A force despatched across the Danube in boats obliged Tömöri, after a day's skirmishing, to retire still further to the west.

The two middle weeks of August were the really critical period of the campaign. The Hungarian king, council, magnates, and generals had been wrangling at Buda and Tolna over the question of the defence of the realm; while Tömöri, from across the Danube, kept sending them messages of the continued advance of the Turks which he was impotent to impede. The obvious thing for the Hungarians to do was, of course, to move southward and defend the strong line of the Drave, but petty jealousies prevented this. The most they would consent to do was to advance to the plain of Mohács, on the west side of the Danube, some thirty miles to the north of the point where the Drave unites with it.[6] The inhabitants of Esseg, on the south bank of the Drave, realized that they had been abandoned, and made haste to send the keys of their town to the Sultan, in token of submission, as he slowly approached in a driving rain. When Suleiman reached the Drave, he could scarcely believe his eyes when he found that its northern bank had been left undefended, but he was prompt to avail himself of a God-given opportunity. On August 15 he "gave orders to throw a bridge of boats across this river and personally supervised the work." [7] As the Turkish historian Kemal Pasha Zadeh rapturously declares, "They set to work without delay to get together the materials necessary for

[5] Quoted in Hammer, V, 437.

[6] István Brodarics, "Clades in Campo Mohacz," in Simon Schard, ed., *Historicum Opus* (Basileae, 1574), II, 1185–86. The "Clades" is printed also in Antonio Bonfini's *Rerum Ungaricarum Decades Quatuor cum Dimidia* (Francofurti, 1581), pp. 757–774.

[7] Quoted in Hammer, V, 438.

this enterprise. All the people expert in such matters thought that the construction of such a bridge would take at least three months, but yet, thanks to the skilful arrangements and the intelligent zeal of the Grand Vizir, it was finished in the space of three days." [8] (The Sultan's diary makes it five.) After the army had crossed over, Esseg was burned and the bridge destroyed. It was a bold step to take; for though the invaders were thereby partially protected from the arrival of Hungarian reënforcements from Croatia, they were also deprived of all means of escape in case of defeat by their Christian foes. To quote Kemal again: "When the army had passed the Drave, the Pasha of profound conceptions thought that the best course to follow was to destroy the bridge, in order that, all other means of safety being intercepted, his soldiers should remain firmly and immovably on the field of combat, and that the idea of flight not presenting itself to their minds, the possibility of retreat should not even show itself in the mirror of their imagination struck with fear." [9]—Almost precisely seven years earlier Hernando Cortés, on the opposite side of the globe, in his campaign against the Mexican Aztecs, had taken a similarly desperate course when he scuttled his ships in the harbor of Vera Cruz.

Meantime the Hungarians were slowly assembling on the plain of Mohács. King Louis had a bare 4,000 men with him when he arrived there; but fresh detachments came continually dribbling in, and others were known to be rapidly approaching. But they were a motley host, whose mutual jealousies made it wellnigh impossible for them effectively to combine. There was much difficulty over the choice of a commander-in-chief. King Louis was

[8] Kemal Pasha Zadeh, *Histoire de la campagne de Mohacz*, tr. and ed. by A. J. B. Pavet de Courteille (Paris, 1859), p. 74.
[9] Kemal Pasha Zadeh, p. 79.

obviously unequal to the task; the Palatine Stephen Báthory had the gout; and so it was finally decided to give the place to Archbishop Tömöri, the memory of whose past successes in border warfare against the Moslems was enough to stifle his own protestations that he was not the man for the task.[10] Soon after his appointment, and when the Turks had already crossed the Drave, the Hungarians held a council of war to determine the strategy most expedient for them to adopt. The more cautious of them advocated a retreat toward Buda-Pesth; then the Turks would have no choice but to follow, for Buda was their announced objective and they were staking everything on success. Every day's march forward would take them further from their base, while the Hungarians if they retired would be sure to be joined by reënforcements. John Zápolya was but a few days distant with 15,000 to 20,000 men; John Frangipani was coming up from Croatia; the Bohemian contingent, 16,000 strong, was already on the western frontier of the realm. But unfortunately the bulk of the Hungarians, including Tömöri himself, refused to listen to such reasoning as this. They were filled with an insane overconfidence.[11] The gallant but rash and turbulent Magyar nobility clamored for an immediate fight. They distrusted the king. Many of them were hostile to Zápolya, and unwilling to have him share in the glory of the victory which they believed certain. It was accordingly decided to give battle at once; and the Hungarians, who could choose their own ground, elected to remain on the plain of Mohács, in a place which would give them full play for their cavalry. Apparently they forgot that the enemy, whose horsemen were much more numerous than their own, would derive even greater advantage from the position they had chosen.

The relative size of the two armies which were about

[10] Joannes Cuspinianus, *Oratio Protreptica* (Viennae, n.d.), fol. A iv verso.　　　[11] Brodarics, p. 1187.

to encounter one another has been a fertile source of discussion ever since. One thing only is certain; the contemporaneous estimates on both sides are ridiculously exaggerated. Tömöri told King Louis, on the eve of the battle, that the Sultan had perhaps 300,000 men; but that there was no reason to be frightened by this figure, since most of the Turks were cowardly rabble, and their picked fighting-men numbered only 70,000! [12] Even if we accept the statement that Suleiman left Constantinople at the head of 100,000 men, we must remember that less than one-half of them were troops of the line. It seems likely that his losses through skirmishing and bad weather, as he advanced, must have more than counterbalanced his gains through reënforcements received along the route. If we put the Janissaries at 8,000, the regular cavalry of the bodyguard at 7,000, the Asiatic feudal cavalry at 10,000, the European at 15,000, and the miscellaneous levies at 5,000, we get a total of 45,000 Turkish fighting troops, besides the irregular and lightly armed akinji, possibly 10,000 to 20,000, who hovered about the battlefield but were never expected to stand the charge of regular soldiers. It is also very doubtful if Suleiman still had anywhere near the 300 cannon with which he is said to have left Constantinople in the previous April.

The actual size of the Hungarian army is almost equally difficult to estimate—principally because of the reënforcements which continued to arrive until the day of the fight. In the grandiloquent letter which the Sultan despatched a few days after the battle to announce his victory to the heads of his different provinces, he puts the number of his Christian foes at approximately 150,000, but it seems probable that the true figures were less than one-fifth as large: perhaps 25,000 to 28,000 men,[13] about equally divided

[12] Brodarics, p. 1188.
[13] Cuspinianus says King Louis was reported to have 30,000 cavalry (*Oratio Protreptica,* fol. A iv verso).

between cavalry and infantry, and 80 guns. Part of these troops were well drilled professional soldiers, many of them Germans, Poles, and Bohemians; there was also the Hungarian national cavalry, made up of the brave but utterly undisciplined nobles. And they had, besides, large numbers of heavy-armored wagons, which could be chained together to make rough fortifications, or even pushed forward, like the modern tank, to pave the way for an infantry or a cavalry charge. It was originally a Bohemian device developed a century before, from classical prototypes, by the Hussite general John Ziska, but it was more valuable for defence than offence. When one of the Polish mercenaries advised the Hungarians to intrench themselves behind a rampart of these wagons and await the enemy's attack, they scornfully refused. Francis Perényi, the witty bishop of Grosswardein, when he found that all counsels of caution had been rejected, is said to have predicted that "the Hungarian nation will have 20,-000 martyrs on the day of battle, and it would be well to have them canonized by the Pope."[14] The prophecy proved all too true.

The plain of Mohács, some six miles in length, is bounded on the east by the Danube. At the northern end is the town, while to the south and west there is a line of low hills, then covered with woods, which furnished an admirable screen for the Turkish advance. Apparently neither side expected a combat till well after noon of the day on which it occurred, and actual fighting did not begin till after three. The story of the details of the battle itself varies widely in the different contemporaneous accounts that have come down to us, but the main outlines seem reasonably clear. The combat opened with a tre-

[14] A. Vámbéry, *Hungary*, p. 287; Brodarics, pp. 1188–89. The figure here in Brodarics, alike in the edition of 1574 and that of 1581, is 2000, which is an obvious misprint. Brodarics adds, "the army did not yet exceed this number."

mendous charge of the heavy-armed Hungarian cavalry against the centre of the Turkish line emerging from the woods. It pierced the opposing ranks, and soon after appeared to be so decisively successful that orders were given for a general advance of all the Hungarian forces. But the Turkish centre had been withdrawn on purpose, in order to lure their enemies on to their destruction. By the time they had reached the Janissaries and the Sultan's standard, they were held up. There were furious hand-to-hand combats between the Christian leaders and the members of Suleiman's bodyguard; at one moment Suleiman himself was in grave danger. But the Turkish artillery was far more skilfully handled than that of their opponents; [15] the Hungarians were mowed down in droves; most important of all, the concentration of the Christians in the centre gave their numerous foes a splendid opportunity, of which they were prompt to take advantage, to outflank their enemies, particularly on the westward. Within an hour and a half, the fate of the battle had been decided. The Hungarians fled in wild disorder to the north and east. Such, apparently, are the principal facts. But as we are following the story of the battle from the Turkish standpoint, it will be worth while to supplement these data by a few passages from the history of Kemal Pasha. He gives Ibrahim all the credit for the feint by which the Christians were enticed to disaster: "The young lion," he declares, "no matter how brave, should remember the wisdom and experience of the old wolf.[16] . . . When the Grand Vizir seized his redoubtable sword, ready to enter the lists, he looked like the sun, which sheds its rays on the universe. In combat, he was a youth, ardent as the springtime: in council, he was an old man, as ex-

[15] Cuspinianus, fol. B recto, speaks of the lack of expert direction for the Hungarian artillery.
[16] Kemal Pasha Zadeh, p. 84.

perienced as Fortune in numerous vicissitudes." [17] When the battle began, he continues, "the air was rent with the wind of the fury of the combatants; the standards shone forth in the distance; the drums sounded like thunder, and swords flashed like the lightning. . . . While the faces of the miserable infidels grew pale and withered before they felt the flame of the blades . . . the cheeks of our heroes, drunk with lust for combat, were tinged with the color of roses.[18] . . . With all these murderous swords stretched out to lay hold on the garment of life, the plain seemed like a fiend with a thousand arms; with all these pointed lances, eager to catch the bird of life in the midst of slaughter, the battlefield resembled a dragon with a thousand heads." [19] And then, when the rout began, he concludes: "At the order of the Sultan the fusiliers of the Janissaries, directing their blows against the cruel panthers who opposed us, caused hundreds, or rather thousands of them, in the space of a moment, to descend into the depths of Hell." [20]

The slaughter which followed the battle was indeed fearful. The Turks took no prisoners, and few of the defeated escaped. The Sultan's diary is even more than usually laconic. For August 31 it reads "The Emperor, seated on a golden throne, receives the homage of the vizirs and the beys: massacre of 2000 prisoners: the rain falls in torrents"; and for September 2; "Rest at Mohács; 20,000 Hungarian infantry and 4000 of their cavalry are buried." [21] On this occasion his figures seem to be corroborated, in round numbers at least, by the Christian accounts of the disaster. Mohács indeed was the "tombeau de la nation hongroise"; never has a single battle proved so fatal to the life of a people. In addition to the annihilation of

[17] Kemal Pasha Zadeh, p. 82.
[18] Kemal Pasha Zadeh, p. 88.
[19] Kemal Pasha Zadeh, p. 90.
[20] Kemal Pasha Zadeh, p. 97.
[21] Quoted in Hammer, V, 439.

its army, almost all of its leaders had perished. King Louis, after fighting bravely, turned to flee when all was lost, but his horse, in trying to climb the steep bank of a small stream, fell backwards into the waters below and buried his rider under him. Tömöri and his second in command were also killed, together with two archbishops, five bishops, many magnates, and the greater part of the Hungarian aristocracy; the flower of the nation, both lay and clerical, had been sacrificed on the fatal day. Suleiman's announcement of his victory to his governors is couched in more expansive language than is his diary, but the impression conveyed in the following sentences from it is substantially correct, as seen from the standpoint of the Turks. "Thanks be to the Most High! The banners of Islam have been victorious, and the enemies of the doctrine of the Lord of Mankind have been driven from their country and overwhelmed. Thus God's grace has granted my glorious armies a triumph, such as was never equalled by any illustrious Sultan, all-powerful Khan, or even by the companions of the Prophet. What was left of the nation of impious men has been extirpated! Praise be to God, the Master of Worlds!" [22]

After Mohács organized resistance practically ceased. On the day following the battle John Zápolya with his army reached the left bank of the Danube; but he made haste to withdraw as soon as he learned of the catastrophe. On September third the Ottoman army resumed its advance; on the tenth it entered Buda. Apparently the keys of the town had been sent out in advance to Suleiman in token of submission by those who had been unable to flee (Kemal Pasha assures us that only "humble folk" had remained within the walls),[23] and the Sultan, in return

[22] Kemal Pasha Zadeh, p. 152. The last two sentences are from the Koran, sura vi, verse 45.
[23] Kemal Pasha Zadeh, p. 108.

promised them that they should be spared the horrors of a sack. But his troops got out of hand, and he was unable to keep his word. As his diary tersely puts it (September 14), "A fire breaks out in Buda, despite the efforts of the Sultan: the Grand Vizir seeks in vain to extinguish it": [24] as a matter of fact the entire city was burnt to the ground with the exception of the royal castle, where Suleiman himself had taken up his residence. There the Sultan found many treasures which he carried back with him to Constantinople: especially the great library of Matthias Corvinus, one of the most celebrated in Europe, and three bronze statues from Italy, representing Hercules, Diana, and Apollo. But the trophy which appealed most strongly to the Ottoman imagination was two huge cannon which Mohammed II had been obliged to abandon on the occasion of his unsuccessful siege of Belgrade in 1456. They had apparently been exhibited at Buda for years past as a proof of Hungarian valor, and the Turks were overjoyed to be able to take them back to the Porte.[25] We also read of the Sultan's delight in the pleasures of hunting and falconry in the royal preserves, and of music and feasting in the royal palace.[26] Meantime the akinji had spread out in every direction, plundering, burning, and murdering even beyond the Hungarian border into Austria; the Sultan's diary expressly states that he had forbidden them to do so,[27] but he apparently made no effort to give effect to his commands. In the midst of the celebrations of his victory he was seriously considering the question of the disposition he should make of the prize that he had won.

There can be little doubt that it was generally expected that he would occupy and garrison all the territory he had gained, and add it to his empire, like Belgrade and Rhodes;

[24] Quoted in Hammer, V, 440.
[25] Kemal Pasha Zadeh, pp. 109–113.
[26] Hammer, V, 440; Kemal Pasha Zadeh, pp. 115–116.
[27] Quoted in Hammer, V, 440.

and it is significant that Kemal Pasha takes so much trouble and space to explain why he decided not to do so. But there were plenty of good reasons why he should rest content, for the time being at least, with the great victory he had won and the terrible destruction he had wrought. His army had suffered cruelly from the wet weather; it was, as we have already pointed out, essentially a summer force, and winter was approaching fast. Buda was much farther from Constantinople than Belgrade, and just so much nearer the lands of his foes. It would need a stronger garrison to hold it than he could well afford. John Zápolya was at large, with a considerable force; in fact, he occupied Buda shortly after Suleiman left it. The Sultan's presence was urgently demanded at Constantinople, and there were rumblings of rebellion in Asia Minor. On the whole it seemed wiser to be satisfied with what had already been achieved. To quote Kemal again, "The time when this province should be annexed to the possessions of Islam had not yet arrived, nor the day come when the heroes of the Holy War should honor the rebel plains with their presence. The matter was therefore postponed to a more suitable occasion, and heed was given to the sage advice; 'When thou wouldst enter, think first how thou wilt get out again.' "[28]

On September 13, accordingly, the Sultan ordered the construction of a bridge of boats across the Danube from Buda to Pesth, and seven days later the vanguard of the Turkish army passed across it. On the night of the twenty-third the bridge apparently broke into three parts, two of which were swept away, so that the last detachments had to be ferried over in boats.[29] The next day Pesth was burnt, and on the morrow the Ottoman army started homeward, keeping for a time on the left bank of the river, in order

[28] Kemal Pasha Zadeh, p. 131.
[29] Hammer, V, 440.

to lay waste fresh territory. There was apparently great shortage of provisions, and sometimes the inhabitants would gather to defend their homes. On these occasions they were invariably slaughtered in the end, though once it would appear that their resistance was sufficient to cause the Turks to lose almost as many men as they had at Mohács. Opposite Peterwardein the Sultan recrossed the river and struck his old line of march back to Constantinople, which he entered in triumph on November 13. He had been absent less than seven months. "After the pearl of the sea of glory had been replaced in the treasure-box of happiness, and the shining star of the skies of power had returned to the constellation of nobility, the Sultan of the world found repose in delicious sojourning in his palace. May the friends of his authority be always happy, and the foes of his empire defeated! May his banners float victorious until the day of the Resurrection, and his armies continue to triumph until the sounding of the last trump! May God always protect the edifice of his greatness!"[30]

[30] Kemal Pasha Zadeh, p. 143.

∾ V ∾

The Siege of Vienna and Its Aftermath

The first six years of the rule of Suleiman had seen him win an uninterrupted series of notable victories. Indeed his triumphant return after Mohács marks in some respects the climax of his whole reign. So far it had proved impossible to defeat him. During the next six years he was to extend his offensive still farther into Christian territory, but he was also to experience his first serious reverses.

In the year following his return from Mohács, his chief immediate care was the suppression of two insurrections in Asia Minor. The first, in Cilicia, was put down by the local authorities.[1] The second, in Karamania and the districts to the east of it, was more serious; and Ibrahim had to be despatched with a force of Janissaries to insure the final defeat of the rebels in June, 1527.[2] Meantime the Sultan had remained at Constantinople; partly, perhaps, because he did not wish to lower his own prestige in the eyes of his subjects by seeming to be obliged to deal personally with revolts; but more probably because he was principally interested in the course of events in Hungary. He could not fail to recognize that the mass of his subjects were disappointed that he had not annexed his recent conquests there to his own dominions. The fact that his border governors had followed up his victory by capturing Yaicze and Banialuka—two advanced outposts which the Hungarians had held inside the Bosnian frontier since the time

---

[1] Hammer, V, 92–93.   [2] Hammer, V, 93–97.

of Matthias Corvinus—seemed to beckon him on to fresh activity on the Danube.[3] And, finally, a golden opportunity was offered him by the state of affairs in Hungary itself.

When Louis of Bohemia and Hungary fell, childless, on the plain of Mohács, his two kingdoms were left without a sovereign. The question of the succession to the vacant thrones affected all Europe. The obvious candidate for both places was Ferdinand of Hapsburg, Archduke of Austria, brother and imperial vicar of the Emperor Charles V, whose ancestral domains bordered Hungary on the west. Moreover Ferdinand, as we have already seen, was doubly brother-in-law to Louis, and there were former treaties between the two houses which gave him strong claims to the succession. In September, 1526, he hurried to Linz to direct his candidacy for the two monarchies which had so suddenly been laid vacant.[4]

In Bohemia his success was surprisingly prompt. His reputation as a ruler was not good; his sister was unpopular; there were a number of other candidates in the field, and the Bohemian nobles totally refused to recognize that any one had any rights whatsoever to the crown, which they declared to be elective under any terms they should decide to impose. But the Austrian agents met all these difficulties with ready skill. They ceased to claim, and hastened to promise. Bribery was also employed with gratifying results, and the archduke was finally proclaimed king on October 24.[5] But Hungary proved a far more difficult problem. Here Ferdinand had a competitor who

[3] Iorga, II, 405; Hammer, V, 102.

[4] *Urbunden und Actenstücke zur Geschichte der Verhältnisse zwischen Österreich, Ungarn und der Pforte im XVI. und XVII. Jahrhunderte,* ed. Anton von Gévay, 11 pts. in 3 vols. (Vienna, 1838–42), Vol. I, pt. 1, pp. 11–21.

[5] Franz Bernhard, Ritter von Bucholtz, *Geschichte der Regierung, Ferdinand des Ersten,* 9 vols. (Vienna, 1831–38), II, 395–425.

was not only in the field but also already the master of the greater part of it. Even during the lifetime of King Louis, John Zápolya, the powerful voivode of Transylvania, had been accused of aspiring to the crown, and now the opportunity for which he had longed seemed at last to be within his grasp. He had been the leader of the party opposed to the Court. Most of his chief opponents had perished at Mohács; he was now left in command of the only considerable force of Hungarian troops that still remained in the field. Above all, he could count on the deep national dislike of Germans, and could appeal to a law which had been passed in 1505 excluding all foreigners from the Hungarian throne. Against Zápolya Ferdinand had the able assistance of his sister, the widowed queen, who refused to preserve her own position by accepting his rival's proposal of marriage. He also had the support of the only official who had the legal right to summon the Diet, the Palatine Stephen Báthori, one of the few survivors of Mohács, and an old enemy of the voivode. All this, however, counted for little against the strength of the Transylvanian opposition. A Diet met at Stuhlweissenburg. The Palatine was not present. Zápolya was elected king and crowned on November 10; an envoy sent to protest was nearly murdered. It was in vain that in the following month a rival Diet elected Ferdinand.[6] Zápolya entered Buda in triumph. England and Venice recognized him, France seemed eager to support him, and the Pope gave him words of encouragement. He was master of nine-tenths of the kingdom; Frangipani brought him the allegiance of Slavonia, and a vigorous thrust at that moment would unquestionably have driven Ferdinand out of the country.

A year later, however, the whole situation had been reversed; for Zápolya was not the man to take advantage

[6] Bucholtz, III, 178–184.

of the position he had won. He was persuaded by the
king of Poland to accept a six months' truce with his
adversary, from which he had everything to lose and
nothing to gain. All negotiations, of course, failed. The
voivode disappointed his adherents by his failure to make
any effective military preparations, while Ferdinand, who
had plenty of the traditional Hapsburg virtue of tenacity,
collected a small but efficient body of regular soldiers.
When his commanders took the field, they had a bare
11,000 men, but they captured one town after another
with surprising ease. Nowhere was any real resistance
offered. Frangipani was killed by a stray shot, and the
Hungarian nobles flocked to make their peace with the
conqueror. Zápolya's forces were worsted in a battle near
Tokay on September 26, 1527. He fled into Transylvania,
but even there the people turned against him. Once more
defeated by the Austrian commanders, he finally took
refuge in Poland. On October 7, Ferdinand, in his turn,
was chosen king of Hungary at Buda, and was crowned
at Stuhlweissenburg on November 3.[7] By the end of the
year he was undisputed master of the greater part of the
kingdom. The old Hapsburg dream of a great Central
European state, created by the union of Austria, Bohemia,
and Hungary, seemed about to be realized.

Whether Ferdinand would be able to maintain himself
in his newly acquired territories was another question, for
the time was ripe for the arrival of *un troisième larron*.
To such desperate straits had the voivode been reduced
that he appealed for aid to the enemy of Christendom.
Hieronymus Laski, a Polish nobleman of high rank, who
had already had diplomatic experience at the Porte in the
service of his own sovereign, volunteered to try to obtain
it for him, and arrived at Constantinople on December 22.[8]

[7] Bucholtz, III, 187–212.
[8] Heinrich Kretschmayr, "Ludovico Gritti," in *Archiv für österreichische
Geschichte*, vol. LXXXIII, 1 (1896), p. 14.

Laski's first interviews with the lesser vizirs were not encouraging. The Sultan's ministers, like their master, were riding the high horse, and took pains to let the envoy know it. "You have come," he was told, "too late; if you wished to be pleasing in our eyes, you should have come before the coronation of your king. How did your lord dare enter Buda, a place where the horse-hoofs of our Emperor have trod? . . . It is our law that where once the head of his horse has entered, that place by perpetual title is to be regarded as belonging to our master. . . . Brother, you have come as if from a servant; if you have not brought tribute, there is no use in talking any longer." [9] Clearly another means of approach must be found, and Laski obtained it by bribing a brilliant Venetian named Ludovico Gritti.[10] The latter was the bastard son of a former bailo at the Porte who had been made Doge of Venice in 1523. Born in Constantinople in 1480, Ludovico had been taken back by his father to Venice in 1496, and had been given an excellent education in the Italy of the High Renaissance. Since his illegitimate birth debarred him from employment by the Venetian government, he returned in 1507 to his native city, where he speedily made a great name for himself in the world of commerce. At the time of Suleiman's accession he occupied a unique position. He had a magnificent establishment, and gave sumptuous entertainments; he was one of the few whom distinguished visitors at Constantinople "had got to see." He also kept a foot in the Venetian as well as in the Turkish world, and was a principal means of communication between them. Most important of all, he had won the friendship and confidence of the Grand Vizir, and Laski knew it. Laski also knew that the Venetians had been much alarmed by the most recent extension of the power of the House of Hapsburg as a result of the battle of

[9] Hammer, V, 104–105.
[10] On Gritti see Kretschmayr's monograph (as above).

Pavia, and that Gritti, like the rest of his compatriots, was eager to put an end to it. He approached the magnate at the psychological moment. In return for an annual pension of three or four thousand ducats and the income of a rich Hungarian bishopric, Gritti obtained for Laski an interview with Ibrahim on December 28.[11]

From that moment onward Laski's prospects grew rapidly brighter. Ibrahim, indeed, did not spare him certain unpleasant truths. "We killed King Louis," he said. "We occupied his royal residence: we ate in it; we slept in it. That kingdom is ours. How foolish are they who say that kings are kings because of their crowns. Not gold nor gems command; but iron—the sword—by which obedience is assured." But in the end, Laski's own diplomatic skill and Gritti's support turned the scale in favor of the envoy. The friendship of Zápolya might well be advantageous to the Turks, and they realized it; and so it was finally arranged that Suleiman should concede the title of king of Hungary to the voivode. From the Ottoman point of view he was simply bestowing on Zápolya the lands that he himself had conquered in 1526. All demand for tribute was dropped. The Sultan granted Laski two audiences, in which he showed himself most gracious, and when the envoy departed (February 29, 1528) Gritti was left in charge of the voivode's interests at Constantinople.[12]

News of Laski's success soon reached Ferdinand, who realized at once that he could not hope to retain his recent conquests from Zápolya if the latter should be supported by the Turks. There was only one thing to do: namely, to send a Hapsburg embassy to Suleiman to treat for peace or at least a truce. In May, 1528, after some difficulty in obtaining a safe-conduct, John Hoberdanacz and Sigismund Weichselberger presented themselves at the Porte.

[11] Iorga, II, 406; Kretschmayr, pp. 14–15.
[12] Kretschmayr, pp. 15–16.

Though they came in fact as suppliants, they had apparently been instructed to speak and act as if they were masters of the situation, and they irritated Ibrahim profoundly by demanding that the Turks at once give back all the places they had occupied in Hungary. "I am surprised," was the scornful retort of the Grand Vizir, "that your master has not also asked for Constantinople!" Thenceforth the cause of the envoys was hopeless. Gritti did everything possible to hamper them, and the Sultan grew more and more unfriendly. In a final audience, he menacingly declared, "Your lord has not yet experienced our friendship and our proximity, but he shall feel them soon. Tell your lord plainly that I myself with all my power am coming to give back to him in person the strong places he has demanded of me. Warn him, therefore, to have everything ready to receive me well." It was the most hostile of dismissals; and a little later, when the envoys were preparing to depart, they were cast into prison on the advice of Gritti, who assured Ibrahim that they had only come as spies. It was several months before they regained their liberty, and they were so frequently delayed on their journey homeward that even in January, 1529, King Ferdinand was ignorant of the result of their mission.[18]

By midsummer of 1528, then, it must have been reasonably clear that Suleiman soon intended to launch a third great expedition up the Danube, this time as the ally, or perhaps better the protector, of Zápolya, against Ferdinand and the power of the House of Hapsburg. There is no reason to be surprised that he delayed his departure until the following year. The season was already too late to embark on an enterprise whose ultimate goal, Vienna, was so remote. Moreover the Sultan fully realized that in

[18] Bucholtz, III, 229–243; Kretschmayr, p. 17; Gévay, vol. I, pt. 2, pp. 36–52.

challenging Ferdinand he was also indirectly bidding defiance to the Emperor Charles V. On May 10, 1529, however, he left Constantinople, at the head of a much larger army than that of 1526. The Christian chroniclers talk vaguely of 250,000 to 300,000, though it is doubtful if there were more than 75,000 fighting men, and it seems clear that four-fifths of them were cavalry. Ibrahim was again seraskier, and the artillery is given, as before, at 300 guns. The rains, which in the preceding campaign had been a nuisance, were this year so continuous and torrential that they seriously affected the outcome of the campaign. Suleiman did not reach Vienna till a month later than he expected, and that month may well have made just the difference between failure and success. The Sultan's comments on the bad weather in his diary are constant and bitter.[14] At Mohács, on August 18, he had been joined by Zápolya, whose prospects had speedily revived when it became known that he had won the favor of Suleiman.[15] He brought with him 6,000 men. The Sultan received him with great pomp, and presented him with four robes of honor and three horses caparisoned with gold. But Suleiman, in his diary, takes great pains to point out that he regarded him merely as a vassal. He explains that the gifts were only bestowed in recognition of the voivode's homage; and he emphasizes the fact that Zápolya twice kissed his hand.[16] At Buda a feeble resistance was offered by a few hundred Austrian mercenaries; but they soon surrendered after a promise of good treatment, which was shamefully violated by the Janissaries. Zápolya was permitted to make a royal entrance there on September 14; but he was obviously dominated and controlled by the Turkish soldiers and officials who escorted him, and Lu-

[14] Suleiman, *Tagebuch*, ed. and tr. W. F. A. Behrnauer (Vienna, 1858), pp. 15–18.
[15] Hammer, V, 112–116.
[16] *Tagebuch*, pp. 16–17 (Aug. 18–19).

dovico Gritti was left behind as the Sultan's representative.[17] Gran, Dotis, Komorn, and Raab either surrendered or were evacuated. Pressburg, which alone seemed likely to offer serious resistance, was by-passed. On September 18 the akinji swarmed across the Austrian frontier, and swept like a hurricane through the open country. On the twenty-seventh the Sultan himself arrived before Vienna.[18] Two days later the investment was complete.

Ferdinand had had plenty of time to prepare, but it proved difficult to find means. His ancestral lands granted grudging subsidies, but he could do nothing without help from outside. His brother Charles was anxious to aid him, but was unable to gain peace with Francis I till August 5, too late to set free the imperial troops in Italy. Ferdinand's best hope was the princes of the Empire, then assembled at the Diet of Spires, and thither he at once repaired, to assure them that if Austria were conquered it would be Germany's turn next. But the Diet hesitated. The problem that occupied its chief attention at the time was that of the Lutherans. The Saxon Reformer had recently come out with a pamphlet, "On the War against the Turks," in which he sought to correct any misconstruction of his earlier words on the subject by exhorting all princes to stand by the Emperor for the defence of Christendom. The tract was somewhat halfhearted: one could not help feeling that Luther still regarded Rome as a more serious menace than the Ottoman; [19] nevertheless it ultimately served to help persuade Catholics and Protestants to unite

---

[17] Hammer, V, 116–118.

[18] *Tagebuch*, p. 23.

[19] Luther's views on the Turks may be readily consulted in the collection *Geist aus Luther's Schriften*, 4 vols. (Darmstadt, 1828–31), "Türken," IV, 486–490, nos. 9262–9275. His analysis of the nature and extent of the Turkish peril is excellent. His ideas may well be compared with those of Erasmus as expressed in his *Consultatio de Bello Turcis inferendo* (Basileae, 1530). Neither had any doubt that the Christians were endangered more by their own sins and corruptions than by the arms of the Ottomans.

in voting a *Reichshilfe* or quota for the defence of the Empire.[20] The collection of the troops took many weeks. Had not the Sultan been delayed by the rains, they could scarcely have arrived on time; but three days before Suleiman reached Vienna, sufficient reënforcements had appeared on the scene to raise the numbers of the garrison from about 12,000 to nearly 20,000 men.[21] The greater part of them moreover were professional soldiers, veterans who loved war. Count Nicholas von Salm, who had already fought the Turks, and had recently distinguished himself at the battle of Pavia, was in chief command. Ferdinand was at Prague during the crucial weeks of the campaign.

The siege of Vienna appeals strongly to the imagination. Never since the battle of Tours, almost precisely eight centuries before, had Christian Europe been so direfully threatened by Mohammedan Asia and Africa. Had the verdict on either occasion been reversed, the whole history of the world might have been changed. And the cause of the Moslem defeat in both cases was fundamentally the same; the invaders had outrun their communications. This is well demonstrated in the case of Vienna by the fact that the long distances and heavy rains had forced the Turks to leave behind them the bulk of their heavy artillery, which had been such a decisive factor in the siege of Rhodes. The lighter cannon, which was almost all that they succeeded in bringing with them, could make little impression on the city walls. Only by mining operations could they hope to open a breach for a general assault.

The Vienna of 1529 was not much more than what is today contained within the *Ring* or *Ringstrasse*.[22] On the

---

[20] K. C. Schimmer, *The Sieges of Vienna by the Turks*, tr. and ed. Francis Egerton, Earl of Ellesmere, new ed. (London, 1879), pp. 14–15.

[21] Schimmer-Ellesmere (p. 19) says 20,000 infantry, 2,000 horse, and 1,000 armed burghers.

[22] See the plan in Schimmer-Ellesmere.

northeastern side it was protected by what is now called the Donau Canal, or southern arm of the Danube, and on the southeastern by its little tributary the Wiener-Bach. The city was surrounded by a medieval wall, considerably strengthened during the weeks before the Turks arrived, and the defenders possessed an admirable watchtower in the tall spire of St. Stephen, whence all the movements of the besiegers could be observed; Count von Salm spent much of his time there. The Turks soon saw that the most promising place to attack was the "Kärnthner Thor" or Carinthian Gate, on the south side of the city, to the west of the Wiener-Bach, and there they concentrated the mass of their forces. The Sultan's headquarters were his splendid red tent, pitched on a hill, three or four miles away. Mining and countermining operations were vigorously pushed during the early days of October. Several times the besiegers were encouraged to launch assaults, which were invariably repulsed. On the other hand, the constant sorties of the garrison were generally unsuccessful.[23] October 12 was the critical day of the siege. On that morning the walls had been breached by mines, and the Turks had delivered the most furious of their attacks. Only with great difficulty had it been beaten off, and the garrison was deeply discouraged; that very afternoon it despatched the most pressing of its messages to hasten the arrival of relief. But the Turks were in even worse case. At the Divan which they held that same day, the preponderance of opinion was in favor of withdrawal. The season was ominously late; supplies were getting short; the Janissaries were murmuring; powerful Christian reënforcements were known to be at hand. Ibrahim besought his master to go home. One more last attack was launched on October 14; but despite the unprecedented rewards that had been offered in case it should be successful, it was de-

[23] Schimmer-Ellesmere, pp. 27–35.

livered in such half-hearted fashion that it was fore-
doomed to failure from the first. That night the Turks
massacred some 2000 of the prisoners that they had taken
from the Austrian countryside; they burnt their own en-
campment; on the fifteenth they began to retire.[24] Their
retreat was cruelly harassed by enemy cavalry, and truly
horrible weather pursued them all the way to Constantinople. It was cold comfort that Zápolya came out
from Buda as the Sultan passed by to compliment his
master on his "successful campaign." All that the Sultan
had "succeeded" in doing was to expel Ferdinand from
his Hungarian dominions; and we need not take too seriously the statement in his diary that since he had learned
that the archduke was not in Vienna, he had lost all interest in capturing the place![25] The fundamental fact remained that Suleiman had been beaten back before the
walls of the Austrian capital by a force a third the size of
his own, or perhaps less. His prestige, about which, like
all Orientals, he was abnormally sensitive, had suffered a
serious blow. Obviously he must take immediate measures
to regain it.

He began by a dramatic effort to throw dust in the eyes
of his own subjects and to make them believe that he had
really returned victorious. The "Feast of the Circum-
cision" of his four sons (June 27, 1530) furnished him the
opportunity to give public entertainments on the grandest
scale. They lasted three weeks and were marked by the
most lavish display. For the common people all sorts of
amusements were provided; the soldiers, the dignitaries of
law and theology, and the officials all had their part in
the ceremonies and the distribution of gifts. The Doge

---

[24] Moritz Smets, *Wien in und aus der Türken-Bedrängniss* (Vienna,
1883), pp. 23–25.
[25] *Tagebuch*, pp. 26–27.

of Venice, Andrea Gritti, who had been invited to be present by a special embassy, declined, on the ground of old age; but two envoys extraordinary were sent in his stead; and they, together with the Doge's son Ludovico and the resident bailo, made four representatives of the republic to atone for the absence of those of other Western states. Characteristically Oriental is the story that, after all was over, Suleiman asked Ibrahim whether the entertainments which he had just witnessed or those which had been given at the wedding of the Grand Vizir seemed to him the more magnificent. Ibrahim with ready wit replied: "A festivity like mine has never been seen since the world has existed, nor ever will be seen again." When his master asked in surprise, "Why so?", he added, "Your Majesty had no guest equal to mine, for I was honored by the presence of the Emperor of Mecca and Medina, the Solomon of our time." "Be a thousand times praised," replied the Sultan, "for having thus recalled me to myself!" [26]

The problem of "saving his face" in the eyes of the outside world, and especially of the European powers, was obviously both more important and more difficult. The Sultan, however, was furnished with an excellent opportunity to attack it by the arrival at Constantinople of a fresh embassy from Ferdinand on October 17, 1530. It was headed by a Croatian nobleman named Niklas Jurišić and a certain Count Joseph von Lamberg. They had a suite of twenty-four persons and a Latin interpreter, and the object of the mission was to obtain a truce with the Turk. It is not difficult to see why Ferdinand was so anxious to be relieved of the threat of another Ottoman invasion. He had been deeply discouraged by the epilogue to the siege of Vienna. With the forces that had assembled there after Suleiman's withdrawal, he ought to have been able to take the offensive, drive Zápolya out of Hungary, and

[26] Hammer, V, 137–145; 461.

possibly recapture Belgrade; but the greater part of his troops refused to move. Most of the princes whom they served were intensely jealous of the power of the House of Hapsburg. They were willing to bear their share in the defence of the Empire, but they had no wish to participate in a dispute between Christian rivals for the Hungarian throne; in fact the Bavarian Wittelsbachs were ardently praying for the success of Zápolya. Nor could Ferdinand count on the support of his brother Charles. The latter, indeed, had made a satisfactory peace with France, and had come to terms with the Pope, who crowned him Emperor at Bologna on February 24, 1530.[27] Just two months later he returned to the Empire, after an absence of nine years, to deal with the Lutherans. That was the problem which, at the moment, was uppermost in his mind; at all costs he must restore the religious unity of Western Christendom. Obviously he could not do that and confront the Turkish peril at one and the same time. Heresy must be extirpated before the Moslem could be fought. It was essential to get a respite from the direction of Constantinople; and Charles gave his approval to his brother's effort to obtain it.

The arrival of the envoys afforded Suleiman and Ibrahim the very opportunity that they desired. The ambassadors were honorably received and entertained at the Sultan's expense. Nevertheless, like many subsequent Christian diplomatic agents at the Porte, they were practically kept prisoners in their quarters, and nine full days were suffered to elapse before they were granted their first interview with the Grand Vizir. When at last he consented to receive them, Ibrahim was more haughty and toplofty than ever. He always spoke of their master as "Ferdinand" pure and simple; and he was particularly careful not to call Charles "Emperor"; that title he re-

[27] R. B. M., III, 260.

served for the Sultan.[28] He amazed his listeners by the accuracy and extent of his information about recent events in Western Europe. He commented at length on the battle of Pavia, the treaty of Madrid, the sack of Rome, and the Peace of Cambray, and then favored the envoys with what was now the accepted Turkish version of the Vienna campaign. His master, so he said, had not come to Austria to capture a city, but to fight with Ferdinand, and as the latter had remained in hiding he had returned to Constantinople. For a long time the ambassadors were unable to get a word in edgewise. When at last they succeeded in telling Ibrahim that Ferdinand desired to be recognized as lawful king of Hungary, but would be willing to pay a "pension" to the Sultan and his Grand Vizir in return for their consent, and their promise to abandon Zápolya, Ibrahim threw open the window and pointed proudly to the Castle of the Seven Towers, where Suleiman's treasures were stored. He also took pains to add that no personal bribe could induce him to betray his sovereign. Yet, despite all his arrogance and boastfulness, his tone had not been wholly unfriendly, nor is there any reason for doubting his statement that the Sultan was entirely willing to make peace, provided he could determine the conditions of it. The trouble was that neither side would yield on the main point at issue. Ferdinand would not give up his claims to Hungary, and Suleiman forbade any discussion of the cession of Buda; in view of what had thus far occurred, he can scarcely be blamed for so doing. After a purely formal audience with the Sultan, which was followed by a state dinner, Jurisić and Lamberg left Constantinople in November, having accomplished nothing. The affair as a whole had strengthened Suleiman's position and regained him much of the prestige which he had lost a year before. His rival had come to him as a suppliant,

[28] Hammer, V, 146.

and had been told that he could not have peace save on the Sultan's own terms.[29]

Diplomatic triumphs, however, were not enough. If the memory of his failure to take Vienna were to be wiped out, Suleiman must win a great battle in the field. And this time he proposed to measure swords with Charles V, the great enemy in the background, the fame of whose doings kept constantly reaching him, and whom he knew to be in the Empire and so, for the first time, within reach. The sailors of the two great rivals had already fought each other all over the Mediterranean. The course of events in the Danube valley during the past ten years had been closely linked with the Hapsburg-Valois struggle in the West. Charles had constantly declared that it was his ultimate intention to march against the Turk, and his recent coronation as Emperor at Bologna furnished a final cause for war. The title of Emperor (in Turkish Padishah) implied something supreme over all other potentates. There really could be but one, and Suleiman was determined to settle by wager of battle who that one should be.[30] It is significant that in his diary he entitles his forthcoming expedition "The campaign against the King of Spain." [31]

The Sultan left Constantinople on April 26, 1532. As usual, it is impossible to form an accurate estimate of the size of the forces under his command, but it seems probable that they were even larger than the army of 1529; possibly as many as 100,000 fighting men. In any case, it was large enough to strike terror into the hearts of the first Christians with whom it came into contact. Before it had reached Belgrade, Ferdinand again attempted to

[29] The Austrian documents concerning this embassy are printed in Gévay, vol. I, pt. 3; the report of the ambassadors appears on pp. 74–89.

[30] It is, however, worth noting that Suleiman wrote a letter, in 1559, to Ivan the Terrible of Russia, in which he addressed him as Czar. Cf. Hammer, VI, 118.

[31] Hammer, V, 157, 476.

stay its advance by fresh negotiations for peace.[32] The increased prestige of the Sultan is clearly revealed by the terms which the Christian envoys had been instructed to offer. The annual "pension" in return for Suleiman's recognition of Ferdinand's right to call himself king of Hungary was now to be no less than 100,000 ducats.[33] If this proposal failed to appeal, they were even to consent to the cession of the kingdom to Zápolya, provided the latter would promise to remain unmarried and bequeath all his possessions to the House of Austria.[34] It was a humiliating contrast to Ferdinand's peace-offers of the previous year. No wonder that Ibrahim was more haughty than ever in his replies. Again he asked the envoys how their prince could possibly call himself king of Hungary after it had been twice conquered by the Sultan, who in his last expedition had been unable even to find Ferdinand, and had seen that he was no king, but "only a little fellow of Vienna, and worth small attention. . . . Therefore," he continued, "our lord has nothing to do with him on this occasion, but is seeking only for the king of Spain . . . who has done much more harm to Christendom than the Turk, for he has destroyed Rome and imprisoned the head of your faith." Finally, the two ambassadors were admitted to pay their homage to the Sultan in an audience of great magnificence, where they were mortified at being set below the representative of the king of France.[35] The answer that was delivered to them was unmistakable in its intent:

Know that by the grace of God and of our prophet Mohammed and of all the saints, I with all my nobles and slaves and my innumerable army have come from my great residence.

[32] Documents relating to the embassy of Leonardo, Count of Nogarola, and Joseph von Lamberg in Gévay, vol. I, pt. 4.

[33] Gévay, vol. I, pt. 4, p. 5. The ambassadors were, however, to start their offer at 20,000 ducats.

[34] Gévay, vol. I, pt. 4, pp. 6–9.

[35] Gévay, vol. I, pt. 4, pp. 27–42.

For a long time now it has been the case that the poor Christians in your territories have been deceived by being persuaded that they were about to set out against the Turks. And every year they are deceived in this way, and their treasures are extracted from them on this pretext, and frequent Diets and meetings are held for this object. Therefore I have determined to set out against the king of Spain, and your orators have come to the frontiers of the kingdom of Hungary, and have delivered their message to my supreme standard-bearer Ibrahim Pasha, whom God preserve and increase. And he has himself reported everything to me, from which I have learned your desire. Know that my intention is not directed against you, but against the king of Spain. This has been so since I began with my sword in the kingdom of Hungary. When we arrive at his German boundaries, it is not fitting for him to abandon his provinces and kingdoms to us and take flight, for the provinces of kings are as their very wives, and if these are left by their fugitive husbands as a prey to foreigners, it is an extraordinary and a disgraceful thing. The king of Spain has for a long time declared his wish to go against the Turks; but I by the grace of God am proceeding with my army against him. If he is great in heart, let him await me in the field, and then, whatever God wills, shall be. If, however, he does not wish to wait for me, let him send tribute to my Imperial Majesty. But you have sent your ambassadors to seek peace and friendship with me. If anyone seeks peace from us in truth and good faith, it is proper that we should not refuse him. And when we seek peace from anyone, it is with truth and good faith. Know that we have given your envoys free speech according to our custom, and we have said everything openly to them. Written in our great and honorable imperial quarters at Esseg, on July 12, 1532.[36]

Obviously, then, the Turkish advance was not to be arrested by offers of peace. For the moment at least, the Sultan was determined to meet the Emperor, if possible

---

[36] Gévay, vol. I, pt. 4, pp. 87–88; Bucholtz, IV, 100–101.

on the field of battle. Charles realized, too, that Europe looked to him to defend it against the Moslem in its hour of direst peril. When he had returned into the Empire in 1529, his chief interest, as we have already seen, had been the suppression of the Lutherans; but the heretics had proved unexpectedly difficult. They had drawn up the articles of their faith, the Confession of Augsburg, in 1530, and the Emperor had condemned it, though not so vigorously as the more ardent Romanists had hoped. On February 27, 1531, the Protestant leaders at Schmalkalden had formally concluded a "League for the Defence of the Gospel." Clearly the Lutherans could not be dealt with offhand. They were a far more serious problem than the Emperor had expected, and meantime the Turkish peril grew increasingly imminent. The inference was obvious. He must make terms, temporarily at least, with the heretic, in order to get his support against the Ottoman. A truce was accordingly arranged with the Lutherans at Nuremberg in June, 1532, and formally proclaimed on the third of the following August. The Protestants were given the Emperor's private assurance (in view of his relations with the Catholic Electors he dared do no more) that all suits against them in the Imperial Court would be dropped (on no other condition would they consent to bear aid against the Turk); and the final settlement of the religious question was indefinitely postpone.—Thus ended one of the decisive crises in the history of the Lutheran Reformation. It is indeed one of the strangest ironies of fate that the cause of Protestantism should have owed so much to the "Commander of the Faithful."

In the meantime large Christian forces were beginning to assemble at Vienna. It is impossible to estimate their total strength, for many of them did not arrive till the crisis was past, but it is safe to say that if Suleiman had elected to attack the Austrian capital, he would have been confronted by one of the largest armies—possibly the very largest—that Western Europe had ever been able to collect. Ferdinand's own domains had responded nobly to his call; the Imperial contingents were even larger than had been expected; Charles had hurried his Spanish and Italian veterans across the Alps. One thing alone was lacking, the presence of the Emperor himself, the man whom Suleiman had set forth to seek. Charles, however, had elected to remain at Ratisbon, two hundred miles farther up the Danube. He had arrived there on the last day of February, and did not leave till September 2.[37] It would be interesting to know whether or not the Sultan had discovered where his chief foe really was. The fact remains that instead of following the river route, as every one had expected him to do, he struck across country, to the south of Vienna, as if to encounter an enemy farther westward. On his way thither he was held up at the little town of Güns, near the Hungarian frontier, some sixty miles south-southeast of the Austrian capital. The Turkish vanguard, under the command of Ibrahim, had reached there on August 5. Four days later Suleiman himself arrived.[38]

The commander at Güns was Niklas Jurisić, the former ambassador. He had with him a handful of cavalrymen, with whom he was about to depart for the general muster at Vienna at the time that the Turks arrived; and not more than 700 of the inhabitants could be counted on to aid in the defence. He had no cannon, few muskets, and only a limited amount of powder. Yet rather than desert the rest of the population of the town and the mass of fugitives from the open country who had taken refuge there, he decided to hold the place as long as he could, if

[37] M. de Foronda y Aguilera, *Estancias y Viajes del Emperador Carlos V* (1914), pp. 361–364.

[38] Iorga, II, 415–416; Martin Rosnak, *Die Belagerung der königl. Freystadt Güns im Jahre 1532* (Vienna, 1789), pp. 16–27.

only to delay the advance of the invaders. And his defence was one of the most heroic in the annals of Christian warfare. The Turks utilized their artillery to excellent effect. They erected a "mount" or wooden bulwark opposite the walls. They exploded mines, and made wide breaches in the defences. Yet every one of the ensuing assaults was beaten off. On August 28, Jurisić replied to a summons to yield, that the town belonged to his King, not to him, and that he would surrender it to no one as long as he lived; also that he would pay no money in tribute, since he had none. After this performance had been twice repeated, another attempt was made to storm the fortress, this time with such fury that the assailants succeeded in getting possession of one of the breaches; whereupon the unarmed population, in horror at the dreadful prospect awaiting them, set up such a shriek of despair that the Turks, mistaking it for the cries of reënforcements, were seized with a sudden panic and fled. Three hours later a herald announced to the garrison that in recognition of their bravery the Sultan had decided to spare them. Their commander was summoned to the tent of the Grand Vizir to discuss the conditions of capitulation. As all means of further resistance were exhausted, Jurisić complied. Ibrahim received him with marked honor and granted him favorable terms. The surrender was to be but nominal; the only Turks it admitted to the place were a handful who were stationed there to man the breaches and keep out the rest. Neither Suleiman nor Ibrahim had yet realized how small had been the force that had detained them.[39]

The Sultan must have been in grave doubt what to do after he had wasted almost the whole of August before Güns. There was incessant rain, and the season was getting ominously late. Vienna was now garrisoned by much

[39] Rosnak, *passim;* Hammer, V, 160–164.

larger forces than those who had defied him three years before. He had loudly announced that he had come to cross swords with Charles V; and Charles, whether Suleiman knew it or not—and "that is the question"—was still at Ratisbon. In view of all the facts, as well as the uncertainties, of the situation, it can be no matter of surprise that the Sultan elected to turn southward and ravage the Austrian province of Styria. To do so was in one sense to admit defeat. On the other hand it enabled him to say, as he had done in the case of Ferdinand in 1529, that the enemy whom he had come forth to fight was not to be found, and that therefore he had no further interest in prolonging the struggle. Henceforth the Turkish campaign really degenerated into a great raid. Almost all fortified places were left unmolested; the sole object seemed to be to lay waste the largest possible areas of the countryside.[40] The Sultan's diary contains a number of significant entries. For example, on September 15: "Halt—in order to gather together again the army which was widely dispersed: fog so thick that it was impossible to tell one from another"; and on the twentieth, at the passage of the Drave, "The three army corps arrive at once at the entrance to the bridge, and there was confusion and tumult. The Grand Vizir and the other pashas take their stations on the bridge; and after the Grand Vizir had sat his horse for an entire day to make the army defile before him, the Sultan presents him with a richly caparisoned steed and a sum of money."[41] The army, like all raiding forces, was obviously getting out of hand, and Suleiman must have been glad when he reached Constantinople on November 21. "Five days of feasts and illuminations. . . ," reads his diary; "the bazaars remain open all night and Suleiman goes to visit them incog-

[40] Hammer, V, 165–175.
[41] Quoted in Hammer, V, 481–482.

nito." [42] Doubtless he wanted to know if his subjects had
been deceived into thinking that he had really returned
victorious. The official Turkish version of the campaign
continued to be that the Sultan had gone forth to meet
his greatest Christian rival in the field, but that it had
proved impossible to have a battle, because the Emperor
had remained in hiding. The fact that Charles had stayed
in Ratisbon until after the Turks had turned aside into
Styria lent a certain verisimilitude to this story, but it is
unlikely that either Europe or the Turks took it seriously.
The outstanding fact remained, that, however good his
excuses, Suleiman had failed to accomplish what he had
set out to do. He had not really succeeded in "saving his
face"; [43] though, as the sequel will show, he continued to
keep up the bluff.

Under all the circumstances it was fairly obvious that
neither side would be averse to a cessation of hostilities.
The Emperor was anxious to get away to Italy and Spain.
He finally reached Vienna on September 23, two days
after the Turks had crossed the Drave, and stayed there
till October 4. By that time there could be no possible
doubt that Suleiman was going home. On November 6
Charles was in Mantua, and on April 22, 1533, he reached
Barcelona. [44] The Sultan, on or before his return to Constantinople, received the unwelcome news that Andrea
Doria, the Emperor's Genoese admiral, had captured the
town of Coron, on the southwestern promontory of the
Peloponnesus, ravaged the adjacent coasts, and finally
returned to Genoa, with 60,000 ducats' worth of Turkish
cannon. [45] A campaign against Persia was also imperative
in the immediate future. We cannot wonder that Suleiman made haste to grant the safe-conducts which Fer-

[42] Quoted in Hammer, V, 483.
[43] Hammer, V, 175–176.
[44] Foronda y Aguilera, pp. 365–374.
[45] R. B. M., III, 299.

dinand demanded of him before the end of the year 1532 for a new embassy to treat of peace.[46]

Hieronymus of Zara, who headed the mission, was an elder brother of Niklas Jurisić, the former ambassador and defender of Güns. He reached Constantinople on January 10, 1533. Within four days of his arrival he had not only had an interview with the Grand Vizir but also an audience with the Sultan himself, and found them both far more ready to treat than had any of his predecessors. Yet both Ibrahim and Suleiman insisted on the recognition of their supremacy. Before negotiations could begin, Ferdinand must first send the keys of the city of Gran in token of submission.[47] Ferdinand's envoy needed fresh instructions before he could consent to this, and accordingly sent his son Vespasian back to Vienna with a Turkish chaush to learn his master's decision.[48] An immediate truce was concluded, and the military commanders on both sides were duly notified. As this was the first time that any Ottoman diplomatic representative had ever come to Austria, King Ferdinand made a point of receiving the chaush with all possible ceremony. He promptly accepted the terms demanded by the Turks, but reassured his Hungarians with the remark that, if necessary, it would be easy to make other keys for the gates of Gran. At his brother's desire, he also despatched as a second envoy a certain Cornelius Schepper, who, though not officially accredited by Charles, was yet instructed to represent his interests.

While he was waiting for his son's return, Hieronymus of Zara had been treated with marked honor at Constantinople. Suleiman had expressly directed that, if he so desired, he should be allowed to attend services on holy

[46] Hammer, V, 178.
[47] Hammer, V, 178–179; Marino Sanuto, *Diarii,* vol. LVII, coll. 574–576.
[48] Gévay, vol. II, pt. 1, p. 72.

days in the Christian quarter of the city, and that he should be given horses and an escort if he wished to go about and see the sights. When at last his son got back and he formally presented the keys of Gran, the Grand Vizir smiled and motioned him to keep them. Nevertheless, in the lengthy discussions which followed, Ibrahim, who is described by the ambassadors as being below middle height, swarthy, with a long face and half a dozen prominent teeth in his under jaw, showed himself even more talkative and boastful than ever. Sometimes he would expatiate on the events of recent history, and lay down the law on topics of every sort. Sometimes he would ply the envoys with questions, such as which was the better country, France or Spain? Why was Spain not so well cultivated as France? Was there any city in it as fine as Paris?[49] He spoke with lofty contempt of the Emperor, who when

he was in Italy threatened to bring war against us, and promised that he would quiet the Lutheran faction and force it to the old rite. He came into Germany; there, as far as the Lutherans were concerned, he did nothing. An Emperor should not begin anything which he cannot finish, or promise anything that he cannot perform. He told the world that he would have a Council, and he has not had one. We are not of that kind. . . . .[50] If I wanted to, I could well make them have a Council. And the Christians should not excuse themselves, one of them because he had the gout, another a headache, and give other reasons still why they could not come. . . . If I wished, I would put Luther on one side and the Pope on the other and force them both to hold a Council.[51]

Most extraordinary of all was the language used by the Grand Vizir about his relations to his own all-powerful

[49] Gévay, vol. II, pt. 1, pp. 20–21.
[50] Gévay, vol. II, pt. 1, p. 23.
[51] Gévay, vol. II, pt. 1, pp. 26, 27.

sovereign. "Though I am the Sultan's slave," he assured his hearers,

whatsoever I do is done. I can at a stroke make a pasha out of a stableboy. I can give kingdoms and provinces to whomsoever I choose, and my lord will say nothing against it. Even if he has ordered a thing himself, if I do not want it, it is not done. And if I order a thing to be done, and he has ordered to the contrary, what I wish and not what he wishes is done. The making of war and the granting of peace are in my hand. I can distribute all treasures. He is not better dressed than I; my fortune remains intact, for he pays all my expenses. He intrusts to me his power, his kingdoms, his treasures, everything both great and small, and I can do with them whatsoever I please.[52]

Thus spake the too successful favorite, forgetting that, as Ludovico Gritti said, possibly with intention, in a later interview, if Suleiman "should send one of his cooks to kill Ibrahim Pasha, there would be nothing to prevent the killing." [53]

The sensitiveness of the Turks on the matter of their dignities was in fact the principal reason why Schepper failed to obtain from them the peace which Charles had instructed him to seek; they were as determined as ever to maintain their prestige. At his first interview, the envoy was asked if he bore a letter from the Emperor. When he produced one, the Grand Vizir rose to receive it, saying, "He is a mighty lord, and we should honor him accordingly." Then, in Oriental fashion, he showed his respect by pressing the letter to his forehead and lips before putting it reverently down—to the great edification of Schepper. An examination of its contents, however, soon made trouble. Many of Charles's titles, of which

[52] Gévay, vol. II, pt. 1, p. 21.
[53] Gévay, vol. II, pt. 1, p. 31.

he had a list quite as long as the Sultan's,[54] aroused the wrath of the Grand Vizir.

This letter [said Ibrahim] is not written by a modest and prudent prince. Why does he enumerate with such arrogance the titles that are his, and those that are not his? Wherefore does he presume to style himself to my lord as King of Jerusalem? Is he ignorant of the fact that my mighty Emperor and not himself, Charles, is Lord of Jerusalem? . . . In the same way he calls himself Duke of Athens, which is now Sethine, a small town, and belongs to me. For what reason does he usurp things that are mine? If my master should write down all the provinces that are his, where would be the end to it? Nor would he usurp those of other people, as Charles does. It is not princely to write with such lack of dignity. I do not believe that this letter is from the Emperor Charles, or that he knows anything about it. Besides, in his letter he makes Ferdinand the equal of my lord, the mighty Emperor. He does well to love him so much, but he ought not to show disrespect to my lord. My lord has many governors who are much more powerful than Ferdinand, and have more land and wealth and subjects than he.[55]

And there were other minor points of difficulty besides the matter of dignities and titles. Not the least of these was the conduct of the garrison which Andrea Doria had installed at Coron, and which declined to observe the truce which Hieronymus of Zara had arranged in the previous January. But Schepper insisted that the Emperor had no interest in a truce, unless he could have a lasting peace, to which the Grand Vizir replied that if Charles wished for peace, he should despatch a specially accredited ambassador to ask for it.[56] For the moment it was obvious that no further progress could be made.

---

[54] Gévay, vol. II, pt. 1, pp. 160–107.
[55] Gévay, vol. II, pt. 1, pp. 25–26.
[56] Gévay, vol. II, pt. 1, p. 27.

No such difficulties stood in the way of a settlement with Ferdinand, which was sincerely desired by both sides. To the scandal of all good Moslems, Suleiman went in person to the house of Gritti, who had by this time become the recognized representative of the Sultan in all matters pertaining to Hungary; and he passed three hours there in earnest consultation with him and with Ibrahim.[57] The final audience to the ambassadors also lasted three hours. There was no trouble this time on the score of dignity, as the envoys consented to repeat with docility the form of address which the Grand Vizir had dictated to them:

King Ferdinand, your son, regards all things belonging to him as belonging to you, who are his father, and he regards all things belonging to you as belonging to him, for he is your son. He did not know that you wanted to have Hungary for yourself; had he known this, he would never have waged war over it. . . . But since he understands that you, his father, have that kingdom as your own, he is exceeding glad, and wishes for you, as his father, good health, for if you have good health, he has no doubt that you, his father, will aid him, your son, to acquire this realm and others besides.[58]

Since the representative of Ferdinand had thus publicly consented to abase himself and his master sufficiently to satisfy the utmost demands of Turkish pride, the arrangement of terms made little trouble. Suleiman granted peace to Ferdinand "not for seven years, for twenty-five years, for a hundred years, but for two centuries, three centuries, indeed forever, if Ferdinand himself does not break it." The Sultan would treat him as a son, and be a friend to his friends and a foe to his foes. Suleiman did not quite abandon Zápolya; it was provided that the voivode and

[57] Gévay, vol. II, pt. 1, pp. 28–29.
[58] Gévay, vol. II, pt. 1, p. 36.

Ferdinand should come to an arrangement in regard to the division of the kingdom, and Gritti was to go to Hungary to supervise the territorial delimitations. Whatsoever settlement should be made must be confirmed by the Sultan himself.[59] The envoys bade their formal farewells on July 14, 1533; but the letters which they were to carry to Charles and Ferdinand were not given them till three weeks later, and they did not leave Constantinople till August 6.

Such was the rather inconclusive end to the great expedition on which Suleiman had set forth, with an uninterrupted record of notable victories, against Vienna four years before. Twice had he decided to retire, with his announced object unachieved. On the other hand, there can be no doubt that the name and fame of the Turks were better known in Western Europe, and the imminence of the Turkish peril was far better realized there in 1533 than in 1529. Whether or not Oriental grandiloquence had successfully maintained the Sultan's claim to be the "mightiest sovereign on the face of the earth" is a matter of opinion. In any case, one of the greatest monarchs of Western Christendom had found himself in such desperate straits, four years before Suleiman had started out to besiege Vienna, that he was not ashamed to beg for the aid of the Commander of the Faithful.

[59] Gévay, vol. II, pt. 1, pp. 38–39.

ᨦ VI ᨦ

Relations with France to 1536

If there was any one country in Europe whose history
and traditions seemed to designate it as the leader in war
against the Moslem, that country was France. In 732 she
had turned back the Arabs and the Berbers at the battle
of Tours. She was, above all others, the land of the crusades. The enthusiasm which had made them possible
had originated in France, at the Council of Clermont,
and had been inspired by a French priest, Pope Urban II.
The majority of those who took part in the first one were
Frenchmen. In the second, which was initiated by a
French preacher, St. Bernard of Clairvaux, we find a
French sovereign, Louis VII, and in the third, Philip
Augustus and Richard Coeur de Lion, who was more
than half a Frenchman. The fourth, which turned aside
against Constantinople, was largely French; and, finally,
the efforts of the crusaders closed with the two fruitless expeditions of Saint Louis the Ninth, the last and noblest of
them all. Two of the most famous crusading orders, the
Knights Templars and the Knights of St. John of Jerusalem, were chiefly French; the latter, as we have already
seen, had continued to fight the Moslem until a much
later date. Against the Ottoman Turks France had more
than once shown traces of her earlier zeal. The French
took the leading part in the expedition that ended so
disastrously at Nicopolis. Even the hard-headed Louis XI
professed to be alarmed by the danger to Christendom.
Charles VIII regarded the conquest of the kingdom of

Naples as but a prelude to the taking of Constantinople, and Louis XII had continually encouraged the preaching of the Holy War. The king of France was, indeed, *le Roi Très Chrétien*.

Francis I was not unmindful of these traditions. After his great victory at Marignano, he had frequently expressed his desire for a peace among Christian princes and a league against their common foe. Although he was doubtless less in earnest than he wished to be thought, and was particularly anxious to have the Pope grant him a share of the clerical revenues for the purpose, the idea of a crusade was one which would naturally appeal to his lively imagination. Even his repeated assertion that the sole reason why he desired to be elected Emperor was that he might lead a united Europe against the Moslem may not have been wholly insincere.

But his defeat by Charles V in the imperial election of 1519 and the subsequent outbreak of war between the two sovereigns put an end to any plans of this kind, however vague, which King Francis may have previously entertained. After Sultan Selim had conquered Egypt in 1517, and had begun to reorganize the country, he had at once confirmed the commercial rights which the Catalans and the French—who were classed together— had previously enjoyed there. A basis was thus furnished for a closer understanding with the Porte, should it ever prove desirable, and Francis did not forget it.[1] When once his great struggle with the Emperor broke out, he bent all his energies to the defeat of the Hapsburgs. Although the Knights of St. John had always been primarily a French order and a glory to France, and their Grand Master, Villiers de L'Isle Adam, was a Frenchman, the king did not move a finger to aid "his good city of Rhodes," or show any interest in the subsequent fortunes

[1] Charrière, I, 121–131.

of the Knights. In the beginning of 1525 we find him considering the plan of an attack on the Austrian provinces of Styria and Carniola by Christopher Frangipani in conjunction with Turkish troops from Bosnia. This design was betrayed to Ferdinand, who defeated it by arresting Frangipani, and released him only on his promise to abandon the Moslem. Still, we have no proof that as yet the "Eldest Son of the Church" had any thought of a step so utterly at variance with his own traditions and previous attitude, so scandalous in the eyes of the whole Christian world, save possibly of the hard-headed Venetians, as actually to ally himself with the arch-enemy of his faith.

His defeat at Pavia, however, on February 25, 1525, made him throw all scruples to the winds. When the battle was over, he found himself a prisoner in the hands of his rival's generals, while his country seemed destined to be the helpless prey of Spaniard, German, Netherlander, and Englishman, and of the traitor Constable of Bourbon. Obviously it was a case for desperate measures; and in his extremity he resolved to beg for the aid of the one sovereign powerful enough to check the victorious Emperor, the Sultan Suleiman the Magnificent. So secretly, however, was the step taken, that for a long time the story of it was shrouded in mystery. Even today we know but little about it, and that little we owe chiefly to the notices of Turkish historians and to the loquacity of the Grand Vizir. It seems probable that the first French mission to Constantinople was despatched, almost as soon as the news of Pavia was known, by the Queen-Mother and Regent Louise of Savoy. The name of the envoy has not come down to us. He had with him a suite of twelve persons bearing rich gifts, including a ruby seal ring which, if we can trust the word of Ibrahim, who showed the ring to Hieronymus of Zara eight years later, had been worn by Francis at Pavia.[2] If this be true, the king himself must have been privy to the plan. The mission never reached its destination, for it was set upon and murdered in Bosnia, apparently by order of the local sanjak bey. The outrage seems to have been committed chiefly for the sake of plunder; still, when we remember the interests of King Ferdinand in that region, it is permissible to suspect that the enmity of the House of Hapsburg may possibly have been in some measure responsible for a crime which would not have been out of keeping with the political morals of the day.

In the month of December of that same year a second French envoy, John Frangipani, presumably a relative of Christopher, reached Constantinople. He was intrusted, besides verbal messages, with a letter from the Regent, and another which appears to have been written in secret by Francis from his prison in Madrid, and which the envoy carried hidden between the soles of his shoes. Neither of these letters has ever been found, but the contemporaneous authorities [3] make it clear that both of them begged the aid of the Sultan in effecting the deliverance of the king of France and attacking the power of the House of Hapsburg. In any case, they gave Suleiman a perfect opportunity to assert and emphasize his supremacy, and he was quick to take advantage of it. The letter which he gave Frangipani to take back with him, when the latter left Constantinople on February 8, 1526, is one of the finest specimens of Oriental style that has come down to us. It reads as follows:

By the grace of the Most High, whose power be forever exalted! By the sacred miracles of Mohammed (may the blessing of God be upon him!), who is the sun of the skies of

[2] Gévay, vol. II, pt. 1, p. 27.

[3] J[on] Ursu, *La Politique orientale de François Ier, 1515–1547* (Paris, 1908), pp. 31–35, notes.

prophecy, star of the constellation of the Apostles, chief of the company of prophets, guide of the hosts of the elect; by the coöperation of the holy souls of his four friends, Abu Bekr, Omar, Othman, and Ali (may the blessing of God on High rest on them all!), and of all God's chosen people, I who am the Sultan of Sultans, the sovereign of sovereigns, the dispenser of crowns to the monarchs on the face of the earth, the shadow of God on earth, the Sultan and sovereign lord of the White Sea and of the Black Sea, of Rumelia and of Anatolia, of Karamania, of the land of Rum, of Zulkadria, of Diarbekir, of Kurdistan, of Azerbaijan, of Persia, of Damascus, of Aleppo, of Cairo, of Mecca, of Medina, of Jerusalem, of all Arabia, of Yemen, and of many other lands which my noble forefathers and my glorious ancestors (may God light up their tombs!) conquered by the force of their arms, and which my August Majesty has made subject to my flaming sword and my victorious blade, I, Sultan Suleiman Khan, son of Sultan Selim Khan, son of Sultan Bayezid Khan: To thee who art Francis, king of the land of France.

You have sent to my Porte, refuge of sovereigns, a letter by your faithful agent Frangipani, and you have furthermore intrusted to him sundry verbal communications; you have informed me that the enemy has overrun your country and that you are at present in prison and a captive, and you have here asked aid and succors for your deliverance. All that you have said having been set forth at the foot of my throne, refuge of the world, my imperial knowledge has comprehended in detail, and I have taken complete cognizance of it.

There is nothing wonderful in emperors being defeated and made prisoners. Take courage then, and be not dismayed. Our glorious predecessors and our illustrious ancestors (may God light up their tombs!) have never ceased to make war to repel the foe and conquer his lands. We ourselves have followed in their footsteps, and have at all times conquered provinces and citadels of great strength and difficult of approach. Night and day our horse is saddled and our sabre is girt.

May God on High promote righteousness! May whatsoever He will be accomplished! For the rest, question your ambassador and be informed. Know it to be thus. Written in the first decade of the moon of Rebiul-akir, in the year 932 [February, 1526] from the residence of the capital of the Empire, Constantinople, the well supplied and the well guarded.[4]

Though the tone of this letter, if lofty, was highly favorable, it will be observed that the Sultan was careful to avoid any specific statement as to what he was willing to do. Such was the established custom of the Porte, which, averse to binding itself in writing, preferred to communicate the essential things by word of mouth.[5] Moreover the situation in Western Europe had greatly altered in the weeks between Frangipani's arrival at Constantinople sometime before December 6, 1525,[6] and his departure in the following February. On January 14, 1526, the Emperor had laid down the terms on which Francis was to be liberated in the famous treaty of Madrid,[7] and though the French king did not return to his own territories till the following March, it must have been evident at the Porte before Frangipani left which way the wind was blowing. Europe was now thoroughly alarmed at the overwhelming preponderance of the House of Hapsburg, and was determined to maintain the sovereignty and territorial integrity of France as the outward and visible symbol of her escape from it. The League of Cognac, formed to serve just that purpose, was not officially concluded till May 22, but the forces which went to compose it were in operation months before.[8] When Frangipani first reached Constantinople, the state of affairs had been much more desperate. There had been talk of the Sultan's launching a great attack around the

[4] Charrière, I, 116–118; *Calendar of State Papers,* Spanish, vol. III, 1, no. 489, p. 801.
[5] Ursu, p. 34.
[6] Sanuto, *Dairii,* vol. XL, col. 700.
[7] R. B. M., III, 241–242.
[8] R. B. M., III, 243–249.

head of the Adriatic against the imperial dominions in Milan,[9] and it had also been proposed to deliver a vast naval assault on the coasts of Apulia.[10] But now, two months later, conditions were very different. The king of France, with the promise of the support of most of the rest of non-Hapsburg Europe, was no longer a negligible quantity. It appeared that after all he might be able to maintain himself in the West. The Sultan would not be obliged to interfere in those remoter regions to save him. He could accomplish what he had been asked to do equally well by a diversion; in other words, by the very attack on Hungary to which Suleiman's own ambitions were driving him. "The bey of France," as Kemal Pasha Zadeh puts it, "and the Sultan's promise to deliver him from the supremacy of the bey of Spain, were among the principal causes which determined Suleiman to undertake the expedition." [11] In other words, the real answer to Pavia was to be Mohács.—Moreover the Sultan was shrewd enough to perceive that though Francis had come to him as a suppliant—the letter quoted above is proof that he proposed to make the most of the fact—there might ultimately be great advantages which he could hope to obtain from the French king's alliance. Over and above the fact that they had a common enemy in the House of Austria, it would give added prestige to the Ottomans—comparatively recent arrivals on European soil—to enter into official relations with a power as ancient and respected as France. They would thus gain a patent of legitimacy for their conquests in the Balkan peninsula. The friendship between the two powers, which lasted, with some intermissions, for nearly three centuries, was based, much like its

---

[9] Gévay, vol. I, pt. 3, p. 44 (report of Lamberg and Jurisić, February 23, 1531).

[10] Ursu, p. 34.

[11] Kemal Pasha Zadeh, *Histoire de la Campagne de Mohacz*, p. 24. See also Ursu, pp. 37–38.

successor the Franco-Russian alliance of fifty years ago, on a community of interests as opposed to certain other powers—a bond which insured its continuance in spite of every difference of religion, civilization, traditions, and ideals. It was denounced as "the impious alliance," "the sacrilegious union of the Lily and the Crescent," but despite its ill odor it was destined to survive, because it was so obviously useful to both the high contracting parties.

Certainly Frangipani had no reason for dissatisfaction with his reception at Constantinople. Though he had brought no gifts, he was amply rewarded and was treated with marked honor. When he ventured to complain of the murder of his predecessor, the Pasha of Bosnia was at once summoned to the Porte to justify himself. This he succeeded in doing, though probably the support of Ibrahim was all that availed to save him; it is at least significant that it was at this juncture that the famous ruby ring of King Francis passed into the possession of the Grand Vizir, who declared that he had bought it! [12] We may also note, in passing, that wide publicity was given at the time to a curious but generally accepted Turkish legend to the effect that a very lovely daughter of a certain king of France had been captured by corsairs and presented by them to Murad II, that she had subsequently become the mother of Mohammed II, and had been converted to Islam.[13] If this were true, the reigning houses of France and Turkey were now connected by ties of blood!

On his way home Frangipani had the ill luck to permit knowledge of the contents of the Sultan's encouraging letter which he bore to reach the ears of Lope de Soria, the imperial representative at Genoa, who sent his master

[12] Gévay, vol. II, pt. 1, p. 27.
[13] Kemal Pasha Zadeh, pp. 164–165.

the whole story on July 15.[14] Of course Charles was prompt to make all possible capital out of the fact that the Eldest Son of the Church and the Commander of the Faithful were now united against him; and he continued to do so till the end of his days. But Europe was in no mood to be easily shocked. Frangipani got safely back to his master, who at once (July, 1526) despatched him again to the Sultan, with a cordial letter of thanks for his proffered aid.[15] It is not certain that the envoy ever reached Suleiman; if he did, it must have been in Hungary, at the close of the Mohács campaign. In any case, we know that two years later the Sultan sent back a formal confirmation of the ancient privileges of the French merchants in Egypt.[16] At the same time, however, he politely but firmly declined to permit an ancient Christian church in Jerusalem, which had been converted into a mosque, to be restored to the use of those who had first worshipped there.[17]

The Mohács campaign proved a grievous disappointment to the king of France. He had regarded it at the outset as an expedition which must needs ultimately curb the power of the House of Hapsburg, but its actual result had been precisely the reverse. The death of King Louis had made Ferdinand of Austria undisputed lord of Bohemia, and gave him at least a chance at the throne of Hungary. The territories of the House of Hapsburg had already been greatly enlarged, and promised to be so still more. So confident, in fact, was Ferdinand, after the Sultan had retired, that he despatched George Frundsberg and his German mercenaries across the Alps to help the Imperialists to sack Rome.[18] Moreover, by the summer

---

[14] Ursu, p. 35.
[15] Ursu, p. 36.
[16] Charrière, I, 121–129.
[17] Charrière, I, 129–131.
[18] R. B. M., III, 245.

of 1527 the French king was beginning to be doubtful whether after all he really needed the alliance of the disreputable Ottoman whom he had addressed as a humble suppliant two years before. The League of Cognac was doing even better than had been expected of it. Everywhere, save in Italy, the Imperialists were checked. Henry VIII was beginning to contemplate the possibility of divorcing Catharine of Aragon, and consequently showed signs of drawing near to France.[19] The inference was obvious. The Eldest Son of the Church must loosen the ties that bound him to the Commander of the Faithful, and attain his anti-Hapsburg aims through the help of Christian allies. The years 1527 and 1528 are filled with the stories of his efforts to win the friendship of John Zápolya and the king of Poland; but as these only indirectly concern the life of Suleiman, it will profit nothing to enlarge upon them here.[20] Hieronymus Laski, whom we have already encountered, and Antonio Rinçon, a Spanish traitor who had gone over into French service, were the principal go-betweens. In general it may be said that they succeeded well: particularly with the voivode, who in return for an annual subsidy of 20,000 ducats promised to adopt as his heir the second son of the French king. None of these negotiations was destined to bring Francis any permanently important advantage; but it is worth noting that in the course of them neither Zápolya nor King Sigismund showed himself anywhere nearly as squeamish about direct relations with the Porte as did he. The voivode, in fact, who was the protégé of the Sultan and was courted by the French monarch, inevitably found himself acting for some years as an intermediary between them.[21]

[19] R. B. M., III, 247.
[20] Charrière, I, 158–169.
[21] Ursu, pp. 40–50.

Francis, in fact, had got himself into a thoroughly false position, and his conduct of Eastern affairs was marked by a duplicity seldom equalled even in that unscrupulous age. He had no real fondness for the Turk, whom he had only approached as a last resort when he was in desperate straits, and with every effort to keep his doings secret. Now that things were looking a little brighter he was anxious to disavow him—at least until they should grow dark again. His political interests and his religious duty as Eldest Son of the Church pulled him in opposite directions. No sooner had he resolved to devote himself to the one than he was obliged by the current of events to pay heed to the other. He was like the man who borrows money from a shady banker and cuts him in the street. The attitude of the Sultan was totally different. In his case political and religious interests did not conflict; they coincided. In waging war on the Hapsburgs he was attacking at once the enemy of his empire and the foe of his faith; he had no scruples or doubts. He punctiliously fulfilled all his promises to Francis, though there can be no doubt that he had taken the measure of the man; he was proud, frank, honorable, from first to last; he never played the suppliant. While the French king was perpetually short of funds, Suleiman always seemed to have unlimited treasures at his disposal. On one occasion, when things were looking bright for Francis in the West, and he had consequently concluded a truce with Charles and had urged the Turk to follow his example, Suleiman loftily replied, "I will certainly do so, when the Emperor has restored to my ally, the French king, the lands of which he has unjustly deprived him." [22]

The nature of the relations between the two was admirably illustrated by the events of 1529–32. The advance of the Sultan on Vienna was one element, at least, in in-

[22] R. B. M., III, 267; Ursu, pp. 111–112.

ducing Francis to sign the Peace of Cambray, in which he bound himself, among other things, to unite his forces with those of Charles against the Moslem. He had been practically sure for six months before of a reasonable settlement with the Hapsburg; why proclaim to the world his shameful treaty with the Ottoman? And yet, on the other hand, he was really more than ever in need of Turkish aid at the moment, for in July, 1528, the Genoese Admiral Andrea Doria had deserted him and gone over to the Imperialists; Francis could no longer claim to control the western basin of the Mediterranean. But for the time being he felt safe in the West and consequently continued openly to disavow the Sultan; in 1530 a French fleet of thirteen galleys actually took part with the Imperialists under Andrea Doria in an attack on the Algerian port of Cherchell.[23] Yet, on the other hand, Francis was careful all the time to keep in touch with Suleiman. Their dealings were doubtless secret and indirect; but there is contemporaneous evidence of all sorts to prove that the French remained in good odor at the Porte. The Sultan had given them his word, and he would not go back on it.

After the Emperor's return into Germany in 1530 another phase began. The French king had not been unfriendly to Protestantism in his early years, feeling, probably, that it would be safer to play with the heretic than with the Moslem. He had now begun to pin his faith on the League of Schmalkalden and the hopes that it offered of weakening Charles's power in the Empire. The one thing that would be certain to compose the religious differences there would be another Turkish invasion. So in early 1532 Antonio Rinçon was once more despatched to Constantinople to try to dissuade the Sultan from embarking on the expedition which was to be

[23] R. B. M., III, p. 297.

checked at Güns.[24] If Suleiman must needs attack the Hapsburg, let him do so in Italy, so that the French king could reconquer Genoa and Milan. Illness, and the intrigues of the Imperialists, prevented the envoy from finding the Sultan until the latter had reached Belgrade. There Rinçon was received with marked honor and was given precedence over the envoys of Ferdinand, whom he met on the same errand.[25] The Turkish historian declares that "his Highness the commanding Pasha [i.e., Ibrahim] spoke to the ambassador of France like a friend, to the others like a lion." The Sultan himself notes two audiences in his diary,[26] and in his letters of reply he addressed Francis as a Padishah and an equal. On the other hand, he could not be expected to listen to the suggestion of the king of France that he should abandon an expedition on which he had got so far. He politely excused himself for his refusal to do so on the ground that, if he halted, his people would say that he had done so out of dread of Charles of Spain. In the end the fears of Francis were justified by the event. The most tangible result of Suleiman's great expedition was the Religious Peace of Nuremberg,[27] which postponed the outbreak of religious war in Germany till 1546.

Ostensibly, during the year 1533, the Franco-Turkish alliance hung fire. On December 24, 1532, the imperial ambassador at Venice wrote his master that he believed that Suleiman "considers himself hoaxed by the Most Christian King, and will place no confidence in him for the future." He also said that in his opinion "the Sultan did evacuate Hungary with much greater loss in men than was reported at the time, perhaps as much as one-third of his

[24] Ursu, pp. 65–69.
[25] Ursu, pp. 69–72; Hammer, V, 158–159.
[26] Quoted in Hammer, V, 478.
[27] July 23, 1532. Jean DuMont, *Corps universel diplomatique* (Amsterdam, 1726–31), vol. IV, 1, pp. 87–88.

army." [28] For the present at least, Suleiman had had enough of Austro-Hungarian campaigns. He made peace with Ferdinand, as we have already seen, in June, 1533; moreover in the autumn of that same year he sent Ibrahim on to prepare the way for an invasion of Persia, and followed himself in the summer of 1534. Clearly for the time being his chief attention was to be directed to the southeast. Francis on his side was still officially at peace with Charles, and was plotting further to strengthen his position in the West by negotiations with sundry Christian potentates. In October, 1532, he had made a treaty with Henry VIII, whom he was sporadically supporting in the matter of the latter's divorce.[29] The avowed purpose of this treaty was "to render abortive the damned conspiracies and machinations of the Turk, ancient enemy and adversary of our holy faith." This could be flaunted in the face of those who still entertained suspicions of Francis' relations with the Moslem, while its real object, of course, was a league against the Emperor. Just a year later, starting off on the opposite tack, he approached Pope Clement VII, who was induced by the prospect of a marriage between his niece Catharine and Francis' son Henry to desert the cause of the Hapsburgs.[30] The two policies were mutually exclusive, for by this time the king of England had bidden the Papacy defiance; but Francis was determined to have a foot in every camp, and he even continued his negotiations with the German Lutherans. The only evidence in this period that Suleiman and the French king were still in touch was the Sultan's order to his piratical sea-captain Barbarossa to put his fleet at the disposal of his Most Christian ally in order to enable him

[28] *Calendar of State Papers, Spanish,* vol. IV, 2, no. 1036, pp. 572–573 (letter of Rodrigo Niño).
[29] Charrière, I, 234–235.
[30] R. B. M., III, 262.

to reconquer Genoa and the Milanese.[31] This, however, was deeply significant. From Suleiman's standpoint it was an exceedingly shrewd move, for it was a bait to induce Francis to abandon his policy of duplicity and make open war on Charles. More important still, it presaged the transference of the most important part of the struggle against the Emperor from land to sea, from the plains of Hungary to the basin of the Mediterranean. It seems probable that the wily Rinçon was primarily responsible for it, and it naturally was highly pleasing to Francis. Should the Sultan make good his word, the French king would henceforth have much more immediately effective aid against the Emperor, in case he should need it, than remote diversions in the Danubian lands.

In July, 1533, Francis received official representatives of Barbarossa in friendly fashion at Le Puy.[32] Six months later he sent Rinçon back to visit the corsair in North Africa, and later to interview Ibrahim in Asia Minor, on his way to Persia.[33] This time the French king made no effort to conceal his relations with the Porte, which were now common knowledge to all the great powers of Western Europe. At the same time Barbarossa, who was then in his sixty-seventh or sixty-eighth year, was commanded by the Sultan to go and consult with the Grand Vizir in Syria. Thence he returned to Constantinople in the late spring of 1534, where Suleiman, with Ibrahim's full approval, gave him formal command, as pasha and grand admiral, of the entire Turkish fleet, with over a hundred ships and 10,000 soldiers.[34] The Sultan had already agreed to the terms arranged between France and the Porte by Rinçon and Ibrahim in Asia Minor. He defended his conduct to the imperial

[31] Ursu, p. 72.
[32] Ursu, p. 77.
[33] Ursu, pp. 79–80.
[34] Gévay, vol. II, pt. 2, p. 35; R. B. M., III, 305.

representative, Schepper, on the ground that "he could not possibly abandon the king of France, who was his brother." [35] On May 28, 1534, sixteen days before Suleiman departed for Persia, Barbarossa set out from Constantinople with all his fleet, and in the next few weeks he treated the Adriatic coasts of Italy to such a ravaging as they had seldom experienced before. [36] Henceforth the story of the Franco-Turkish alliance and that of the naval war in the Mediterranean and North Africa are almost inextricably fused; and we can postpone most of our consideration of the further development of the former until a later chapter.

One final matter, however, remains to be mentioned here, if only to round off the diplomatic side of the story to the point to which we have brought it. A Franco-Turkish alliance having been made, it was fitting that the high contracting parties should exchange ambassadors, and in the winter of 1534–35 Francis had determined to take the momentous step of sending his country's first resident representative to the Sultan's court. This time he selected one of his own secretaries, a cultured gentleman, named Jean de la Forêt, to undertake the task. On February 11, 1535, he gave him full instructions as to how to deal with Barbarossa and with Suleiman. With the former his main duty was to ask for vigorous aid in the reconquest of Genoa. The latter was to be induced to consent to a "general peace," but only on condition that Charles should agree to all of the French king's just demands; in other words, the cession of Genoa, Milan, and Flanders, and the recognition of Zápolya as king of Hungary! If the Emperor should refuse, he must be made to yield by war, and if Francis were to bear an efficient part in it, the Sultan would have to grant him a subsidy of a

[35] Gévay, vol. II, 2, p. 47.
[36] Ursu, p. 85.

million ducats. If Suleiman could not afford this, it was hoped that at least he would begin to fight at once himself, and order Barbarossa to attack Sardinia and Sicily.[37]

Agreeably to his instructions La Forêt first visited Tunis, where Barbarossa had established himself in the preceding year. Thence he passed on into Asia Minor, and finally caught up with the Sultan at Honan in Azerbaijan in the month of May. Thenceforth he kept close to Suleiman till the end of the Persian war, which lasted much longer than had been expected; they did not get back to Constantinople till the early weeks of 1536. On their arrival they found that the situation in the West had altered greatly to their disadvantage. The outstanding fact, of course, had been the capture of Tunis (July 21) from Barbarossa, by the naval and military forces of Charles V;[38] the Imperialists were once more dominant in the Mediterranean. Suleiman could not help feeling that the French king had failed to live up to his engagements. "How can I trust him," he asked La Forêt, "when he always promises more than he can perform?"[39] Nevertheless, when he learned that Francis had invaded Piedmont in the beginning of February, he made up his mind that the French king might be of some use to him after all, and promised to coöperate by launching an attack across the Straits of Otranto against the kingdom of Naples; Barbarossa also was expected to play a part. On the other hand, Francis was unwilling to advertise the full extent of the intimacy of his relations with the Moslem to the rest of the Christian world, and so instructed La Forêt to try to obtain for public consumption a treaty of primarily commercial significance, whose main object was to veil the close political and military collaboration

[37] Charrière, I, 255–263; Ursu, pp. 88–92.
[38] Cf. *below*, p. 217.
[39] Ursu, p. 95; Gévay, vol. III, pt. 1, pp. 18–19 (report of Francis, Baron von Sprinzenstein, to Ferdinand I, probably early in October, 1537).

between the Commander of the Faithful and the Eldest Son of the Church. This the envoy succeeded in doing in February, 1536. It was the first official treaty between France and the Ottoman Porte, and has served as the model for many similar and subsequent conventions of Christian powers, not only with the Turks but also with other Asiatic nations.[40]

Its main provisions, as we have already indicated, are concerned with the trading privileges of the French in the Ottoman Empire; they have gone down in history as the "capitulations," and they are but the logical consequence and fulfilment of the privileges granted by Selim the Terrible to the French merchants in Egypt when he conquered it from the Mamelukes in 1517. They gave the French the right to sail, buy, and sell throughout the Ottoman Empire on the same terms as did the Turks; they recognized the validity of the jurisdiction, both civil and criminal, of the resident French consuls over all Frenchmen there, and obliged the Turks to lend armed force, if necessary, for the execution of the consular judgments. The treaty also provided for complete religious liberty for the French in the Ottoman Empire; it gave them the right to keep guard over the Holy Places, and therewith a sort of protectorate over all Christians resident on Turkish soil; it permitted them to dispose of their property by will, and provided equitably for the cases of those who died intestate. Henceforth France began to enjoy a special and preponderant position in the Ottoman Empire. If other nations wished to send their ships there, they must sail under French colors, for the French king was the only Christian sovereign whom the Sultan would consent to treat as an equal. The "capitulations," in fact, really made Turkey into a sort of

[40] Charrière, I, 283–294, with note on the date of the treaty on pp. 283–284.

French crown colony, whither she could export her goods; they were also a principal cause of the prosperity of Marseilles.

Suleiman's military record in 1536 was not so spotless as it had been ten years before. On the other hand, the Turks, under his leadership, had now definitely made their entry into the diplomatic society of Western Europe. They had begun to count, in international relations, as they had never done before, and the Sultan's reign was but a little more than one-third over! If he kept on at the present rate there was no telling where he would stop! But before we pursue the story of his subsequent treaties and campaigns, we must devote a couple of chapters to his internal government, his court, his private life and his favorites, and to the manners and customs of his subjects.

∾ VII ∾

The Government

We have already noticed the fact that though Suleiman has gone down in Christian annals as "the Great" or "the Magnificent," he was known to his own people as "El Kanuni" or "the Legislator"; his reign marks an epoch in the constitutional as well as in the military and imperial progress of the Turks. The constitutional side of the picture must not be overdrawn. Suleiman was primarily a warrior, and it has been well said of him that he was a legislator only by contrast to his immediate predecessors, who were even more men of the sword than of the pen than was he, and scarcely legislated at all. Moreover the laws which he drew up and which have come down to us aim rather to define the existing state of affairs than to introduce radical innovations. But for that very reason they provide one of our best sources of knowledge of the conditions prevalent in the vast and heterogeneous empire over which he ruled.

It will be worth while to spend a paragraph in discussing the background against which those conditions rested. The Turks were by nature a most conservative people, who often looked back with longing to primitive times, and who found it difficult to accommodate themselves to the changes which their incredibly rapid expansion since the days of Osman demanded. Originally they had been a pastoral, nomadic, pagan folk on the Asiatic steppes; their chieftain had called himself Khan; their lives had been regulated in accordance with the adet, or body of unwritten tribal custom: primitive no doubt, yet never wholly forgotten. Then there had come the gradual conversion to Islam, with all the contacts with a vastly superior if somewhat decadent civilization which that implied. The sheri or sacred law of the orthodox Moslems took precedence over the adet; the rulers adopted first the Arab title of Emir, or Commander, and later that of Sultan; on the other hand, they were constantly at pains to remind themselves that they also were still Khans. The next step was the capture of Constantinople, and the rich heritage of Graeco-Roman tradition and magnificence which came with it; Mohammed II was prompt to appropriate it all—except of course the Christianity. He took the additional titles of Kaisar-i-Rum, i.e. Roman Emperor, and Padishah (a word of Persian origin which means Vice-regent of God) [1] to impress men with the fact that he was the successor of Augustus and of Constantine; even the contemporaneous Byzantine chroniclers referred to him as "Basileus"—the title that had been used by the Greeks for the Great King of ancient Persia and later for the Roman and Byzantine Emperors. He was no doubt a Turkish, a Moslem Basileus; but by no means all of his predecessors had been Greeks or orthodox; the main thing was that he was held worthy to continue the line; and, as we shall later see in more detail, the change from the Byzantine to the Ottoman regime was in many respects much less radical than is generally supposed. And then, finally, under Selim had come the conquest of Syria and of Egypt, and the assumption of the title of "Guardian and Protector of the Holy Cities."—Obviously the task of governing an empire which had expanded so rapidly and included such a great variety of peoples within its boundaries was going to be one of enormous difficulty, particularly as the

---

[1] Originally "lord who is a royalty"; cf. *Encyclopedia of Islam, s.v.* "Padishah."

Turks were by nature averse to change. Suleiman had little to guide him. The last important "law-book" at his disposal was the so-called *Kanun-Nameh* of his great-grandfather Mohammed II, and that was now in large measure out of date.

According to Occidental definition, Suleiman was a despot, but he was by no means an absolute despot; on the contrary, there were numerous important limitations to his power. Of these the most definite and significant was unquestionably the sheri or Sacred Law of Islam, which he was powerless to abolish or even alter. He must regulate his life according to its precepts; it restricted his conduct in war and in peace; it limited his revenues; it even protected his Christian subjects who behaved themselves and paid the kharaj or land tax incident on non-Moslems, from any attempt at forcible conversion. Less specific, though scarcely less important, was the incubus of the long tradition and unchanging manners of a people who loved, above all things, to "go on in the same good old way." Suleiman might transgress the urf, or expressed will of previous Sultans, or even the ancient primitive customs or adet, but he must not lightly remove what he could not replace with something that was universally conceded to be better. It was in the nature of things impossible that he should be an innovator, or a "radical reformer." Over and above all this, there were the vast distances and lack of means of communication which prevented him from exercising effective personal control over the areas remote from Constantinople. Only in the regions adjacent to the capital was it possible for him to make his authority immediately and directly felt.

On the other hand, it should be observed that the same laws and traditions by which the Sultan's authority was to some extent limited served also, in a measure, to fortify and support it. They helped, among other things, to guarantee it against the perils of a disputed succession. "The majority of the legists," so runs the Kanun-Nameh of Mohammed II, "have declared that those of my illustrious children and grandchildren who shall ascend the throne, shall have the right to execute their brothers, in order to insure the peace of the world; they are to act conformably." [2] The son whom the Sultan selected to succeed him had the undoubted privilege of putting to death all his brothers and nephews, provided he could do it. If he could not, and if one of those brothers succeeded in doing the same by him—as Selim the Terrible did by Achmed—well, it was the will of God; and such was the respect for the "blood of Osman" that the Turks, at least in the period of their greatness, rallied ultimately around the prince who had gained the throne, no matter what the methods by which he had contrived to attain it. The power of the Commander in chief was not to be endangered by rival claimants.

No despot, however absolute, can manage everything himself. The carrying out of his instructions and the decision of minor questions must, of necessity, be delegated to subordinates. Our next problem, therefore, is to examine the institutions through which Suleiman ruled. All of them are comprehended in two main groups, which have been respectively christened by a distinguished recent authority on Suleiman's government as the "Ottoman Ruling Institution" and the "Moslem Institution of the Ottoman Empire"; they correspond very roughly to our modern conception of "State" and "Church" in a country where there is a state church. It was not until after

[2] Joseph von Hammer-Purgstall, *Des osmanischen Reichs Staatsverfassung und Staatsverwaltung*, 2 vols. (Vienna, 1815), I, 98.

Suleiman's death that even the Venetians, shrewdest and most observant of all the Christian visitors at the Porte were fully able to comprehend their duality, their similarities, and their contrasts; very possibly the great Sultan may have taken pains to see to it that they were not more fully informed. But it may be worth while to quote a few comments from the reports of two famous bailos— Marcantonio Barbaro and Gianfrancesco Morosini—resident respectively in Constantinople from 1568 to 1573 and from 1582 to 1585, on the government of the Ottoman empire as they envisaged it.

Barbaro tells us:

It is a fact truly worthy of much consideration, that the riches, the forces, the government, and in short the whole state of the Ottoman Empire is founded upon and placed in the hands of persons all born in the faith of Christ; who by different methods are made slaves and transferred into the Mohammedan sect. Then whoever will carefully direct his attention to this principal consideration, will come more easily to an understanding of the government and nature of the Turks. . . .

Other sorts of persons are not ordinarily admitted to the honors and the pay of the Grand Signor, except the above-mentioned, all Christian-born. . . .

The Emperor of the Turks has ordinarily no other ordinances and no other laws which regulate justice, the state, and religion, than the Koran; so that, as the arms and the forces are wholly reposed in the hands of persons all born Christians, so, as I have already said, the administration of the laws is all solely in the hands of those who are born Turks, who bring up their sons in the service of the mosques, where they learn the Koran, until being come of age they are made kazis of the land.[3]

[3] Marcantonio Barbaro, report of 1573, in Albèri, *Relazioni*, 3rd ser., I, 314, 316, 322–323.

Morosini follows:

There are two sorts of Turks; one of these is composed of natives born of Turkish fathers, and the other of renegades, who are sons of Christian fathers, taken violently in the depredations which his fleets and galleys are accustomed to make on Christian territories, or levied in his own territory by force of arms from the subjects and non-Moslem taxpayers (carzeri) of the Signor, who while boys are by allurement or by force circumcised and made Turks. . . . Not only does the greater part of the soldiery of the Turks consist of these renegades, but in yet greater proportion all the principal offices of the Porte are wont to be given to them, from the grand vizir to the lowest chief of this soldiery, it being established by ancient custom that the sons of Turks cannot have these positions. . . .

To the native Turks are reserved then the governing of the mosques, the judging of civil and criminal cases, and the office of the chancery; from these are taken the kazis and the kaziaskers, the teachers (hojas), and their Mufti, who is the head of their false religion; and the kazis are like podestàs, and render justice to every one, and the kaziaskers are like judges of appeal from these kazis. . . .

The renegades are all slaves and take great pride in being able to say, "I am a slave of the Grand Signor"; since they know that this is a government or commonwealth of slaves, where it is theirs to command.[4]

The two most striking things in the above descriptions are that those to whom the Sultan intrusted the actual conduct of his government regarded themselves as being his slaves, and that the vast majority of them were of Christian parentage and traditions. It will be worth while to devote a few paragraphs to a further consideration of these facts.

The Ottomans deliberately elected to have the service

[4] Gianfrancesco Morosini, report of 1583, in Albèri, 3rd ser., III, 263–264, 266, 267.

of their Sultans, from the lowest menial in the Imperial Palace to the Grand Vizir at the head of the government, performed by a great family of some 80,000 slaves, who at the time of their entrance into it were practically all non-Moslems. Over each one of them the Sultan had the unquestioned power of life and death; they must obey his slightest wish; such property as they owned went automatically to their master when they died; and yet it is evident that the vast majority of them felt honored in the end by the condition to which they had been consigned. They were recruited principally in two ways; by capture in war, and by the system that was known as the devshurmeh, and in both the selection was made with the utmost care. By Mohammedan law the Sultan was entitled to one-fifth of all those taken prisoner on the field of battle, and special agents were detailed to see to it that he was given the ones most suitable for his purposes. Even more systematically planned was the so-called devshurmeh, or process by which the most promising youths were hunted out and taken from those portions of the empire from which tribute was due. These included certain parts of Asia Minor, the Black Sea lands, and the Balkan Peninsula, but the last-named proved by far the most fruitful soil. Every four years or oftener "a body of officials more skilled in judging boys than trained horse-dealers are in judging colts" [5] were sent out from Constantinople to the regions in question, to choose and bring back with them a certain number of the best youths they could find, to be inducted into the Sultan's great slave-family, and used there for whatever purpose they proved best fitted. Save in exceptional cases the recruits were between twelve and twenty years old; the ages preferred were between fourteen and eighteen. No family ties were suffered to interfere with the inexorable work-

[5] Lybyer, p. 51.

ings of the system. Parents who had sons of whom, both physically and intellectually, they had every reason to be proud, would be likely to lose them all, while their neighbors, who had produced poorer stuff, might well be left untouched. Certainly at first sight the whole practice seems utterly atrocious, if envisaged from the standpoint of the West. But if we approach the question without prejudice, it is at least fair to say that it had certain partially compensating advantages. If the mother was heartbroken at being forced to part with her best-loved son and see him take service with Moslems, she could console herself with the thought that it was wholly possible that he might some day attain to great wealth and power. There is plenty of good contemporaneous evidence to prove that many parents regarded the process rather as a privilege than as a burden. A passage from the third letter of Ogier de Busbecq, imperial ambassador at Constantinople from 1555 to 1562, is worth quoting in this connection:

I have my doubts [he says] as to whether the man who first abolished slavery is to be regarded as a public benefactor. I know that slavery brings with it various disadvantages, but these are counterbalanced by corresponding advantages. If a just and mild form of slavery, such as the Roman laws ordained, especially with the State for master, had continued, perhaps fewer gallows and gibbets would be needed to keep those in order who, having nothing but life and liberty, are driven by want into every conceivable crime. Freedom when combined with extreme poverty has made many a man a rascal; it causes temptation such as few can resist. Nature has denied to many the power of self-control, and the knowledge which is indispensable for acting aright; they need the support and guidance of a superior as the only means of stopping them in their career of vice. They are like savage animals, and require chains to prevent their becoming dangerous.

In Turkey the class which is likely to go astray is controlled by a master's authority, while the master is supported by the slave's labor. . . . We never attain the grandeur of the works of antiquity. What is the reason? Hands are wanting, or, in other words, slave labor. I need not mention what means of acquiring every kind of knowledge the ancients possessed in learned and educated slaves.

And then, at the end of the paragraph, he betrays his Occidental predilections by adding, "However, please consider that these remarks are not meant very seriously." [6] Certainly the practice could not be reconciled with Western ideals.

Yet it is not difficult to see why the Ottomans adopted it. In the first place, it conformed to one of the best-established principles of all true despotisms, namely, to rely on servants and ministers imported from afar, who could bear no part in local quarrels and factions; it reminds one of the tenth-century Slavic guard at Cordova of the Caliph Abd-ar-Rahman an-Nasir, and of the Turkish guard of the Abbasside Court of Baghdad. Secondly, it was a great missionary undertaking. By its means, unlimited possibilities were offered for the conversion to Islam of the most promising scions of the non-Moslem families of regions recently conquered. And yet it is interesting to note that the conversion was not ordinarily accomplished by compulsion. The policy seems to have been merely to isolate the new arrivals from Christian society and ideals, to give them every opportunity to become acquainted with the beauties and advantages of Islam, and to rely on environment and the influence of the majority to do the rest. Of course if the novice had any ambition to rise, conversion was the first requisite. It was impossible to attain to any post of prominence or importance in the army or government without open

[6] Busbecq, I, 210–211.

profession of the Mohammedan faith, and there is evidence that its adoption was speedier and more sincere at the upper rungs of the ladder than at the lower. But it is not probable that any member of the Sultan's slave-family failed to succumb, outwardly, at least, in the end. How many continued to be Christians at heart is a matter of opinion, but there is reason to believe that insistence on orthodox Mohammedanism—an insistence which was probably first stressed in Suleiman's time—often resulted in hypocritical outward conformity.

We pass from the composition and personnel of the "Ruling Institution" to the ways in which it discharged its more important functions. Of these the first was the conduct of war; for "the Ottoman government had been an army before it was anything else. . . . Fighting was originally the first business of the state, and governing the second." [7] Though the preponderance had perhaps been shifted to the governmental side of the picture by the time of Suleiman the Magnificent, the traditional primacy of the army was never forgotten; the fact that the Sultan personally accompanied his armies on almost every one of their great campaigns, and took the larger part of his slave family with him, speaks volumes in this connection. "In fact, army and government were one. War was the external purpose, government the internal purpose, of one institution, composed of one body of men." [8]

The backbone of the Ottoman army was of course the Janissaries, or "new troops"; all of them were members of the Sultan's great slave-family, and were recruited as described above. Suleiman realized the supreme importance of having a large body of crack infantrymen as a nucleus for his forces, and there is evidence that the 12,000 whom he had inherited from his father were irregularly increased

[7] Lybyer, p. 90. [8] Lybyer, p. 91.

before the end of the reign. It is, however, quite inadmissible to assume that the 48,316 members of his slave-family, who are said to have accompanied him on his last campaign, were all members of the corps.[9] The Janissaries were picked for their physical strength and fitness, and for their love of fighting. They labored, however, under the serious disadvantage that they had no weapon wherewith to thrust. "The Ottoman's idea of arms was from the first limited to a sabre and a missile." The Janissaries had scimitars and bows, but they had no spears. At the very time when the pikeman formed the core of the Spanish infantry whose supremacy on the field of battle was the dominant fact in the military history of the Western Europe of the day, the Turk lacked any weapon to correspond. "In the sieges of Rhodes and Malta the Hospitallers constantly cleared the slashing Janissaries out of the trenches with half-pikes." [10]

The Janissaries were subjected, both in peace and in war, to the most rigorous discipline. Until the time of Suleiman they had been forbidden to marry. Apparently there was some relaxation of this restriction during his reign, and at a later date, when children of Janissaries began to be admitted to the corps, its old-time pugnacity declined; the old recruits, collected in the traditional way, were far sterner stuff than their offspring. But the Janissaries also enjoyed many privileges. The Sultan's own name was inscribed on the roll of the first of the one hundred and sixty-five ortas, or companies, into which they were divided, and Suleiman insisted on receiving

[9] As does C. W. C. Oman, *History of the Art of War in the Sixteenth Century*, p. 759. Officially it would seem that the number of the Janissaries remained, down to the nineteenth century, at 12,000, but it is clear that many others had by that time been permitted to enjoy the privileges and exemptions of the corps, and to use its name.

[10] These quotations are from an article by Major J. W. DeForest in the *Atlantic Monthly* for April, 1878, p. 507, entitled "The Russians on the Bosphorus."

his pay with them; [11] this last was a shrewd move, for it made them proudly conscious of the fact that he was one of them, and greatly increased their devotion to his person. They could not be punished for misconduct save by their own officers; even the Grand Vizir lacked any authority over them. Everything served to enhance their *esprit de corps*. In battle they guaranteed the Sultan's personal safety, and were the terror of his foes. In time of peace, they were, to put it mildly, exceedingly difficult to keep in hand, and the necessity of giving them occupation was a subsidiary reason for the initiation of more than one of Suleiman's campaigns. They regarded the periods which elapsed between the death of one Sultan and the accession of his successor as intervals during which they were virtually free to do their own will; Suleiman was indeed fortunate that he had been able to gather the reins of authority into his own hands within eight days of the death of his father. They demanded and received from him an unprecedentedly large donation on this occasion, and had often to be pacified, later in the reign, by liberal gifts. They often had a decisive voice in the matter of the succession to the throne in case there were rival claimants. The circumstances of Selim's accession will be recalled; in case of doubt the candidate who commanded their allegiance was virtually certain to win; Suleiman again was exceedingly lucky in being Selim's only son. In later years, Suleiman himself was to have tragic experience, within his own family, of the power of the Janissaries. [12]

The body of cavalry which most closely corresponded to the Janissaries, and like them was under command of the Sultan and not of the seraskier in time of war, was the Spahis of the Porte. Their organization was much looser

---

[11] Ignatius Mouradgea d'Ohsson, *Tableau général de l'Empire Othoman*, 7 vols. (Paris, 1788–1824), VII, 354–355.

[12] Lybyer, pp. 91–93, and references there.

and more ancient than that of the Janissaries, but they were also regarded as a part of the Sultan's great slave-family or kullar. The so-called feudal Spahis, the akinji and azabs were in quite a different category, and far less closely in contact with Suleiman. Nevertheless selected members of the imperial slave-family were assigned to the command of the units into which they were divided, to make sure that they did not get wholly out of touch. The magnificent discipline of a Turkish army, which elicited such unbounded admiration from all who beheld it, was doubtless chiefly exhibited by the Janissaries and the Spahis. Certainly a wilder troop than a marauding band of ravaging akinji would be difficult to imagine; and yet when they were called in they never failed to respond. The thing that really gave the Turkish army its power and reputation in Suleiman's day was the inspiration of the constant presence of the Sultan in its midst. The moment that it came to be the custom, under his son Selim, for the Sultan to delegate the supreme command, in order to spare himself the rigors of campaigning, the Ottoman military power and empire began to decline. The system had its disadvantages. The indispensability of the Sultan's presence with his troops rendered it impossible for him to divide his army, or to fight on two fronts at once. It forced him to make peace with the Hapsburgs when a campaign against Persia became imperative. It was unsuited to the needs of a rapidly expanding empire, and limited the possibilities of Ottoman conquest. Yet it was in the army and the direction of it that Sultan Suleiman and his great slave-family were to be seen at their most successful and their best.[13]

Suleiman was the undisputed head of the government of the Ottoman empire. If the sacred Moslem law and the

[13] Lybyer, pp. 98–113.

conservative traditions of his people set limits to what he could do, there was no rival authority or institution of any kind to challenge or imperil his power; every official was appointed, directly or indirectly, by him and could at any moment be dismissed by him; each was expected, as long as he held his place, to do his utmost to aid in the carrying out of his master's will. The most able and intelligent members of the kullar were trained for the highest offices of the state, both central and local. The judiciary, which was the only department of the government service to be removed from the sphere of influence of the slave-family, and was wholly staffed by Moslems born, was also entirely under his control. He continued the practice, initiated by his great-grandfather, of granting appointment and investiture to the Greek Patriarch, and he issued orders to the latter's flock to render him suitable obedience. In all parts of his empire, and over all the different peoples and creeds that inhabited it, his authority, in theory at least, was absolute.[14]

To Suleiman belonged also the sole power to issue laws. The sacred Moslem law, or sheri, as we have already pointed out, was wholly beyond his power to alter or annul; and the sheri was originally intended not only to regulate the government of the Ottoman state of the time in which it was first adopted, but also the conduct of its individual members. But the origins of the sheri stretched back for over seven centuries, and times had changed. Its fundamental principles must indeed be left intact, but in the matter of their application it would be possible to supplement them and give greater latitude. Indeed it was essential to do so, unless the modern Ottoman was to lose touch with the precepts of the Koran, and be untrue to the faith that he professed. Suleiman saw the need and

[14] Lybyer, pp. 150–151.

resolved to meet it; and the jurists and theologians rendered him great service by giving him their expert opinions on just how far he could go without actually transgressing the law. They classified the provisions of the sheri into different groups, in accordance with the measure of the obligation to obey them. They strove, whenever possible, to aid their master by elastic interpretations. Suleiman made the best possible use of their assistance. Not that he was ever in danger of transgressing the sacred law; he was far too devout a Moslem for that; but he realized that it was imperative that its precepts be accommodated to the needs of a society vastly different from that which gave it birth. Before the capture of Constantinople, the Sultans who had attempted to supplement the sacred law had issued firmans or ordinances; beginning with Mohammed II, they had adopted the Greek word κανών or rule, which became in Turkish kanun, as the name for their legislation; it is but one of countless instances of the debt owed by the Ottomans to Byzantium. The Moslem was ever a judicious copier.[15]

The amount of Suleiman's legislation, and the areas that it covers, will seem far too insignificant to the Western mind to justify his Turkish title of "El Kanuni"; but he at least did much more than any Sultan since Mohammed II to reconcile the fundamental precepts of the sheri with the conditions under which the sixteenth-century Ottoman lived. Most of his laws are concerned with matters of land-tenure, taxation, and the regulation of markets and prices. Criminal procedure also demanded and received revision. Recently conquered Egypt, too, which was in terrible confusion, was given what virtually amounted to a new constitution—the Kanun-nameh Misr. Suleiman did not hesitate to emphasize the necessity of obeying those parts of the sacred law which were un-

[15] Lybyer, pp. 152–159.

popular, such as its ban on the drinking of wine, or those which were personally obnoxious to him, such as its disapproval of musical instruments and silver-plate. It is also true that the Sultan put forth much of his legislation without adequate personal knowledge of those whom it principally affected. The whole thing was done too much *de haut en bas,* with the result that many of the best laws which Suleiman enacted were not properly enforced. Bribery and corruption were effectively employed to shield those most unfortunately affected by his legislation, and it all had to be done over again, within fifty years of his death, in the reign of Achmet I. But there can be no doubt that the great Sultan was earnestly desirous to maintain fairness, justice, and good order, and to bring the fundamental precepts of the ancient law of Islam into accord with the wholly different circumstances under which his life and that of his subjects was lived.[16]

According to the Kanun-Nameh of Mohammed II, the Ottoman empire was to be organized on the basis of a division into four departments, recalling the four posts of the regulation Turkish army tent; it was a pretty illustration of the primacy of the military consideration in the Ottoman mind. Of these four, only three concern us here; the other may be better discussed in connection with the "Moslem Institution" and judicial affairs. We now take up in order the vizirs, the Defterdars, or heads of the treasury, and the Nishanji and Reis Effendi, or secretaries of state.[17]

In the earlier days there had been but one vizir. In the time of Suleiman the number rose for the first time to four. The word means "burden-bearer," or, according to

---

[16] Lybyer, pp. 159–163, 276–277.

[17] Lybyer, pp. 163–187; Alfred Rambaud, in Lavisse and Rambaud, IV. 753.

another derivation, "decider" or "judge"; and the Grand Vizir, who dominated the others, fully deserved his title. He was in fact a sort of Vice-Sultan; and as long as he continued to enjoy his master's confidence, he was virtually supreme, under him, in every department of the government service. He had little leisure; for in addition to representing the Sultan as head of the military and civil administration, as presiding officer of the Divan, and as supreme judge, he made the majority of the important appointments, and he had to receive great officials and participate in numerous state ceremonies. So heavy were the responsibilities that the term of office was usually short, but Suleiman was fortunate in finding three really notable men, whose tenure was unusually long: Ibrahim from 1523 to 1536, Rustem from 1544 to 1553, and again from 1555 to 1561, and finally Mohammed Sokolli, who took office in 1565 and lasted on for thirteen years after Suleiman's death into the reign of his grandson until 1579. All of these, be it noted, were Christian renegades; and all of them also were the Sultan's kul, who might be executed, if he so desired, at a moment's notice. It was a fascinating and a dangerous job. Under a strong monarch, like Suleiman, the system worked well; for a Sultan such as he, who kept in touch with everything that was going on, could safely delegate much to subordinates. But the great increase of the authority of the Grand Vizir which marked his reign was to prove disastrous for his weaker successors. On the one hand it enabled the Sultans to spend their lives in idleness and debauchery; on the other, the position of the Grand Vizir was so perilous and insecure that he dared not formally take over to himself the duties and functions which his master was no longer capable of fulfilling.[18]

We pass to the administration of finance. There can

[18] Lybyer, pp. 163-167.

be no doubt that Suleiman's revenues were larger than those of any of his Christian contemporaries. They were considerably greater at the close of his reign than at the beginning, and have been estimated, toward the last, at an annual value of from seven to twelve million ducats. The bullion content of a ducat was 3.93 times that of the present American gold dollar; the relative purchasing power of money in the sixteenth century and today is a matter on which it is impossible to pronounce.[19] But there is plenty of evidence that, with all his wealth, the Sultan often found himself in need of more; the new methods of obtaining funds which were introduced during his reign are the best possible proof of it. The only levies authorized by the sacred law were a tithe of the produce of the lands of believers; a special poll tax on all adult male non-Moslems, and the kharaj or land-tax on conquered territories. But since then a host of new imposts had been added. The whole system of export and import duties at Constantinople had been taken over bodily from the Greeks: a great variety of new levies, differing from region to region, had been laid on fields, produce, mines, markets, etc., on celibates, and also on the permission to wed. Unrest in the provinces was sure to be punished by heavy fines, and Suleiman got much money from the confiscation of the property of high officials and other persons of great wealth. The simultaneous development of the machinery for collecting the taxes gives additional evidence of the rapidity of the increase of the Sultan's revenues. New commissions were being constantly brought into existence to deal with newly invented taxes. They were added from time to time as the need arose, but there was never any systematic reor-

---

[19] Cf. on this question Francisco López de Gómara, *Annals of the Emperor Charles V*, ed. R. B. Merriman (Oxford, 1912), pp. 138–139, and R. B. M., III, 32, note 1.

ganization of the Ottoman treasury as a whole. At the head of it there remained indeed the four great Defterdars (the word means "keeper of books," that is, tax books), each of them in charge of the collection of the revenues of one of the great portions of the empire; but under them there had come into being by the end of the reign upwards of twenty-five bureaus, some of them to deal with collecting, others with disbursements, some with the finances of a certain locality, others with those of some category or class. Most of these bureaus were resident in the regions committed to their charge and not in Constantinople, and instead of sending the funds they collected back to the capital, they often disbursed them themselves: doubtless, in theory at least, according to definite instructions, but also, in most cases, without adequate supervision. It is not an exaggeration to describe them as wellnigh independent bodies. In order to make sure of its money the government had recourse to tax-farming. The Defterdars would sell the revenues of certain regions for lump sums to important magnates, who in turn would resell them to others, and the process was often repeated until in the end it might well be "not Ottomans, but Christians and Jews who applied the screws to the unfortunate subjects. The amount wrung from them might easily be double what the government received." Comparisons with the financial expedients of Charles V and Philip II in Spain will be found profitable. In general it would seem that the increasingly intimate contacts of the Ottomans with the Occident had served to make them forget the noble simplicity of the system of taxation prescribed by the Koran.[20]

Less information has come down to us in regard to what Western writers have characterized as the "chancery" of the Ottoman government; by the end of Suleiman's reign it might perhaps be more accurate to describe it as

[20] Lybyer, pp. 167–182.

the "secretaryship of state for foreign affairs." Originally the head of it was the Nishanji, whose sole duty was to authenticate the Sultan's edicts; but before Suleiman's death he had been practically—though not officially—superseded by the Reis Effendi, who, under the direction of the Sultan and Grand Vizir, had an important voice in the conduct of international relations. In the times at which the Sultan intrusted everything to the Grand Vizir, the latter found that he had more work on his hands than he could possibly perform, and consequently, in turn, tended to give more and more autonomy to the Reis Effendi. This development did not reach completion till the reigns of the great Sultan's weaker successors, who delegated everything to subordinates and lived a life of luxury and ease, but the origins of it stretch back to Suleiman's day. It is worth noting that the numerous clerks of the chancery, as well as of the treasury, who had been mostly Greek and Christian at the time of Suleiman's accession, tended more and more, as time went on, to be recruited from among the Turks. The amount of secretarial labor increased apace, and it became more and more essential to intrust it to those who were familiar with the Turkish language and traditions. It was a significant evidence of the truth of the dictum that when Turks dismount from their horses, they become bureaucrats and scribblers; it was also an augury of approaching decline.[21]

A few words remain to be added in regard to local government, and the condition of the non-Moslems in the Ottoman Empire. The central authority made itself much more effectively felt in some regions than in others. In Greece, Bulgaria, Servia, Bosnia, and Dobrudja, as well as in the greater part of Asia Minor, it really kept things under its authority; but the inhabitants of Mol-

[21] Lybyer, pp. 182–187; Léon Cahun, *Introduction à l'histoire de l'Asie: Turcs et Mongols* (Paris, 1896), p. 82.

davia, Wallachia, Georgia, and most of Kurdistan ultimately succeeded, by means of paying tribute, in retaining their own princes, while those of Albania and Monte-
negro, intrenched behind their mountains, remained practically independent of control by Constantinople in Suleiman's day, as did also, though in a somewhat different
fashion, the Berber states of North Africa. And it is fair
to add that the Ottoman regime was not unpopular. It
had the good fortune to follow, both in Asia Minor and
the Balkans, on the heels of a period of anarchy and confusion; it brought in with it a sort of *Pax Romana*. Despite
the grossness of many of its customs and the burdensome-
ness of its taxation, the Greeks of Rhodes preferred it to the
rules of the Knights of St. John; the Eubœans and the
Greeks of the Morea liked it better than that of the Venetians; and the Serbs and Hungarians compared it favorably with the dominion of the Austrian Hapsburgs. It
was far less intolerant than the governments of the Western Christian nations. If non-believers paid the extra imposts that were demanded of them, they were always
permitted to worship God in their own way.—The
"Grand Dragoman of the Porte," translator, host, the man
whom all travellers and merchants arriving in Constantinople must immediately get in touch with, and to all
intents and purposes, a minister of state, was always, in
Suleiman's time, an Orthodox Greek.[22]

The regular name for an administrative district of the
Ottoman Empire was a sanjak, and the official selected
from the Sultan's kullar who had charge of it was called a
sanjak bey; the head of a group of districts was known as
a beylerbey; and each was provided with ample assistance
by an adequate staff of lieutenants, bookkeepers, and
clerks. The most important beylerbeys were those of Anatolia and Rumelia; the former in time of peace was nor-

[22] Lavisse and Rambaud, IV, 767–769.

mally resident in Constantinople; the latter was frequently there and had his regular place in the Divan. Like all officials of the Turkish empire, their principal functions were those of wartime. On them fell the duty of collecting the feudal Spahis of their respective areas, and bringing them to unite with the imperial forces at the proper time and place. When the fighting was in Europe the army of the beylerbey of Rumelia had the right of the battle-line, and that of the beylerbey of Anatolia the left; when in Asia, the order was reversed.[23]

Of all the subject peoples of the Ottoman Empire, the Greeks were those with whom its authorities were brought into most intimate contact. But it was a Greek people sadly depleted of intellectual and social leaders. The stars of its intellectual firmament, such as Bessarion and Gemisthos Plethon, had fled westward before and after the capture of Constantinople to complete the triumph of the cult of the classics in the Italy of the Renaissance. Most of its ancient magistrates found it expedient to go over to Islam. Rival candidacies for its chief ecclesiastical dignities, from the patriarchate downward, gave the Turks an admirable opportunity, of which they were prompt to avail themselves, to undermine, while they still professed to support, the constitution of the Byzantine Church. All that was left was the small trader, apparently almost contemptible; forbidden to bear arms, or to arm the ships in which he sailed; yet not unwelcome at the Porte because he had to pay double duty. At the same time he was better off than the Italians, who had, in turn, to pay twice as much as he. Competition was to be keen, in later years, from the merchants of those Western countries such as France, to which capitulations granted special privileges; even more from the Armenians; and most of all from the

---

[23] Lybyer, 103–105; Lavisse and Rambaud, IV, 755–758. The word "sanjak" originally meant "flag," or "banner."

Jews expelled from Spain, many of whom subsequently established themselves at Constantinople and Salonika. But the Greeks were quite able to maintain themselves. It was through commerce that they kept alive the memory of their glorious past. It was through commerce, at a much later day, that they were to prepare themselves to regain their freedom.[24]

The Slavs of the Danube valley were in less happy case. Most of them were on the grand route of the Ottoman invasions into the northwest; they were burdened with every kind of extra taxation, and when the Turkish armies passed through their lands, they were compelled to do everything within their power to facilitate the Ottoman advance. The inhabitants of the more mountainous regions on the Adriatic were left, comparatively speaking, undisturbed; and many of them emigrated and took service, under the name of stradiots, with the Venetians, the French, the Emperor, and the king of England. Further eastward, the Wallachians and Moldavians vainly attempted to regain their independence, with the aid of the Poles and the Russians and occasionally with that of Ferdinand; but Zápolya was in a position to defeat their intrigues. Several Ottoman expeditions despatched into the regions in question, in the course of Suleiman's reign, furnished an argument for submission to Turkish control which the inhabitants found increasingly potent, while the Khan of the Crimean Tatars also rendered Suleiman valuable aid in keeping these territories in hand. The remoter parts of Asia Minor and the subject portions of Arabia all had special systems of government of their own; but whatever the local arrangement, the authority of the Sultan was in the last analysis supreme.[25]

[24] Lavisse and Rambaud, IV, 769–773. George Finlay, in his *History of Greece under Ottoman and Venetian Domination* (1856), draws a much darker picture.

[25] Lavisse and Rambaud, IV, 772–776.

The administration of justice is the only department of the government service which we have left untouched, and the reason is that it was in the hands of a very different set of people from the Sultan's kullar, or slave-family of renegade Christians, who dominated everything else. Since law and theology are closely fused in the Koran, it was essential that the control of them be placed in the hands of Mohammedans born, and the so-called "Moslem Institution" of the Ottoman Empire was the body to which, under the Sultan, the double task was intrusted.

A few more words must be added, at this point, to explain the nature of this "Moslem Institution." Aside from the fundamental difference between its personnel and that of the Sultan's kullar, it has been contrasted thereto as church is contrasted to state. But Islam had no hierarchically organized body of clergy, such as was to be found in all the Christian nations of the West; any devout Mohammedan who was "in any way lifted above the level of the ordinary believer" [26] could justly regard himself as belonging to the great body whose primary duty it was to preserve and strengthen the law and the faith of the Prophet, though the importance of the role that he played in it depended primarily on his intellectual abilities, and his knowledge of the Koran and of the Sacred Law. The so-called "Moslem Institution" was primarily, then, like a great Ottoman national university, which all true believers might enter, practically free of charge; but of which only the most distinguished graduates could aspire to attain office. The juristic side demanded far higher abilities than did the theological. It is the juristic side that invites our chief attention here.

The body of those who had "satisfied the intellectual requirements" of the "Moslem Institution" in its capacity

[26] Lybyer, p. 199.

as a society of scholars, was known as the ulema or class of learned men. The ulema was divided into two main groups—the muftis who elected to become juristic counsellors to the great officials, central and local, of the kullar, and the more active category, from kazis to kaziaskers, who may be compared to the practicing judges of today.

A mufti was assigned to every sanjak bey and beylerbey, and also to the resident judge in every important city; there were between two and three hundred of them in official status and they were all appointed for life. Whenever a question arose which involved a knowledge of the sacred law, the mufti was consulted and gave his professional opinion or fetva, which usually settled the case. But the mufti of Constantinople was in a class by himself; for the Sultan and his chief ministers were constantly asking his advice on matters of the highest public importance. Unlike the other muftis he was not regularly chosen from the class to which he belonged, but was usually advanced by the Sultan from the ranks of the kazis and kaziaskers; since the time of Mohammed II he had been called the Sheik-ul-Islam ("Ancient of Islam"). Many Christian writers have compared his position to that of the Pope, but the parallel should be drawn with reservations. The Sheik-ul-Islam took precedence indeed over all other government officials, save the Grand Vizir. In a sense he was even the superior of the Sultan himself, since he was the exponent of the sheri, which the Sultan was powerless to change. "He represented justice and the image of God." He alone could formally pronounce whether or not a war which the Sultan had declared was "holy," and incumbent on all true Moslems. On him alone devolved the solemn responsibility of declaring whether or not the Sultan had violated the sacred law, and whether or not he could, in consequence, be rightfully deposed. On the other hand, he had no power of initiative whatsoever. He could not speak unless his opinion was asked; his sole duty was to decide, when appealed to, what the law demanded should be done; his verdicts were given somewhat as are those of the Supreme Court of the United States. And the most despotic of Sultans did not venture to ignore them. They might disregard the fetvas of the lesser muftis, though they risked, by so doing, the allegiance of the faithful, but the sentence of the Sheik-ul-Islam could not be transgressed. It was by the Sheik-ul-Islam that Selim the Terrible was restrained from following up his massacres of Moslem heretics by whole-sale extermination of the Christians within his boundaries. "Conversion, tribute, or the sword" was the formula in the Koran and in the sacred law; provided the Christians paid their kharaj and poll tax, they could not lawfully be disturbed in the exercise of their faith; the great mufti was positive on the point; he informed the Patriarch of his decision, and furnished him with arguments for the protection of his flock which Selim dared not neglect. And, as we shall see more fully in the ensuing chapter, it was through the answer given by the Sheik-ul-Islam to a hypothetical question which was propounded to him on purpose, that Suleiman finally convinced himself, in 1553, that he was justified in putting his eldest son Mustapha to death.[27]

The muftis as a class really wielded enormous power in the Ottoman state. They were less highly paid than many other less important officials; they were never outwardly conspicuous; yet they embodied and fortified that conservatism and changelessness which are the basis of the faith of Islam. The prime object of their fetvas was to make sure that the customs and practices of the age in which they lived did not violate the fundamental principles of the sacred law; they looked backward, not

[27] Lybyer, pp. 199–215.

forward. It was chiefly due to their influence that Ottoman civilization remained practically stationary for more than three centuries after the death of Suleiman the Magnificent—three centuries during which the rest of the world advanced apace.[28]

The judges who presided over the courts where actual cases were tried were divided into various complicated categories; for the Ottomans, like all other Moslems, took pride in the perfection—one might also possibly add, in the intricacy—of their judicial arrangements; but the kazis at the bottom and the kaziaskers at the top are the only ones we need consider here. The kazis were stationed, each in the principal city of the region to which he was assigned, and dealt with the cases that were brought before them with a speed and definiteness which evoked the admiration of Western observers. "Since there is nothing here [that is, in France] so near immortality," writes one of them, "as the processes and extortions of our law, I am ashamed to have to tell of the diligence and promptitude of the verdicts of the courts of a people whom we hold in low esteem." [29] There was doubtless much bribery and corruption, but the courts of the West were by no means wholly free from them; in any case, the Ottoman system got the job done. One is reminded of the saying of the great Spanish jurist Solórzano that "it is better to omit to ascertain and punish some things than to retard everything." [30] The kaziaskers, at the head of the hierarchy, were but two; one for Rumelia, or the Ottoman lands in Europe, one for Anatolia, which was supposed to include all the Turkish territories in Asia Minor and in Africa. Both were resident most of the time in Constantinople, and it is worth noting that cases which con-

[28] Lybyer, p. 215.
[29] Guillaume Postel, *De la république des Turcs* (Poitiers, 1560), I, 127.
[30] Juan de Solórzano Pereira, *Política Indiana* (Madrid, 1647), lib. V, cap. X, paragraph 22.

cerned Moslems were brought before the kaziasker of Rumelia, while those which concerned non-Moslems were tried by the kaziasker of Anatolia. Both of them were highly paid and much overworked, and when not occupied with other official duties, were supposed to sit in justice in their own houses; most of the cases that came before them were sent up on appeal from the minor tribunals, but their courts, like all others in the Ottoman Empire, were also courts of first instance. To them was also delegated the decision of many of the suits brought before the Grand Vizir, who as representative of the Sultan was officially the chief of the ulema, and consequently the highest judicial officer of the land. But the most important of all their functions was that of dealing with the capital cases of great officials which were brought before them in the Divan. That great assembly sat in judgment on important magnates, with whose conduct in office the Sultan had reason to be displeased. Often, indeed, the accused was not present to defend himself; but, in theory at least, no one was ever executed without a trial, and in trials of this kind, the decisive voice usually lay with the kaziaskers.[31]

It will be worth while in closing to devote a paragraph to this Divan, for in it the kullar and the ulema were brought together. It was, in fact, next to the Sultan himself, who was the head of both of its component parts, the supreme expression of the unity of the Ottoman state. On campaigns, it might be held in the tent of the Grand Vizir or even on horseback. On such occasions it was primarily, of course, a council of war, and was shorn of much of its normal ceremony and magnificence. In time of peace it met, with much pomp and circumstance, in the Hall of the Divan at Constantinople. Its sessions there were held on Saturdays, Sundays, Mondays, and Tues-

[31] Lybyer, pp. 220–224.

days. They began soon after sunrise, and often lasted for seven or eight hours. Every possible precaution was taken to see to it that the proceedings were not disturbed. In earlier days the Sultan had invariably presided in person, but Suleiman usually delegated this function to his Grand Vizir, and contented himself with keeping a grated window in the wall, through which he could listen, when he so desired, to the course of the deliberations. Since the members of the Divan had no means of knowing when he was on hand, they found it expedient to conduct themselves as if he were always present in their midst. Some Turkish writers have maintained that the Sultan's absence from the Divan was the primary cause of the decline of the Ottoman Empire in the succeeding period; but in view of the vast increase of business and responsibility which the rapid expansion of his dominions rendered inevitable, we can scarcely wonder that Suleiman seized the chance to relieve himself of such a burdensome task, and he had no compunctions about giving a free hand to the best of his Grand Vizirs. The Divan, when it met in full force and panoply at Constantinople, was at once the highest Council of State, or in modern parlance the cabinet—that portion of its functions being performed by those officers of the kullar who were privileged to attend it, and a supreme court of justice, in which cases of the highest importance were decided by the Grand Vizir and the kaziaskers. Great questions of national policy, such as problems of internal government, the lines of diplomacy, and the making of war and peace, were discussed and settled there; so likewise the weightiest lawsuits of the empire, and the fates of its greatest magnates, received in the Divan their final verdicts. All its decisions, whether political or judicial, were subject, of course, to the approval of the Sultan. Its various officials repaired after the sessions to the Hall of Audience to ask for that approval; if an eminent Grand Vizir was in the saddle, it was seldom refused. The speed with which the Divan dispatched its business was extraordinary. The Turk was a man of few words; anything like the modern practice of filibustering was inconceivable. Though the Divan had no power to make laws, its influence on legislation was not negligible. The kanuns issued by the Sultan were based in large measure on the information he received from its members; it was the means by which he kept in touch with everything that was going on. "It was a training-school of judges, administrators, and statesmen"; it was the capstone of the kullar and the ulema; "under the leadership of the Grand Vizir [it] governed the Otto-man Empire for the Sultan." [32]

[32] Lybyer, pp. 187–193.

๛ VIII ๛

The Seraglio; The Harem; The Sultan
and His Subjects

We have hitherto discussed Suleiman's kullar as the nerve centre of the Ottoman army and government. It remains to consider it as a slave family and a nobility and as the dominant factor of the imperial court.

The coupling of the name "slave family" with that of a "nobility" may first provoke surprise, and a few words to explain the apparent contradiction are necessary to a comprehension of what follows. To begin with, it is essential once more to remind the reader that it was a highly desirable distinction to belong to the Sultan's kullar; no stigma whatsoever attached to it. Its members all wore a special costume which entitled them to the respect customarily due to those closely associated with monarchs. Their bodily wants were cared for, and they were generally exempt from taxation. Even the humblest of them, who never rose beyond the position of servant or under-gardener, was possessed of all these privileges. The 80,000 members of Suleiman's kullar were comparable, in fact, to the nobles of any one of the great Christian kingdoms of the West, with the important difference that the privileges conferred on them were, with a few exceptions, not hereditary. The whole system was based on the principle of advancement by merit. In a very true sense, indeed, the kullar was "a school in which the pupils were enrolled for life." Suleiman, it was said, "sows hope of certain reward in all conditions of men, who by means of virtue, may succeed in mounting to better fortune," [1] but only those who made good progress were promoted and got to the top. For Ottoman political philosophy never contemplated the possibility of permitting any one of the members of the kullar to hand on to his descendants the position or the privileges he had been able to win for himself. His children might indeed be permitted to inherit a portion of his property, though even this was by Suleiman's gracious favor rather than of right; but his dignities and authority were regranted by his master after his death or disgrace to whatever member of the kullar was deemed most worthy to assume them. The Sultans did not propose to have their sovereign authority endangered by the power of great feudal families, as were the monarchies of England, France, and Spain at different periods in the fifteenth century. It was in order to avoid just this peril that the kullar was recruited in the way in which it was. Every member of it was considered to be "his own ancestor" and his tenure of office was terrifyingly insecure. The political pot was perpetually kept boiling. When any one died or was removed, his place was open to the ablest candidate, whose origin might well be totally different from that of his predecessor.

Western observers were much impressed by these things: none more than Ogier Ghiselin de Busbecq, the Imperial ambassador at Constantinople intermittently from 1555 to 1562. He was a fascinating personality, this Busbecq—a great classical scholar, antiquarian, and copyist of ancient inscriptions—a botanist also, to whom among other things we are indebted for the introduction of the

---

[1] Vasco Diaz Tanco, *Libro dell' origine et successione dell' imperio de' Turchi* (Venice 1558), p. 197.

horse chestnut, the lilac, and tulip into Western Europe [2]—but, above all, a charming, open-minded, tolerant, humorous man of the world, and a keen observer of men and events, who was not ashamed to learn and profit by what he saw of the manners and customs of a people which the mass of Western Europe still regarded as barbarous. Here is his description, written to an old friend and fellow-student in 1555, of the Sultan's kullar as he first saw it, when summoned before Suleiman at Amasia in Asia Minor.

The Sultan was seated on a very low ottoman not more than a foot from the ground, which was covered with a quantity of costly rugs and cushions of exquisite workmanship; near him lay his bow and arrows. His air, as I said, was by no means gracious, and his face wore a stern, though dignified, expression.

On entering we were separately conducted into the royal presence by the chamberlains, who grasped our arms. This has been the Turkish fashion of admitting people to the sovereign ever since a Croat, in order to avenge the death of his master, Marcus, Despot of Servia, asked Amurath for an audience, and took advantage of it to slay him.[3] After having gone through a pretence of kissing his hand, we were conducted backwards to the wall opposite his seat, care being taken that we should never turn our backs to him. . . .

The Sultan's hall was crowded with people, among whom were several officers of high rank. Besides these there were all the troopers of the Imperial guard, Spahis, Ghourebas

---

[2] See his *Life and Letters*, I, 107–108; also "Brave Busbecq" by George Sarton in *Isis*, XXXIII (1942), 557–575. Busbecq was much aided in his botanical work by his private physician, Willem Quackelbeen, who accompanied him to Constantinople. Much additional information will be found in the forthcoming eighth volume of Dr. F. Verdoorn's *Chronica Botanica*: Dr. Verdoorn was kind enough to show me several pages of the typewritten manuscript. Busbecq was knighted in 1563, and the original patent of his knighthood is to be seen today in the Houghton Library at Harvard.

[3] Cf. note to page 10, note 9, *ante*.

[Ghurebas], Ouloufedgis [Ulufaje, or paid troops], and a large force of Janissaries; but there was not in all that great assembly a single man who owed his position to aught save his valor and his merit. No distinction is attached to birth among the Turks; the deference to be paid to a man is measured by the position he holds in the public service. There is no fighting for precedence; a man's place is marked out by the duties he discharges. In making his appointments the Sultan pays no regard to any pretensions on the score of wealth or rank, nor does he take into consideration recommendations or popularity; he considers each case on its own merits, and examines carefully into the character, ability, and disposition of the man whose promotion is in question. It is by merit that men rise in the service, a system which insures that posts should only be assigned to the competent. Each man in Turkey carries in his own hand his ancestry and his position in life, which he may make or mar as he will. Those who receive the highest offices from the Sultan are for the most part the sons of shepherds or herdsmen, and so far from being ashamed of their parentage, they actually glory in it, and consider it a matter of boasting that they owe nothing to the accident of birth; for they do not believe that high qualities are either natural or hereditary, nor do they think that they can be handed down from father to son, but that they are partly the gift of God, and partly the result of good training, great industry, and unwearied zeal; arguing that high qualities do not descend from a father to his son or heir, any more than a talent for music, mathematics, or the like; and that the mind does not derive its origin from the father, so that the son should necessarily be like the father in character, but emanates from heaven, and is thence infused into the human body. Among the Turks, therefore, honors, high posts, and judgeships are the rewards of great ability and good service. If a man be dishonest, or lazy, or careless, he remains at the bottom of the ladder, an object of contempt; for such qualities there are no honors in Turkey!

This is the reason that they are successful in their undertakings, that they lord it over others, and are daily extending the bounds of their empire. These are not our ideas; with us there is no opening left for merit; birth is the standard for everything; the prestige of birth is the sole key to advancement in the public service. But on this head I shall perhaps have more to say to you in another place, and you must consider what I have said as strictly private.[4]

A few more words need to be added to Busbecq's description, in order to understand how Suleiman's kullar —or, as we may for the present purposes describe it, his household or court—had come to be constituted in the way in which it was during the great Sultan's reign. In earlier days it had been a much more primitive affair, for the early Ottomans had not been induced to depart from their pristine simplicity by the reports that reached them of the splendors of Baghdad; not till after the conquest of Constantinople had their rulers been persuaded to adopt many of the forms and ceremonial which had so greatly impressed Busbecq. But when they were once established at the Porte, it is interesting to observe how many Byzantine titles and customs were taken over, almost without change, by the Turks. The "order of ceremonies" and titles prescribed by the Kanun-Nameh of Mohammed II is modelled on the rules drawn up in the tenth century by Constantine Porphyrogenitus. The same Mohammed, after he had learned the ways of the Palaeologi, put forth an edict, utterly subversive of Ottoman tradition, to the effect that "It is not my will that any one should eat with my Imperial Majesty; my ancestors used to eat with their ministers; but I have abolished this custom";[5] and Suleiman followed in the footsteps of his

[4] Busbecq, I, 152-155.
[5] Hammer, *Des osmanischen Reichs Staatsverfassung und Staatsverwaltung*, I, 98.

great-grandfather. The Ottoman practice of employing eunuchs to guard the harem and the treasures of the Sultan's palaces owes much to Byzantine precedent, and it is also worth noting that eunuchs sometimes attained to high place under both governments. To the exarch Narses —the victorious general of Justinian, and companion in arms of Belisarius—correspond a thousand years later "Suleiman the Eunuch," one of the Sultan's most successful captains and the fifth of his Grand Vizirs, and Ali Pasha, the Albanian, who won fame on many battlefields in his master's day and was appointed to the chief command in Hungary in 1556.[6] And there are a host of official Turkish titles which are almost precisely analogous to those of Byzantine days: the Grand Vizir to the Great Domestic, the Reis Effendi to the Great Logothete, the Kaziasker to the Stratopedarch, and so on down the list to the huntsmen, stableboys, and kitchen servants.[7] The bakshish distributed to the Janissaries by each Sultan at the time of his accession was the lineal heir of the Roman *donativum*.

On the other hand, the court of the Ottoman Sultans maintained its own individual character in a number of ways which differentiated it sharply from that of their Byzantine predecessors, and indeed from all the other royal and imperial courts of Western Europe. Of these by far the most important was the seclusion of the women who belonged to it. No one of them was permitted to appear at any of its ceremonies or state occasions. They all lived in their harem, which was situated—at least at the beginning of Suleiman's reign—in what was known as the Old Palace, near the centre of the city, at a considerable distance from the Sultan's own residence, which had been built by his great-grandfather on the site of

[6] Busbecq, I, 236–237.
[7] Lavisse and Rambaud, IV, 750.

the ancient Byzantine Acropolis.[8] Practically no one, save
the Sultan himself, was permitted to pass the high walls
that guarded the harem. The men and the women of
Suleiman's kullar were two wholly separate groups; the
sole link between them was himself.[9]

For the women of the Sultan's harem, just as his Grand
Vizirs, vizirs, his Janissaries, Defterdars, Nishanji, Reis
Effendi, and the rest, were all reckoned as a part of his
great slave-family, and were recruited in much the same
way as were its male members. All of them were either
given, purchased, or captured in war, and practically all
of them were the daughters of Christians. There were
about three hundred of them in all—a far smaller number
than in the days of his degenerate successors—and of these
a very large majority were either attendants or else young
girls—new recruits—who were being carefully trained in
the hope that when they had attained young womanhood,
they might have the good fortune to attract the Sultan's
attention. If they failed to do so before they reached the
age of twenty-five, they were usually sent forth to be
married to Spahis of the Porte. The guard of the harem
was intrusted to a body of forty or more black eunuchs,
who were commanded by an official who bore the title
of Kizlar Aghasi, or "Captain of the girls." The Genoese
Giovanni Antonio Menavino, who was only in Constantinople in the days of Suleiman's father and grandfather,
has left us the following description of the ceremonies
accompanying a Sultan's visit to the harem of that time.

When the Sultan [he says] will go to the Seraglio of the
ladies, either in disguise, or, if he prefers it, on horseback, the

[8] Lybyer, pp. 123–124; N. M. Penzer, *The Harem* (London, 1936), p. 17.
Barnette Miller, *Beyond the Sublime Porte*, pp. 25–26, tells us that "with
the reigns of Suleiman I and Murad III, who transferred the royal harem
to the Grand Seraglio in two successive instalments, the Old Palace" . . .
became . . . " a place of banishment of the harems of deceased Sultans."
[9] Lybyer, p. 122.

chief of the eunuchs places the inmates, all finely attired, in the courtyard in a line; and when the Sultan has arrived and the door is shut, he and the eunuch pass along the line saluting them courteously; and if there be one who pleases him, he places on her shoulder in the presence of the rest a handkerchief, and walks on with the eunuch to the garden to look at the ostriches and peacocks, and many other birds which are kept there; and he afterwards returns to the ladies' apartments to sup and sleep; and being in bed he asks who had his handkerchief, and desires that she should bring it to him; and the eunuch immediately calls the girl, and she comes gladly, bringing the handkerchief, and the eunuchs quit the room. Next morning the Sultan orders her a robe of gold, and increases her daily allowance by nine aspers, and gives her two more waiting women to serve her. And sometimes he remains in the Seraglio [i.e. harem] three or four days, sleeping with whom he will, and then returns to his own palace.[10]

But there is grave doubt if the last sentence of this description holds good for Suleiman's time, save possibly at the very beginning. The overwhelming preponderance of contemporary evidence goes to show that he visited his harem infrequently in comparison with his predecessors; and there can be no possible doubt that the harem of his day as a whole was almost negligible in its influence on the policy and administration of the empire when contrasted with those of his successors. Yet there was one woman in that harem who was to become a dominant factor in the long, complicated, and tragic tale of his relations with his Grand Vizirs and with his own offspring. No story of his reign would be comprehensible without some reference to it, and a few introductory words are essential to show the background against which it rests.

[10] Sir William Stirling-Maxwell, *The Turks in MDXXXIII* (London and Edinburgh, 1873), pp. 58–59, translating Giovanni Antonio Menavino, *Trattato de' Costumi et Vita de' Turchi* (Florence, 1548), pp. 181–182.

The principal personality in the harem at the time of the Sultan's accession was undoubtedly his mother, the Sultana Valideh; she lived on for many years into the reign of her son,[11] and until the day of her death in 1533 continued to supervise the younger female members of his kullar. Suleiman's favorite Sultana at that period was doubtless the lovely Montenegrin "Gulbehar" or "Rose of Spring," who had borne him his eldest son Mustafa before he had come to the throne. She had no overweening ambition, and the Grand Vizir, Piri Pasha, inherited from Selim's day, was a gentle soul; all promised to be quiet and peaceful. But soon there came a change. At about the same time (June, 1523) that the ambitious Ibrahim replaced Piri Pasha as Grand Vizir, a charming girl was brought back to Constantinople by Turkish raiders into Galicia. Her smile was so irresistible that she was promptly given the name of "Khurrem," or "the Laughing One," though she is better known to posterity as Roxelana. Her beauty, it would appear, was by no means remarkable, but her slight, graceful figure, her gaiety, charm, and never-failing wit enabled her before long to gain complete ascendancy over the heart and mind of the Sultan.[12] The "Gulbehar" remained officially the first Sultana until Roxelana succeeded in getting her exiled for at least a part of the year to Manissa, in 1534;[13] but after she had borne the Sultan her first child there was no question that Roxelana was nearest Suleiman's heart. In the same year that she contrived to rid herself of her rival, she persuaded the Sultan to give her the position of his lawful wife; seven years later, it appears that Suleiman permitted her to leave the harem and come and live with him in the imperial palace.[14] As Roxelana gained power and prestige, she became increasingly jealous of all possible rivals; she

---

[11] Cf. note to page 27, note 1, *ante*.
[12] Lavisse and Rambaud, IV, 760–761.
[13] Lybyer, pp. 126, 141, note 2.
[14] Penzer, pp. 175–176.

easily induced Suleiman to marry off the most beautiful women in his harem, as a pledge that she had no rivals for his affection. But that was by no means all. Roxelana was not content with merely being the first lady in the land. She aspired to have a voice in the government. And that meant that, sooner or later, she would come into conflict with Ibrahim. A battle royal was imminent.

The Grand Vizir had gone on from glory to glory ever since he had replaced Piri Pasha in 1523. We have already spoken of his earlier triumphs; by the close of the campaign of 1532 he had come to believe that he really ruled the state. In the next three years Suleiman was apparently content to leave everything in his hands,[15] and it is worth noting that in the Persian campaign of 1535 Ibrahim had dared to call himself Sultan as well as seraskier.[16] What share Roxelana's influence had in bringing about the tragedy that was enacted at the seraglio on March 15, 1536, we shall never know. The fundamental fact remains that Ibrahim had become a menace to the Sultan's authority, and, in so far as Roxelana aspired to direct the Sultan's policy, to her own. Many reasons have been adduced to account for Ibrahim's fate—disrespect for the Koran, secret negotiations with the French, and the jealousy aroused by his enormous wealth [17]—but the fact that he had become too powerful was enough. He came, all unsuspecting, to the Sultan's palace, in response to his master's summons. He sat at dinner with him as usual and went to spend the night in an adjacent chamber. The next morning his dead body was found strangled at the seraglio gate. The state of his corpse was good proof that he had made a valiant fight for his life.[18] It is said that splashes of his blood were shown on

[15] Lavisse and Rambaud, IV, 762, note.
[16] Lybyer, p. 83. But see Busbecq, I, 238, who says that "Sultan" is "the title given by the Turks to men of high rank."
[17] Lavisse and Rambaud, IV, 762–763; Postel, III, 48 ff.
[18] Hammer, V, 233.

the walls of the harem for a century after his death, as a warning to those who should dare to try to influence the relations of the Sultan with his women slaves.[19] If this be true, it would seem to indicate that Roxelana was at least partially responsible for the tragic fate of the Grand Vizir.

In any case, the removal of Ibrahim made Roxelana, for the time being, her husband's chief minister. The next three Grand Vizirs were unimportant. Ayaz Pasha (1536–39) is said to have had forty cradles in his palace at the same time, and to have left one hundred and twenty children at his death; he died of the pestilence.[20] His successor, Lutfi Pasha, only lasted till the end of 1540; he was suspected of intrigues with the Germans, but Suleiman was fond of him, and he was pensioned.[21] The last of the trio was Suleiman Pasha, the Eunuch, who followed on, at the age of eighty, and was deposed in 1544; whether the chief cause of his removal was his advanced years or the jealousies of his rivals is not evident.[22] And then, at last, came Roxelana's chance. She persuaded Suleiman to give the vacant office to her son-in-law Rustem Pasha, a Bulgarian by origin, who was already second vizir and had given many proofs of high talent and fidelity; particularly notable had been his services as a financier.[23] But the fact that he had married Roxelana's daughter was the most important of all; it fortified his position and hers, and enabled them to coöperate effectively to win a prospect of the succession for Roxelana's sons.

The chief obstacle to the realization of this daring plan was Suleiman's eldest son Mustapha, the child of the "Rose of Spring." He was handsome, popular, and very able; Suleiman had shown him high favor and given him important

---

[19] Hammer, V, 538–539.
[20] Hammer, V, 304.
[21] Hammer, V, 304, 328.
[22] Hammer, V, 328, 386.
[23] Lybyer, p. 167.

offices; everyone took it for granted that he was destined to succeed his father.[24] But Suleiman was secretly jealous of Mustapha's ambition, which he feared might ultimately imperil his own authority; the fact that the Prince had been an intimate friend of Ibrahim did not help matters.[25] Roxelana perceived what was passing through her master's mind, and was prompt to take advantage of it. In 1553 the Turkish army was sent off on a campaign against Persia. Rustem was in supreme command; for Suleiman, who was then in his sixtieth year, had elected to remain at Constantinople. But presently a messenger arrived from Rustem's headquarters to tell him that the Janissaries were calling for Mustapha to lead them; "The Sultan is now too old to march in person against the enemy," so they were reported to have said; "no one save the Grand Vizir objects to having him yield his place to the Prince; it would be easy to cut Rustem's head off, and send the old Sultan to repose." The Grand Vizir added that Mustapha had lent a willing ear to these seditious words, and begged Suleiman to come and take command of the army in person.[26] The Sultan was at first in grave doubt what course to pursue, and in order to satisfy his religious scruples, he consulted the Sheik-ul-Islam. That he might obtain an impartial answer, he put the case before him as follows:

He told him that there was at Constantinople a merchant of good position, who, when about to leave home for some time, placed over his property and household a slave to whom he had shown the greatest favor, and intrusted his wife and children to his loyalty. No sooner was the master gone than this slave began to embezzle his master's property, and plot against the lives of his wife and children; nay more, had attempted to compass his master's destruction. The question which he (Soly-

---

[24] Hammer, V, 489, note xxxii.
[25] Hammer, V, 538–539.
[26] Hammer, VI, 53 ff.

man) wished the Mufti to answer was this: What sentence could be lawfully pronounced against this slave? The Mufti answered that in his judgment he deserved to be tortured to death.[27]

On receiving this opinion Suleiman hesitated no longer. By midsummer, 1553, he was at the head of his troops in Asia Minor. On September 21, he summoned Mustapha to his headquarters at Eregli. The friends of the Prince suspected danger and begged him to pay no heed to his father's command, but Mustapha proudly replied that if he were to lose his life, he could wish no better than to give it back to him from whom he had received it. At the same time he also plainly showed that he really feared nothing, by establishing his tent next to that of his father and by ostentatiously receiving the salutes of the viziers and the Janissaries on his way to the Sultan's presence.[28] On his entrance he found three mutes awaiting him with the bowstring; they are said to have been the same ones who strangled Ibrahim seventeen years before.[29] Suleiman witnessed the ensuing struggle and execution from behind a curtain, without the slightest sign of pity or remorse.[30]

[27] Busbecq, I, 116–117. [28] Hammer, VI, 55–56.
[29] Lavisse and Rambaud, IV, 763.
[30] Cf. Nicolas von Moffan's *Eine Grausame That* (Augsburg, 1555). There is also a curious little pamphlet, twenty-eight pages long, entitled *The History of the Life and Death of Sultan Solyman the Magnificent, Emperor of the Turks, and of His Son Mustapha*, and "inscribed to the spectators of Mustapha, a Tragedy, acted at the Theatre Royal in Drury Lane," which was published in London in 1739, and sold for sixpence a copy. It is of slight historical value, but was intended to give the spectators of David Mallet's *Mustapha* the background of the events that formed the subject of the play. Officially anonymous, there seems little doubt that it was written by the dramatist himself. John Genest (*Some Account of the English Stage*, III, 574) declares that the play "was never acted," but this is obviously a mistake. *The Gentleman's Magazine*, February, 1739, devotes more than a page to the play, including a verse (p. 96) "To Mr. Mallet, Occasion'd by being at the representation of *Mustapha*." The author of the life of Mallet in the *Dictionary of National Biography* specifically states that "it achieved a great success, and ran for fourteen nights," and Allardyce Nicoll (*Early Eighteenth-Century Drama*, p. 58) supports him.

The Sultan deemed it expedient to pacify the Janissaries with a gift of 500,000 to 600,000 ducats. The silent, sly, and sombre Rustem was also permitted for the time being to retire.[31] His place was taken, for the next two years, by Achmet Pasha, the second vizir, who seems to have been a faithful and hard-working official. But in September, 1555, Achmet was accused of plots and intrigues, and beheaded, on the day of the Divan, in the Sultan's hall of audience.[32] There is no reason to think that he was guilty; Suleiman was doubtless deceived by the palace clique; the real fact was of course that Roxelana had insisted that Rustem should be brought back to power,[33] and this time he remained Grand Vizir till his death from the pestilence in 1561. His second term of office was to witness a family tragedy no less appalling than had the first.

The death of Mustapha left the two sons of Roxelana—Selim and his younger brother Bayezid—as the only rivals for the succession, and they hated each other cordially. Bayezid was obviously by far the better man, and the idol of the Janissaries. Selim was drunken, debauched, and incompetent; but, unfortunately for the peace of the Empire, he was his mother's favorite, and to the day of her death in April, 1558,[34] she did her utmost to persuade his father to make him his heir. The Sultan, alternately swayed by his devotion to Roxelana and by his knowledge of the relative merits of his two sons, did his best to postpone the inevitable catastrophe by giving them commands in different portions of the empire.[35] The spectacle of this family quarrel hurt him deeply; he had by this time lost his Roxelana, and sought to gain God's help and consolation in his great sorrow, by fasting, by sumptuary edicts, and by

[31] Iorga, III, 123.
[32] Hammer, VI, 85–88.
[33] Iorga, III, 126.
[34] Hammer, VI, 99; Charrière, II, 464–465; note.
[35] Iorga, III, 128–129.

public prayers. But it was all in vain. The two brothers continued to slander and insult each other. Both of them moreover had gathered about them considerable military forces, most of which were not regularly enrolled in the Turkish army; and in the summer of 1559 civil war broke out between them on the plains of Asia Minor. Bayezid was decisively defeated in the ensuing battles, and after Suleiman had crossed over from Constantinople to see to the restoration of order, he took refuge in November at the court of the Shah Tahmasp.[36] Before his flight, he had written to his father to assure him of his loyalty and innocence, but his letter was intercepted by an agent of Selim's, and never reached the Sultan. The latter was thus obliged by the force of events to take sides with Selim; his affection for the memory of Roxelana won the day over the interests of the state. Thereafter ensued a prolonged correspondence between Suleiman and Selim on the one side, and Shah Tahmasp on the other, over the fate of the fugitive prince. Embassies bearing costly gifts went to and fro. At first the Shah had hopes that he might make use of Bayezid to persuade the Sultan to give back to him the Mesopotamian lands which the Turks had taken from him in the campaign of 1534–35, but he was doomed to disappointment. The military superiority of Suleiman's armies was an argument that he dared not ignore, and finally, in return for a bribe of 400,000 pieces of gold, he handed Bayezid over to the Sultan's chief executioner, who had been despatched to Tabriz for the purpose, and there performed his terrible office on September 25, 1561. Bayezid's five sons were also disposed of at the same time, and the way to the throne was cleared for the vicious Selim.[37] Roxelana had really been responsible for the execution of the only two of Suleiman's children who were worthy to succeed him.

[36] Iorga, III, 129–130; Busbecq, I, 271–313.   [37] Iorga, III, pp. 130–132.

Rustem died a few weeks after the execution of Bayezid, and was succeeded by the second vizir, Ali-Pasha, a Dalmatian by origin, genial, popular, courteous, generous, and excessively corpulent.[38] One somehow feels that his appointment was an evidence that the old Sultan was weary of internal quarrels, and wanted to have someone for his chief minister with whom everybody could agree. Ali Pasha kept his position for the rest of his life, which ended in 1565, and was succeeded by the Bosnian Mohammed Sokolli ("Falcon's Nest"), a really great statesman, who held office for thirteen years after his master's death. Thus of the nine Grand Vizirs who were appointed by the "Magnificent" Sultan, two were executed, three were deposed, and four died in office. Ibrahim, Rustem, and Mohammed Sokolli were the only ones that deserve to be called great, but they held office, in all, for no less than forty-two years.

A few descriptions of Suleiman by Christian observers —all but one of them Venetians—between 1526 and 1562, may serve to give the reader some idea of the impression he made on those who visited the Porte at different periods of his reign.

The first is by Pietro Bragadino, Venetian bailo at Constantinople from 1524 to 1526. It is dated June 9, 1526, a little more than six weeks after the Sultan had departed on the campaign which gave him the victory of Mohács, and it is much like that of Contarini in 1520.

"He is thirty-two years old," says Bragadino, "deadly pale, slender, with an aquiline nose and a long neck; of no great apparent strength, but his hand is very strong, as I observed when I kissed it, and he is said to be able to bend a stiffer bow than anyone else. He is by nature melancholy,

[38] Busbecq, I, 334; Hammer, VI, pp. 146–147.

much addicted to women, liberal, proud, hasty and yet sometimes very gentle." [39]

Eight years later, in June, 1534, Daniello de' Ludovisi again describes the Sultan as "tall, thin, with an aquiline nose and of an earthy complexion," but adds that he is

healthy, of a choleric and melancholy temperament, given rather to ease than business, orthodox in his faith and of decent life; his intellect, however, it is commonly said, is not very alert, nor has he the force and prudence which ought to belong to so great a prince, seeing that he has given the government of his empire into the hands of another, his Grand Vizir Ibrahim, without whom neither he nor any of his court undertake any important deliberation, while Ibrahim does everything without consulting the Grand Signior or any other person. [40]

Nineteen years afterwards the picture changes again. Bernardo Navagero, writing in February, 1553, describes Suleiman as

above middle height, thin, of a brown complexion, with a majesty and sweetness of expression in his countenance very pleasing to behold. He eats sparingly, very seldom of flesh, and no flesh but that of kid with a red skin. He now drinks no wine, as they say he used to do in Ibrahim's time, only fair water, on account of his infirmities, which are said to be the gout and a tendency to dropsy. At Constantinople he is almost every day in his brigantine, passing over to visit his gardens or to hunt in Anatolia. Adrianople is with him a favorite residence, especially in winter, because he has there a seraglio which opens upon a chase, and he goes hunting almost every day. He has the reputation of being very just, and when he has been accurately informed of the facts of a case he never wrongs any man. Of his faith and its laws he is more observant than any of his house has ever been, and he professes never to break

[39] Albèri, 3rd ser., III, 101.
[40] Albèri, 3rd ser., I, 28,

his word, than which there can be no higher praise. After so many years of experience he understands affairs well, and for the most part conducts them admirably.[41]

The observant and sympathetic Busbecq, in a letter dated at Constantinople on September 1, 1555, gives us further information about Suleiman.

His years [so he writes] are just beginning to tell on him, but his majestic bearing and indeed his whole demeanor are such as beseem the lord of so vast an empire. He has always had the character of being a careful and temperate man; even in his early days, when, according to the Turkish rule, sin would have been venial, his life was blameless; for not even in youth did he either indulge in wine or commit those unnatural crimes which are common among the Turks; nor could those who were disposed to put the most unfavorable construction on his acts bring anything worse against him than his excessive devotion to his wife, and the precipitate way in which, by her influence, he was induced to put Mustapha to death; for it is commonly believed that it was by her philtres and witchcraft that he was led to commit this act. As regards herself, it is a well known fact that from the time he made her his lawful wife he has been perfectly faithful to her, although there was nothing in the laws to prevent his having mistresses as well. As an upholder of his religion and its rites he is most strict, being quite as anxious to extend his faith as to extend his empire. Considering his years (for he is now getting on for sixty) he enjoys good health, though it may be that his bad complexion arises from some lurking malady. There is a notion current that he has an incurable ulcer or cancer on his thigh. When he is anxious to impress an ambassador, who is leaving, with a favorable idea of the state of his health, he conceals the bad complexion of his face under a coat of rouge, his notion being that foreign powers will fear him more if they think that he is strong and well. I detected unmistakable signs of this practice of his; for I observed his face when he gave me a

[41] Albèri, 3rd ser., I, 72–73.

farewell audience, and found it was much altered from what it was when he received me on my arrival.[42]

The last picture of the series is really pathetic. It comes from the pen of Marcantonio Donini, who was secretary to the Venetian bailo from 1559 to 1562.

His Majesty [so he tells us] during many months of the year was very feeble of body, so that he lacked little of dying, being dropsical, with swollen legs, appetite gone, and face swelled and of a very bad color. In the month of March last, he had four or five fainting fits, and he has had one since, in which his attendants doubted whether he were alive or dead, and hardly expected that he would recover from them. According to the common opinion his death must occur soon, in spite of the strong remedies resorted to by his physician, unless indeed the gladness which he feels at the death of his sons and grandsons produce a miraculous effect on his health. On hearing of their death, it is said, he looked up to heaven with joined hands and spoke after this fashion, "God be praised that I have lived to see the Moslems freed from the miseries which would have come upon them if my sons had fought for the throne; I may now pass the rest of my days in tranquillity, instead of living and dying in despair." But there are people who say that either the anger of God will not let the deaths of the innocent grandchildren go unpunished, or that Prince Selim, now that his brother is not there to contest the throne, will soon find means of bringing his father's life to an end. May God bring about that which may be of most advantage to all Christendom.[43]

The course of the Sultan's day, when he was in Constantinople, naturally varied in accordance with the amount of work that he had on hand; but he was always surrounded with a multitude of servants, guards, and attendants, and

[42] Busbecq, I, 159–160.
[43] Albèri, 3rd ser., III, 178–179.

his slightest actions were regulated with a precision which reminds one of the fifty pages of *L'État de la France* which prescribe "L'ordre du lever et du coucher" of Louis XIV at Versailles. His clothes, which he seldom wore more than once, and his arms were brought him in the morning by favorite members of his kullar. His meals were served him in similar fashion on gorgeous plates, his sweetened or perfumed water (for he drank wine seldom, and never in the latter part of his life) in jewelled cups. A doctor was often present to guard against the possibility of poison.[44] If he had no state business to transact, Suleiman would read, after eating, in the "Book of Alexander," or in religious and philosophical treatises, or else amuse himself by watching the antics of dwarfs and the contests of wrestlers or listening to the quips of his jesters. Custom prescribed a nap in the afternoon. When he rose from it the Sultan would usually send for one of his four sumptuously decorated barques, and be ferried across, with one of his chief ministers or favorites, to the Asiatic side of the Bosphorus, to spend an hour in the gardens there. During the day he reclined on two mattresses, one decked with silver brocade and the other with gold; at night he slept on three, which were covered with red velvet. As a precaution against foul play, he changed his bedroom daily; and his chamberlains were kept constantly busy in preparing the one in which he elected to pass the ensuing night. Tall silver candlesticks were placed on both sides of his couch, with their lights so shaded as not to interfere with his sleep. Five armed guards kept watch until the following morning.[45]

On the days when the Divan was being held, the Sultan's time was much more fully occupied. Though he was rarely in attendance himself, he was always in close touch, and the

[44] Iorga, II, 447; Luigi Bassano, *I costumi et i modi particolari de la vita de Turchi* (Rome, 1545), fol. 20.

[45] Iorga, II, 447–448; Navagero in Albèri, 3rd ser., I, 96.

formal audiences in which his chief officials apprised him of the decisions that had been reached inevitably consumed much time. The pomp and ceremony which marked every action of his private life were greatly increased on these occasions, and the marvellously rich ornamentation of the Hall of Audience was the wonder of all observers.[46] Particularly interesting was the manner in which foreign ambassadors were received. A sharp distinction was drawn between the envoys of a friendly country—such as Venice during the greater part of the reign and France after 1536— and emissaries from a hostile power, who had been despatched to the Porte for a specific purpose. The former were treated like free men; but the latter, in order to obtain the pass which was necessary to enable them to reach Constantinople, were forced to accept the status of prisoners, take up their abode where they were commanded to do, and often never saw the Sultan at all; in such cases their business was usually transacted with the Grand Vizir. Even the representatives of friendly states were obliged to wait for at least three days before being admitted to Suleiman's presence. When at last the great moment came, they were obliged to make the deepest of bows; after which the Sultan would rise, as he often did when receiving the humblest of his own subjects, and hold out his hand for the envoy to kiss. The latter was then turned over to a vizir, who dined him, and, if he was a Frenchman, wined him, on a service of silver and gold, before they proceeded to business. If negotiations were prolonged or purposely delayed, as was not seldom the case, the emissary in his leisure hours was given a guide and a guard of honor to show him the sights of the city, and he was always expected to reward those who accompanied him with a liberal bakshish. If his business was happily concluded, the envoy was sometimes invited to sit beside the Sultan himself at dinner on

[46] Iorga, II, 448; Gévay, vol. I, pt. 4, p. 41.

the day before his departure, and he invariably was given one or more richly decorated kaftans, often worth as much as 2000 or 3000 ducats, as a farewell present. The exchange of costly gifts was an outstanding feature of the Turkish diplomatic life of the time.[47]

Every Friday Suleiman went to worship in the mosque; and the ceremonial, on these occasions, was in some respects the most impressive of all. Mounted heralds preceded him, calling out "Stand back; the Sultan comes!" Then followed upwards of four thousand armed Janissaries and Spahis, and after them two chief equerries; then fifteen or twenty richly caparisoned steeds, the chief Aghas of Suleiman's household and their suites, and finally the Sultan himself on horseback. Everywhere there was complete silence, save for the tramp of horses and men; the masses paid their homage without moving, but the Sultan nodded right and left, to Jews and Christians as well as to his own people. He entered, and prayed for almost two hours in his shining kiosk; then he returned, with the same ceremonial, to the Seraglio.[48]

When a letter, written in white ink on black paper, formally apprised him of the death of one of his children, the mourning ritual was always the same, even though the Prince had been murdered at his father's command. The Sultan cast his turban on the ground, divested himself of all his jewels, commanded all the decorations to be taken from the walls, and the gorgeous rugs on the floor to be turned upside down, and forbade all music in the city for the space of three days. Sheep were sacrificed, and alms were distributed to the poor. On the day of the burial, the Sultan followed the coffin to the grave, and a special preparation was placed in the eyes of the horses which drew his chariot, in order to cause them to "weep." In

[47] Iorga, II, 450–451; Menavino, pp. 173–175; Bassano, fol. 55 verso.
[48] Iorga, II, 451; Bassano, fol. 13.

sorrow, as in adoration and triumph, the onlooking multitudes preserved the same unbroken majestic silence.[49]

A few words remain to be added about Suleiman as a patron of architects and scholars. He shares with his great-grandfather Mohammed II the honor of being the greatest builder in the long line of Turkish sultans. Constantinople owes him the famous Aqueduct of the Forty Arches, and in the capital and the adjacent towns he decreed the construction of no less than seven mosques. Most of the latter were built in honor of the members of his family, but the most beautiful of them all, which in some respects surpasses Santa Sophia and was finished in 1556, bears his own name. The main lines of the Turkish mosque are modelled on those of the basilicas of Byzantine days, with their flat cupolas and porticos. The outstanding Ottoman innovation is, of course, the tall pointed minarets, two and sometimes four of them to every mosque, from the balconies of which the muezzins called the people to prayer: it is their delicate outlines that give the visitor to Constantinople his first impression of a city of clustered spires. But the interior of the Turkish mosque is also very different from that of its Byzantine prototype; one feels at once that it was built for worshippers of another faith. Majestic simplicity is everywhere the keynote; white and the more sober colors are predominant; the windows are so arranged that the light is evenly distributed. One is inevitably reminded of the vast wastes of the sunlit deserts of Arabia. Nothing is permitted to distract the attention of the believer from the object of his adoration.—In the development of all these new architectural principles and ideas, the builders whom Suleiman consulted and directed bore a prominent part.[50] It must be remembered, furthermore, that the mosque itself occupied but a comparatively small

[49] Iorga, II, 451–452; Bassano, fols. 33–34 recto.
[50] Lavisse and Rambaud, IV, 766–767.

part of the enclosed space which bore its name, "the rest being taken up by a labyrinth of courtyards and buildings, consisting of auditoriums, where the Koran was read; treasuries, where private individuals" could "deposit their valuables for safe-keeping; academies, medical colleges, children's schools, quarters for students, and soup-kitchens for the poor; insane asylums, hospitals, khâns for travellers, and baths—a little philanthropic settlement, nestling at the base of the lofty temple as at that of a mountain, and shaded by mighty trees." [51] Suleiman's interest in education is attested by the fact that the number of children's schools rose in his reign to fourteen; when the pupils had completed their course, which consisted of reading, writing, and the fundamental principles of Islam, they were led in joyful procession through the streets, as on the days of circumcisions. [52] If they had the talent and so desired, they could go on to one of the eight "colleges," which were built in the enclosures of the eight principal mosques, and were known as the "eight paradises of knowledge." In them were taught ten subjects—grammar, syntax, logic, metaphysics, philology, metaphors, rhetoric, geometry, astronomy, and astrology; it was an Oriental elaboration of the *trivium* and *quadrivium* of the Occident. Most of the graduates became imams, or else teachers in the children's schools; the more distinguished returned to their colleges as professors, or took high places in the ulema. [53]

One of the most brilliant periods in the history of Turkish poetry reached its culmination in the reign of Suleiman. The poets were largely inspired by Persian

[51] Edmondo de Amicis, *Constantinople*, tr. Maria H. Lansdale (Philadelphia, 1896), II, 219–220.
[52] Iorga, II, 434; Bassano, fol. 37.
[53] Lavisse and Rambaud, IV, 764; Barnette Miller, *The Palace School of Muhammad the Conqueror* (Cambridge: Harvard University Press, 1941), may also be consulted with profit.

models, but the Sultan did his utmost to develop an "Ottoman style," and took pleasure in presiding at the competi-
tions in which the prize was awarded to the most successful.
The greatest poet of the time seems to have been Abd-ul-
Baki—known as "the Immortal," and "the Sultan and
Khan of lyric verse"; Suleiman wrote him an ode in which
he called him "the first of Ottoman poets." Very notable
was the freedom of speech accorded to these rhymesters.
Yaya-beg, a Christian captive converted to Islam, dared
openly to lament the execution of Mustapha, and even
ventured to say that "Rustem has given us the misery of
seeing Suleiman still on the throne; how long will this
Satan be permitted to live?" [54]—The reign abounded in
great jurists, theologians, and encyclopedists. One of the latter started a treatise which was to deal with three hundred
and seventy different "sciences," and has left us biographies
of all the most famous Ottoman authorities on the law.
The writing of history began in the latter part of the reign
of Mohammed II, and made rapid strides in the reign of his
great-grandson. The work of Kemal Pasha Zadeh, who
recounted the events of the Mohács campaign, and afterwards became Sheik-ul-Islam, is typical of the period. A
dozen of his contemporaries celebrated the triumphs of
Suleiman in verse and in prose. [55]

The life of the mass of the Turks in the reign of the great
Sultan presents the same kind of contrast to the wealth
and luxury of those in high places which is to be found in
most parts of Western Europe in the period. Their houses
were of wood, scarcely better than huts, for it was a "part

[54] E. J. W. Gibb, *A History of Ottoman Poetry*, III, 1–164, and Lavisse
and Rambaud, IV, 764–765. Of von Hammer-Purgstall's four-volume
Geschichte der osmanischen Dichthunst (Pesth, 1836–38), most of the second
volume is devoted to the poets of Suleiman's reign, with hundreds of ex-
tracts translated into German verse. Four pages are given to Suleiman himself, who wrote under the *nom-de-plume* of Muhibbi, "the Devoted Friend."
[55] Lavisse and Rambaud, IV, 765.

of the Turkish creed to avoid display in the matter of buildings . . . if their habitations protect them from robbers, give them warmth and shade, and keep off rain, they want nothing more." [56] They contained little furniture, and no decorations whatsoever, save rugs, on which the poorer classes slept. Linen was a luxury which few could afford, as was also porcelain. Meals were eaten "with three fingers" (the saying was that the Moors used five and the Devil only two) off wooden plates; there were no forks. Black bread, rice, fruits, and occasional bits of mutton were the staple diet. Fish and tortoises, of which there was an abundance on the Asiatic shores of the Bosphorus, were for the most part avoided as unclean,[57] and wine was never drunk in the house; water sweetened and flavored in various ways was the only beverage there.[58] Public bars, however, were everywhere to be found, and we are told by a contemporary that despite the precepts of the Koran and the edicts of the Sultan the "Turks go in and drink there the whole day long: not a day passes in which drunken Turks are not to be found in the streets." [59] Busbecq adds that

to drink wine is considered a great sin among the Turks, especially in the case of persons advanced in life; when younger people indulge in it the offense is considered more venial. Inasmuch, however, as they think that they will have to pay the same penalty after death whether they drink much or little, if they taste one drop of wine they must needs indulge in a regular debauch; their notion being that, inasmuch as they have already incurred the penalty appointed for such sin in another world, it will be an advantage to them to have their sin out, and get dead drunk, since it will cost them as much in either case. These are their ideas about drinking,

[56] Busbecq, I, 90.
[57] Busbecq, I, 134.
[58] Iorga, II, 428; Menavino, pp. 109–110.
[59] Bassano, fol. 37.

and they have some other notions which are still more ridiculous. I saw an old gentleman at Constantinople who, before
taking up his cup, shouted as loud as he could. I asked my
friends the reason, and they told me he was shouting to warn
his soul to stow itself away in some odd corner of his body,
or to leave it altogether, lest it should be defiled by the
wine he was about to drink, and have hereafter to answer for
the offence which the worthy man meant to indulge in.[60] *Si
peccas, pecca fortiter!*

There were many public baths for men and for women,
and in Constantinople and the other large cities of the
empire they were built of marble and appropriately
decorated. For the price of four aspers, any Turk, male or
female, could spend an hour there, conversing, and eating
and drinking.[61] One of the notable features of the Ottoman Empire of Suleiman's time was the large number of
caravanseries, built by the Sultan or the magnates, not only
in Constantinople but at regular intervals along the principal land routes, as free resting-places for merchants and
travellers; they did much to promote trade. Card-playing
and other Western games were unknown. The young
amused themselves with athletic pastimes such as archery[62]
and the jerid, a game in which the participants hurled
light javelins at one another from the backs of galloping
horses.[63] Their elders took pleasure in watching the mad
antics and dances of whirling dervishes, and listening to
the insolent quips in which they criticized and ridiculed
the leading personalities of the day, not excepting the
Sultan himself.[64] Long walks in the adjacent countryside

[60] Busbecq, I, 88–89.
[61] Iorga, II, 428. Busbecq, I, 231, points out how these baths gave opportunity for the practice of some of the vices with which the Turkish name
is associated in the Occident.
[62] Busbecq, I, 252–255.
[63] Iorga, II, 429, calls it a new form of the discus-throwing of classical
times, but the connection is not obvious.
[64] Iorga, II, 430.

were often taken; on such occasions, rugs were carried and spread out in the pleasantest places, where their owners reclined upon them, and listened to the music of old-fashioned flutes made of reeds.—[65] One of the pleasantest traits of the Ottoman of that time was the universal love of flowers. It was almost a religion for him; even military privilege was obliged to give way to it, for soldiers on the march were strictly forbidden to tread on roses.[66]

Every large city in the Empire was divided into quarters, whose inhabitants combined to pay watchmen to patrol the streets at night. The principal duties of these functionaries were to see to it that all the houses in their respective sections were duly shut up at close of day, and above all to make sure that all fires were extinguished at nightfall, so as to prevent the possibility of such terrible conflagrations as that which had devastated Philippopolis in 1516.[67] Dogs, which were regarded as unclean, and were never privately owned, were permitted to roam the streets so that they might pick up the offal and refuse therein.[68] Deeds of violence were very rare. The spilling of blood was reckoned as an insult to the Sultan, who was the guardian of the public peace, and whom all men were bound to aid in the discharge of this function; there were also armed squads of picked Janissaries who patrolled the streets at night. It seems probable in fact that the Constantinople of Suleiman's time was freer from murders than any other capital in Europe.[69]

Though no law forbade the Turks from having as many concubines as they pleased in addition to their lawful wives, it is unlikely that the average man availed himself of

[65] Iorga, II, 429; Bassano, fols. 48 verso–49 recto.
[66] Iorga, II, 429; Busbecq, I, 107, 111.
[67] Iorga, II, 432.
[68] Busbecq, however (I, 224–227), takes pains to emphasize the fact that the Turks behave kindly to any kind of animal.
[69] Iorga, II, 432–433.

the implied permission to do so. In the first place it was too expensive; moreover there were many cases in which the husband gave his personal promise to remain faithful to his wedded spouse, as for instance if she brought a larger dowry than usual, or if her father was of high rank. The husband, however, could obtain a lawful divorce by a mere statement of his intention; in case the wife desired it, the problem became somewhat more difficult. Adultery was punished publicly and with relentless severity. The guilty woman was led through the streets on an ass for which she herself was obliged to pay; similarly the man was obliged to reward the public executioner for every one of the hundred strokes of the flogging he received, to kiss his hand and to thank him for it.[70] "The endurance of the Turks in undergoing punishment," says Busbecq, "is truly marvellous. They often receive more than a hundred blows on their soles, ankles, and buttocks, so that sometimes several sticks of dogwood are broken on them, and the executioner has to say repeatedly, 'Give me the other stick.' "[71]

Trading, as between Turk and Turk, was notable for its honesty; the precepts of the Koran and the laws of the Sultan prescribed it. Many a merchant had the receipts which had been given him by his co-religionists buried with him in his grave, and every Moslem was in honor bound to state exactly what he had paid for the goods which he offered for sale.[72] In their transactions with Christians the Turks were unquestionably less scrupulous, but their dealings with one another were of exemplary rectitude.

On the other hand, the custom of giving presents or fees was universal; and at the upper rungs of the ladder, it

---

[70] Menavino, pp. 35–37; Busbecq, I, 228–230; Iorga, II, 434; Spandugino, *Petit traicté de l'origine des Turcqz*, ed. Charles Schefer, pp. 255–256.

[71] Busbecq, I, 294.

[72] Iorga, II, 434–435.

developed into a system of officially recognized bribery. The traveller who, on his arrival, was presented with a nosegay by a boy or girl in the street, was expected to toss out two or three coins in return.[73] The Sultan, who, theoretically at least, was accessible to the humblest of his subjects, was always offered some kind of a gift, usually set before him on the end of a pole as he passed on horseback through the streets, by those who hoped to induce him to help them.[74] The bakshish which the Janissaries received at the accession of a new Sultan is but another phase of the same story. Every representative of foreign powers and of the Greek Orthodox church, and all those recently appointed to high station in the Ottoman government, were expected to dole out presents to their friends and to those who had used their influence in their favor. The amounts of the gifts that they gave naturally varied in accordance with the importance of the places that they had attained, but at the top there can be no doubt that they were very large.[75] The passing to and fro of vast sums among the magnates worked havoc in the Turkish government under Suleiman's weaker successors, as did also the contrast between their vast wealth, and the poverty of the mass of the nation. All the property of the wealthier of the kullar who were executed or died childless, as well as that of certain other magnates, went by law, as we have already pointed out, to the Sultan at their deaths. If they had children, and the latter were usually permitted, in Suleiman's time, to have nine-tenths, it was by imperial grace and favor and not of right; and the day was not far off when that grace and favor were to be no longer extended to them.[76] And what was the result? The rich, realizing that they had less and less chance of being able to pass anything on to their

---

[73] Busbecq, I, 87.
[74] Iorga, II, 434.
[75] Iorga, II, 438–439.
[76] Lybyer, pp. 55–56, 178.

sons and daughters, used all their money to enhance the splendor and magnificence of their own establishments. They spent everything they had; and the outward evidences of the chasm that divided their luxurious existence from that of the simple life of the common Turk grew rapidly more and more obvious."—These facts are worthy of serious consideration by those who believe that a principal cure for the evils from which America is suffering today is to be found in "the confiscation of all property once a generation."

[77] Iorga, II, 439–440. It is fair to add that many of them established religious endowments of various kinds, and stipulated that a descendant should be the administrator.

∾ IX ∾

War and Victories in the Mediterranean;
Khaireddin Barbarossa

We remember that Suleiman had started out in 1532 on the expedition which received the surrender of Güns, with the avowed object of measuring swords with the Emperor Charles V, and that he openly expressed his disappointment at having been unable to find him. In the following year and afterwards he was to renew his efforts to try conclusions with the "king of Spain," but henceforth his attempts were to be made for the most part on the sea. The Sultan himself never accompanied his fleets, but he was ably represented by some of the most daring sailors of the day. Under their leadership, and with the occasional help of the king of France, the Ottoman navy was destined to become, for a time, the dominant power in the Mediterranean.

As the Emperor in the early years of his reign could not venture, unsupported, to risk his fleets in the eastern basin of the Mediterranean, it was obvious that Suleiman must seek him out in the western. Events had been occurring in the Barbary states of North Africa during the reign of his father and grandfather which gave promise of enabling him to do so. The great days of the earlier warlike dynasties there were now over. The Beni Merin of Fez and Morocco, the Beni Zeian of Tlemcen, and the Beni Hafs of Tunis had long since passed their prime, and their control over the various governors and petty chiefs along the coast was but nominal. But these same chiefs were practiced in the arts of piracy. The region is particularly favorable to it; the shallowness of most of its harbors and the uncertainty of its treacherous winds offer admirable opportunities of escape to marauders familiar with local conditions. Ever since the fall of Granada in 1492, thousands of fugitive Moors had taken refuge there. They burned for revenge against the Spaniards, and eagerly pointed out to their hosts the vulnerability of the Andalusian shores. So persistent was the raiding in the ensuing years that the Spaniards were obliged to take vigorous measures to put a stop to it, and the obvious one was to carry the war into North Africa itself. The more ardent souls, such as Queen Isabella and Cardinal Ximenes were constantly harping on the necessity of doing this, and longed to reëstablish the authority exercised by Hispania Romana over the province of Mauretania Tingitana.[1] In 1505 the Spaniards had captured Mers-el-Kebir; in 1509 Oran; in 1510 Bugia, Algiers, Tenes, Dellys, and finally Tripoli fell into their hands.

Meantime the Moors of North Africa had not been idle, and they were destined to find aid and effective leadership in the persons of the two famous Barbarossa[2] brothers, Aruj and Khaireddin. These were sons of a potter of the island of Lesbos, who after stormy careers as pirates in the Levant had transferred their operations to the western basin of the Mediterranean. At Tunis, which the Spaniards had prudently avoided, they were well received by the local Hafside ruler; and thence, after some reverses, Aruj succeeded in 1516 in retaking Algiers, although the Peñon, or rocky islet in the mouth of the harbor, continued to defy him. In the next two years he extended his conquests, recapturing Tenes and Dellys, so that his sway

[1] R. B. M., I, 12.
[2] It would appear that Aruj was the only one of the pair to have a red beard, but that it was so vivid and conspicuous that the name was passed on by his Christian foes to his younger brother as well.

covered nearly the whole length of the coast of modern
Algeria, but when he attempted to penetrate inland
and take Tlemcen, the Spaniards sent a strong force against
him, and in 1518 he was defeated and slain.[3] But his brother
Khaireddin, who succeeded him, was soon to show the
world that besides being the equal of Aruj in energy and
daring, he was vastly his superior in statecraft. Recognizing
that his present resources were insufficient to enable him to
defend himself against further attacks by the Spaniards
without outside help, he skilfully appealed to the power
that could best furnish it. Selim the Terrible, on his
triumphant return to Constantinople after the conquest of
Egypt, gave audience to an embassy from the famous
corsair, who forswore his independence, did homage to
the mighty Sultan, and besought his aid.[4] Selim was quick
to appreciate the value of such an opportunity to extend
his authority, even if only nominally, into the western
basin of the Mediterranean. He therefore received Khaireddin's message most graciously and appointed him beylerbey of Africa, in token whereof he despatched him the
horse, the scimitar, and the banner of two horsetails—
the usual insignia of the office. He also sent him munitions
and a force of 2000 soldiers, with permission to levy others
who should enjoy the privileges of Janissaries. 4000 vol-
unteers profited by the chance of serving under a leader
so likely to offer rich prospects of booty.

During the next ten years hostilities continued intermittently. Charles V was too busy in Europe to send adequate aid to the Spaniards, and Suleiman was too much
occupied with the capture of Rhodes and his Danubian
campaigns to give vigorous support to Barbarossa, whose
services he inherited from his father. Khaireddin, moreover, had to contend not only with the Spaniards but also,

---

[3] R. B. M., III, 292–293.
[4] Ernest Mercier, *Histoire de l'Afrique Septentrionale*, III, 23–24.

at first, with his Berber neighbors, whose jealousy had been aroused by his recent promotion. In 1520 the ruler of Tunis attacked him and forced him temporarily to abandon Algiers. Nevertheless Barbarossa was able to win the majority of his encounters with his Christian foes. The year after his return from Constantinople he routed a force of 5000 Spanish veterans, sent across from Sicily under Don Hugo de Moncada to dislodge him.[5] In 1522 he captured Vélez de la Gomera on the shores of Morocco. In 1523 he reëntered Algiers, and in May, 1529, he at last got possession of the Peñon, and built the mole which connects it with the mainland today. The Spaniards had held the islet continuously since 1510 and their possession of it had largely neutralized their enemy's possession of the town.[6] Barbarossa's captains also ravaged the Valencian coasts, and in October, 1529, off the island of Formentera, the most daring of them, the famous Caccia Diabolo, disastrously defeated a Spanish fleet which the Emperor had despatched to intercept him.[7] Exploits such as these were not without their effect on Barbarossa's co-religionists in North Africa. The earlier jealousies were forgotten. All the Mohammedan pirates in the Western Mediterranean, most of them European renegades, flocked to serve under his orders, and he kept a strong force of regular troops under arms, balancing the Janissaries with local elements. His private bodyguard was made up of renegade Spaniards. Thousands of Christians groaned in captivity in the bagnios of Algiers, from which they were drawn forth to row the boats which were to bring in new plunder. Meantime he also extended his authority farther and farther into the interior, and organized a loose but effective system of government of the troublesome native tribes and confederations.

[5] R. B. M., III, 293–294.
[6] R. B. M., II, 257; III, 294–295.

[7] R. B. M., III, 296.

Barbarossa had, in fact, attained such importance by 1529 as demanded vigorous action by his Christian foes, and now at last the Emperor was in a position to take it. The peace of Cambray in August of that year gave him a seven-years' respite in his struggle with Francis I, and fourteen months earlier the great Genoese Admiral Andrea Doria had left the service of the French king and transferred his allegiance to his rival, to whom he remained loyal for the rest of his life. Charles now had a really strong navy, and one of the ablest of living sailors to lead it.[8] The results of these developments made themselves evident in 1530. In July of that year Doria attacked Cherchell, a pirate's nest about fifty miles west of Algiers. Although the expedition was finally repulsed, it was at least good proof that the Christians had assumed the offensive. A year later they captured the town of Honeine (or One) just west of Oran, from which Tlemcen drew its provisions, and installed a Spanish garrison; and in 1532 they beat off a raid of Caccia Diabolo on Sardinia, which Barbarossa had launched in reply.[9] Far more significant than these petty clashes were the operations of Doria further eastward. In 1532 he passed through the Strait of Messina with a fleet of forty-four galleys; and on September 12 he captured Coron, on the southwestern tip of Greece.[10] The enterprise, to which reference has already been made, was doubtless chiefly intended to distract the Sultan's attention from the land campaign which faded away after Güns; but it did far more than that. A Spanish garrison was left in Coron, and with Doria's aid it succeeded in 1533 in beating off a much larger army and fleet which Suleiman had despatched to retake it. The

[8] R. B. M., III, 297.

[9] R. B. M., III, 297–298.

[10] R. B. M., III, 298–299; Hājjī Halifā, *The History of the Maritime Wars of the Turks*, tr. James Mitchell (London, 1831), p. 44.

place was voluntarily abandoned, indeed, by the Christians in April, 1534. It was too remote to be of real value, and the Emperor was doubtless glad when the Turks permitted the garrison to evacuate it, and march out with all the honors of war. That, however, was not the essential fact. The thing that mattered was that the Christians had ventured to carry the naval warfare into the eastern basin of the Mediterranean.

Suleiman was both irritated and alarmed by the capture of Coron, and by no means pleased with the performance of his own fleet. It showed that despite the efforts of some of his predecessors—especially Mohammed II—to create a really powerful Ottoman navy, the Turks on sea were not nearly so formidable as the Turks on land. Yet his need of a strong fleet was only too obvious. His empire was situated on three continents; it was by sea that communication between its separate parts could be most effectively maintained. He was also the fortunate possessor of unrivalled maritime resources: the magnificent harbor of Constantinople, on an inland sea protected by straits at both ends against all attack, excellent shipbuilding material in the adjacent forests, and ample resources in money and men which could be devoted to naval construction according to his own untrammelled will. On the other hand, he had to contend with the fatal drawback that the Turks had never been a maritime or commercial nation. Their trade with foreign lands had been entirely carried on in foreign ships, and even in their own waters it was in the hands of their Christian subjects. To man their galleys they had mainly to depend on Christian prisoners who labored at the oars, and on pirates and renegades who fought and hoisted the sails—all of them undisciplined and untrustworthy material, which had to be stiffened for combat by Janissaries and Azabs. Worst of all was the difficulty of finding officers of a calibre to cope with the

Christian seamen of the West.[11] Such victories as the Ottoman navy had been able to win in the past were due to its size and nothing else. Since the siege of Rhodes, in which it had played but a subsidiary part, it had seldom gone outside the Dardanelles, and the way in which Doria, with greatly inferior forces, had been able not only to capture but to relieve Coron was a crowning demonstration of its inefficiency.

The situation demanded immediate and vigorous action, the more so because Suleiman in 1534 was about to start out on a campaign against Persia, and must leave his own dominions well defended in his absence. The Sultan had kept a watchful eye on the doings of Khaireddin Barbarossa during the previous fifteen years, and was quick to recognize the man that would be indispensable to save him in his hour of need. In August, 1533, just after Doria's relief of Coron, he ordered Barbarossa to leave North Africa in charge of one of his lieutenants and repair to Constantinople to pay homage to his sovereign. Khaireddin obeyed, though in leisurely fashion. He was then in his sixty-seventh or sixty-eighth year, and was not unconscious of his own importance. He made a stately entrance into the Golden Horn, bringing with him forty ships in gala attire. At the next Divan he was received in audience with eighteen of his captains, who, after being given robes of honor, were at once despatched to the shipyards, to improve and accelerate the construction which was in progress there.[12] It was some time before Barbarossa could be given the office for which the Sultan had intended him from the first. The local authorities were profoundly jealous of the sudden rise to prominence of this Algerian corsair, and it speaks volumes for the degree to which Sulei-

[11] J. W. Zinkeisen, *Geschichte des osmanischen Reiches in Europa*, 7 vols. (Hamburg, etc., 1840–63), III, 279–328, is still valuable for the maritime affairs of the Turks, Zinkeisen used largely Venetian sources.

[12] Hājjī Halifā, p. 47.

man, at that time, was dependent on the advice of Ibrahim, that he refused to act without the latter's consent. Barbarossa had to journey overland, in December, into Syria, where Ibrahim was making preparations for the Persian campaign, in order to obtain the formal approval of the Grand Vizir.[13] But when he returned with it, all his difficulties vanished. In March, 1534, he was made Kapudan Pasha, or admiral-in-chief of the Ottoman fleet. The tie that had first been formed sixteen years before, when Barbarossa had sent to Constantinople to ask for the aid of Selim the Terrible, had now been strengthened into a mighty bond, which not only placed the control of the Turkish navy in the hands of the ablest Moslem sailor of the day, but also extended the influence of the Sultan over the western part of North Africa.

In June Barbarossa set forth from Constantinople at the head of a fleet of eighty-four ships; of these, according to the Turkish historian, no less than sixty-one had been built under his supervision at the Porte.[14] For several weeks he ravaged the shores of Southern Italy, where he tried, though in vain, to capture and carry off the beautiful Julia Gonzaga as a present for the Sultan's harem; all this, however, was but byplay. His real objective, and that of the master whom he served, was the kingdom of Tunis, where the tottering Hafside dynasty was maintaining itself with difficulty, and only because it had been willing to call for Christian help. Recently a new prince, Muley Hassan, had begun his reign there by a general massacre of his relatives. One of them had, however, escaped, and had been carried off to Constantinople by Barbarossa; it was on the pretext of winning the kingdom for him that Khaireddin in August landed his Janissaries at Bizerta. So great was the terror inspired by his name, and so universal was

[13] Hājjī Halifā, p. 48.
[14] Hājjī Halifā, p. 49.

the resentment at the cruelties of Muley Hassan, that the latter deemed it prudent to retire into the interior, and Barbarossa entered the city without striking a blow.[15] The pretext of installing the fugitive claimant was now discarded and the country was definitely annexed to the dominions of the Sultan. The Turks had got a new foothold in one of the most important places of the Mediterranean, on the south side of the narrow channel which divides its eastern and western basins; another and most valuable link had been added to their chain of posts which stretched nearly all the way from the Dardanelles to the Atlantic. It was less than one hundred miles distant from the shores of Sicily, whose conquest would be the next obvious step in the resistless progress of the Ottoman arms. It was from Tunis that Sicily had almost been subdued by Carthage; it was from Tunis that it had been conquered by the Saracens in the ninth century, and held by them for two hundred years. It was from Tunis that Pedro the Great of Aragon had launched the expedition that gave the Spaniards their first foothold in Sicily [16] in 1282. It was to be from Tunis that Anglo-American forces were to cross over in 1943 to begin the liberation of Europe.

The peril to Christendom was obvious, and Europe looked to Charles to meet it. In 1534 he had got back to Spain, where the Cortes were eager to contribute funds. He was still, nominally at least, at peace with Francis I, and the Lutherans in the Empire were, for the time being, relatively quiet. Vigorous measures of defence were at once taken in all his Mediterranean possessions, and his fleets were kept ready to sail at a moment's notice. But Charles was not content with mere measures of defence. The new Pope, Paul III, urged him to revive the crusades and drive the foe out of the coign of vantage that he had

[15] R. B. M., III, 305–306.
[16] R. B. M., I, 318–326.

seized, and Portugal, the Netherlands, and the Empire promised to send contingents.[17] But though the Emperor was determined to get the Turks out of Tunis, he hoped, if possible, to accomplish his object without a fight. In the autumn of 1534, he despatched in disguise to Tunis a certain Genoese named Luis de Presenda, who had lived in Fez and knew the languages and customs of North Africa. He was instructed first to get into touch with the dethroned ruler, Muley Hassan, and try with his aid to stir up such a revolt as would result in the expulsion of Barbarossa from his new domains. If this proved impossible, he was to approach Barbarossa himself, and see if he could not be induced to abandon the Sultan; the bribe that was to be offered him was the lordship of all North Africa. Failing here, Presenda was to do his utmost to get Barbarossa assassinated; it ought not to be too difficult to do so, since the intended victim was not infrequently drunk. None of these interesting projects was destined to succeed, for Barbarossa soon discovered them, and Presenda was put to death; but the fact that Charles consented to dabble in such plots is an interesting evidence of his earnest desire, whenever possible, to avoid an appeal to arms. They also go to show that, for the moment at least, the Emperor was little if any more scrupulous in his dealings with the Moslem than was his Most Christian rival, the king of France.[18]

Charles had not sufficient faith in the success of Presenda's mission to abate his preparations for war. In the spring of 1535, there assembled at Cagliari in Sardinia a fleet of 400 sail, bearing upwards of 30,000 troops: some 17,000 of them were Spaniards; 7,000 of them Germans; the rest scattering levies from the Italian states. On June 10 the Emperor and Andrea Doria arrived from Barcelona. Four days later the expedition set sail; on the seventeenth,

[13] Hājjī Halifā, p. 48.
[14] Hājjī Halifā, p. 49.

the troops began to disembark near the ruins of the ancient
Carthage, on the selfsame spot where Saint Louis IX had
landed two hundred and sixty-five years before; the place
roused stirring memories.[19] Barbarossa did not venture to
risk a naval battle with the imposing Christian armament,
or even to oppose its landing. Fifteen of his best ships, fully
armed and manned, were despatched to the westward to
find shelter in the harbor of Bona. The rest, after having
been stripped of their guns, sought refuge in the shallow
salt-water lake, six miles across, which intervened between
Tunis and its only approach from the sea. Their artillery
in the meantime was emplaced on the strong bastions of
La Goletta, the formidable fortress which guarded the
narrow entrance to the lake. La Goletta got its name from
the fact that it was believed "to hold Tunis by the
throat." [20]

Under all the circumstances, it was evident that the
Emperor must capture La Goletta before he could venture
to attack Tunis itself. The siege of the fortress lasted
twenty-four days, and was terribly costly. La Goletta was
desperately defended by some 5000 Turks and an indefinite number of Moors, ably commanded by a famous
corsair popularly known as "Sinan the Jew." But finally,
on July 14, a tremendous bombardment from land batteries and from the fleet paved the way for an assault which
the defenders were unable to repel. Not only did the
capture of La Goletta leave open to the Emperor the road
to Tunis. It delivered into his hands the eighty-two Turkish vessels which had sought refuge in the lake, and it convinced him that by forcing the pace he could not only
capture Tunis but also Barbarossa. For the moment, he
was quite unmindful of the fifteen well armed ships which
Khaireddin was holding in reserve at Bona.[21]

[19] R. B. M., III, 309–310.   [21] R. B. M., III, 311–315.
[20] R. B. M., III, 310.

The march to Tunis along the northern shore of the lake began on July 20. It was terribly hot and the Christians' water supply was ominously short. Barbarossa, foreseeing this, had drawn up his army in crescent formation so as to bar his foe's access to the only wells along the route, but the pangs of thirst rendered Charles's soldiers desperate, and the ensuing fight was soon decided in their favor. By evening Barbarossa had withdrawn his forces to the shelter of the walls of Tunis, whither the Emperor immediately followed them. He doubtless expected more battles on the morrow, but events had meantime been occurring inside the city which spared him the necessity of further fighting. Within the walls were several thousand Christian captives, who, aided by certain renegades and encouraged by the news of Charles's victories outside, determined to make a bold dash for liberty. Under the lead of a Knight of Malta, they burst into the arsenal, armed themselves, and poured forth to attack the Turks and Moors. By the morning of July 21 Tunis was no longer in a condition to defend itself, and the Emperor was able to enter the city without serious opposition. Then followed the three days of ruthless plundering which were the regular rule on such occasions. Muley Hassan was installed in power as the vassal of the Emperor, and given a strong Spanish force to garrison La Goletta. In the second and third weeks of August the Christians sailed away in several different squadrons to Spain and Italy. Ostensibly, at least, Charles had scored an important success, and looked forward on his return to receiving the plaudits of a grateful Europe. But at Messina, in October, he got a piece of news which proved to him that his recent campaign had been, after all, comparatively futile, and that the conquest of Tunis mattered little as long as Barbarossa was at large.[22]

[22] R. B. M., III, 316–318.

For Barbarossa had made good his escape from Tunis, with several thousand of his followers, in the confusion which reigned there during the Christian sack, and had retired in safety to Bona. Andrea Doria, who had remained at La Goletta, had neglected the Emperor's order to occupy the town. When Barbarossa arrived there he found in the harbor his fifteen best galleys fully armed and equipped, and promptly sailed away with them to Algiers; a squadron which Doria had finally despatched to intercept him proved totally inadequate to accomplish its purpose. But Barbarossa was not satisfied with escaping; he longed for revenge. At Algiers he raised the number of his fleet to thirty-two; then, foreseeing that the Spanish dominions would be so absorbed in getting ready to welcome their victorious sovereign on his return that they would be totally unprepared to meet an attack, he flew the flag of Spain from his masthead, disguised his crews as Christians, and in September sailed boldly forth to attack the Balearics. His daring was rewarded with astonishing success. Everywhere he was received with salutes and rejoicings until at last his identity was made known. It was at Port Mahon in Minorca that he struck his hardest blow. Two Portuguese caravels in the harbor there were captured; 5700 prisoners were taken, and 800 others were slain. On the way back to Algiers he also ravaged the Valencian coast at Oropesa, and sailed away with 6000 ducats which he consented to accept as a ransom for his captives.[23] By February, 1536, he was back again in Constantinople, to be warmly welcomed by Suleiman, who had just returned in triumph from Baghdad, and immediately commanded him to supervise the construction of "two hundred vessels for an expedition against Apulia, to the completion of which he accordingly applied himself."[24]

[23] R. B. M., III, 318–319; Hājjī Halifā, p. 53.
[24] Hājjī Halifā, p. 55.

Clearly the quondam pirate had become an officially accredited Admiral—if not more, and certainly the Turks were nothing daunted by the fact that the Emperor had taken Tunis.

The next phase of the story was to see the main scene of the naval conflict transferred for a few years to the eastern basin of the Mediterranean, but there was a lull in the fighting during the whole of the year 1536. For this the renewal of the war between Charles V and Francis I was primarily responsible; and the fact that Barbarossa was absent in Constantinople convinced the Emperor that his North African possessions were for the time being safe.[25] On the other hand, rumors had already reached Western Europe of the great raid that Suleiman was meditating on Southern Italy as soon as Barbarossa had completed the construction of his new fleet, and the prospect was the more serious because the Sultan's alliance with Francis I was now in full running order, and the allies were timing their movements to coincide.[26] Strangely enough, it was at this critical juncture that the Emperor received a secret message from Barbarossa, to the effect that Khaireddin, if reëstablished in Tunis, would be willing to change sides. He was apparently deeply jealous of the famous Lutfi Pasha, the seraskier of Rumelia, whose authority and influence were so great as to threaten his own. It is probable also that he was angered by the execution of Ibrahim, who had loyally supported him in 1533–34. Doubts as to whether or not Barbarossa's proposals had been made with treacherous intent, in order to lull Charles into a false sense of security, and still more the length of time that necessarily elapsed before the principals could

[25] R. B. M., III, 320–321.
[26] Ludwig von Pastor, *The History of the Popes from the Close of the Middle Ages,* tr. F. I. Antrobus *et al.*, 34 vols. (London, 1891–1941), XI, 261 ff.

get into touch, rendered their negotiations abortive for the time being; they were however to be resumed in the near future. Khaireddin for the moment was not wholly loyal to his master, and the Emperor had not enough of the enthusiasm of the true crusader to neglect any opportunity to gain his ends without a fight.[27]

The Turkish raid on Apulia began in earnest in July, 1537. A landing was effected at Otranto, and numerous captives were carried off; Andrea Doria was too weak to offer any effective resistance. But the Turks failed to follow up the advantage they had won. Francis I had apparently promised them to appear in Italy and support them, but when the moment came, he failed to keep his word. A truce at Bomy (July) had already put a stop to his hostilities with the Emperor in the North, and a corresponding one for the South, though not signed till November at Monzon, was already inevitable. It was the same old story; unless he was in desperate straits the French king invariably disavowed his Turkish ally. The result was that in August Suleiman ordered Barbarossa to desist from his attack on Italy and join him in an attempt to capture from the Venetians the island and fortress of Corfu. The Sultan himself had led a powerful army overland, and was now encamped at Avlona.[28] That he should have suddenly decided to attack the one Christian power with which, up to that time, he had maintained amicable relations need not cause us too much surprise. The Venetians had been displeased by the trade privileges granted to France in the "capitulations" of the previous year, and they showed it. They were "famous," wrote the Turkish historian Hājjī Halifā, "for . . . their deceit and perfidy in all their transactions," and "are in reality the most inveterate of all the enemies of the faith." [29] They had also

[27] R. B. M., III, 331–332.   [29] Hājjī Halifā, p. 56.
[28] R. B. M., III, 322.

recently been guilty of various acts of overt hostility in the waters about Corfu. Of these the latest and most flagrant was an attack on a Turkish vessel bearing messages and the governor of Gallipoli, and the murder of all on board, "except a youth who threw himself into the sea, and floated on a plank till he was taken up by one of the ships of the fleet, which conveyed him to Lutfi Pasha. The latter laid the matter before the Sultan, who . . . commanded that Corfu should be besieged." [30] But the place proved unexpectedly strong, and repelled all assaults; on September 15 the Turks withdrew, defeated. [31] Burning for revenge, they transferred their efforts to the waters of the Aegean, and raided most of the Venetian islands there. The republic was ready at last, after long wavering, to unite with the forces of Christendom against the Turk. [32]

The changed attitude of the Venetians, and the enthusiasm of Pope Paul III, who longed to revive the crusades, led to the formation, in February, 1538, of a new "Holy League," by the Emperor, the Papacy, and Venice against the enemy of Christendom. [33] The meeting-place for the different contingents was fixed at Corfu. First to arrive were the Venetians, with fifty-five galleys; next, on June 27, came the twenty-seven that were furnished by the Pope; then Andrea Doria appeared with forty-nine more, on September 7, and finally, two weeks later, a large contingent of *naos gruesas de combate*, despatched by the Emperor from Spain. It is not difficult to guess the reason for Charles's tardiness. If the war was to be fought in the eastern waters of the Mediterranean, he could not possibly derive profit from it, unless—what was virtually unthinkable—the entire Ottoman navy should be wiped out;

[30] Hājjī Halifā, pp. 56–57.
[31] Ursu, pp. 104–105.
[32] R. B. M., III, 322.
[33] Pastor, XI, 276–278.

his interests were still in Western Europe and in North Africa. And so, on the eve of the approaching battle, he made a final effort to detach Barbarossa from the service of the Sultan. On the night of September 20, 1538, at the little town of Parga, opposite Corfu, a representative of the Sultan's Admiral met Andrea Doria and Ferrante Gonzaga, the viceroy of Sicily, who were empowered to treat with him in the name of the Emperor. At first there seemed a real prospect of inducing him to change sides. But Barbarossa refused to budge unless Charles would give him Tunis, where the Emperor was determined to maintain Muley Hassan, and he totally refused to listen to Charles's demand that he burn such portions of the Turkish fleet as he could not bring over into the imperial service. The conference accordingly broke up, having failed to accomplish its purpose. Enough, however, had occurred to make it certain that the Spanish and Venetian contingents would not coöperate effectively in the fight that was now inevitable. The Venetians were keen to attack. The imperial contingents were chiefly anxious to avoid loss.[34]

The Turks had meantime taken up their position just inside the entrance to the Gulf of Prevesa, under the shelter of the guns of the fortress that guards it, close to the site of the battle of Actium. Their fleet was slightly smaller than that of their foes, but it was better manned and more ably led. All the most famous of Barbarossa's corsairs accompanied him, especially the terrible Dragut, who was to follow in his footsteps after his death in 1546. The Christians soon appeared at the mouth of the gulf, but as Barbarossa at first could not be induced to come out and offer battle, a plan was advanced of landing troops, capturing the castle at the harbor's mouth, and blocking up the Turkish fleet within the gulf by sinking a transport at the narrowest part of the entrance. It appears that Doria

[34] R. B. M., III, 322–324.

had originally approved of the scheme; but when the moment for action came, he entirely refused to play the part assigned to him. His reasons can only be conjectured, though one's suspicions are naturally aroused by his previous negotiations with the enemy. In any case the landing operation was abandoned; the Christians kept out in the open sea, and finally Barbarossa was persuaded by the more pugnacious of his subordinates to issue out from his retreat and go forth to seek the foe.

The engagement which ensued on September 27 is usually known as the battle of Prevesa, and the accounts of it are so contradictory that it is almost impossible to reach the truth. Apparently the Christians were about to retire when Barbarossa came out of the gulf; Doria was leading the retreat, and was only with great difficulty persuaded by his allies to return and fight. Certainly he did nothing to support the Venetians. The two main portions of the Christian fleet got separated, and followed different plans of action. The Turks concentrated their attacks on the greatest of the Venetian galleons, which barely succeeded in defending itself; but most of the rest of the action consisted in long-range and generally ineffective cannonading. Only a few of the larger ships were sunk, and even the Turkish historian only claims the capture of two of the Christian galleys; it would seem that the day really passed off without much serious fighting. But when the battle was terminated by a gale which blew up in the late afternoon, the Christians were in full retreat towards Corfu; the Turks could justly lay claim to the victory, and it was appropriately celebrated as such by the Sultan, when he learned of it while hunting in Rumelia.[35] The Christians tried to neutralize the effect of the reverse they had sustained by attacking the strong fortress of Castelnuovo, at the mouth of the Gulf of Cattaro, and capturing it on

[35] Hājjī Halifā, p. 64.

October 27, but they held it for less than ten months before it was retaken by Barbarossa.[36] The episode, moreover, had the effect of increasing the jealousy between the Spaniards and the Venetians, who quarrelled bitterly over the right to garrison it during the short period that it remained in Christian hands. The whole affair was, in fact, a crowning demonstration to the republic that she had made the gravest of errors in breaking relations with the Porte. She at once set to work to re-open them, but did not finally succeed in gaining peace till October, 1540. The terms which the Turks demanded were very harsh: the cession of all the small islands which Barbarossa had captured from her, as well as the unconquered fortresses of Napoli di Malvasia and Napoli di Romania, and also the payment of a war indemnity of 300,000 ducats, besides "presents" of over one-tenth of that amount to her "friends" among the Turkish officials.[37] But she had to submit; there was no other way out. At Constantinople her influence was by this time almost completely supplanted by that of France. As for the Turks, besides the glory and booty and fortresses and islands, they had gained one advantage of even more value still, namely, the control of the sea. From the battle of Prevesa in 1538 to that of Lepanto in 1571, they had made themselves the first naval power in the Mediterranean and a match for all the others put together. In view of their past history, and of their lack of interest in things maritime until after the conquest of Constantinople, this was certainly no mean achievement.[38]

The victory of the Turks at Prevesa and the reëstablishment of good relations with Venice naturally made Sulei-

---

[36] R. B. M., III, 325–328.   [37] Hammer, V, 316–317.

[38] R. B. M., III, 328–329. For a full account of this treaty and the negotiations for it, see T. F. Jones, "The Turco-Venetian Treaty of 1540," in American Historical Association, *Annual Report*, I (1914), 161–167.

man and Barbarossa anxious to carry the naval war into enemy waters, and the next chapter of the story takes us back to the western basin of the Mediterranean. It opens with a series of minor encounters, in which the Christians were on the whole the more successful. In the middle of June, 1540, a prolonged chase of the corsair Dragut was terminated by his capture in the inlet of La Giralata on the northern shore of Corsica. He was carried off to Genoa, and chained to a rower's bench until four years later he was ransomed by Barbarossa. The Turkish reply to this coup was to launch an expedition against Gibraltar. It was organized at Algiers, at the instigation of Barbarossa, and consisted of sixteen ships, which were chiefly manned by Turks. On September 9 they arrived off the fortress, which was just able to hold out against them; but they gutted the town at the base of the Rock, and carried off seventy-three prisoners to Vélez de la Gomera on the Moroccan coast; the Spaniards had to pay 7000 ducats to obtain their release.[39] On the first of the following October there ensued a furious naval battle off the little island of Alborán, 125 miles due east from the strait. After an hour victory declared itself for the Christians, who sank one of the Turkish ships and captured ten more; the enemy, however, made them pay dearly for their success.[40] Despite minor reverses, there could be no question that the Turks had seized the offensive. Never before had the Ottoman power penetrated so far west.

The Emperor all this time had been busy in the Netherlands.[41] Such resistance as the Turks had encountered had been due to the activity of the Spanish naval commanders on the spot, for Charles was anxious if possible to save both himself and them from the necessity of further en-

[39] R. B. M., III, 330–331.
[40] R. B. M., III, 331–332.
[41] H. Pirenne, *Histoire de Belgique*, III, 122–126.

counters with the Ottoman fleet. A new war with France was already probable, and with Barbarossa in command of the entire Turkish navy, the Franco-Turkish alliance would be more menacing than ever. Might it not be worth while to revert to the crooked diplomacy of 1537 and 1538, and make one more effort to win Khaireddin to his side? The ransom of the survivors of the garrison of Castelnuovo gave a pretext for renewing negotiations, and this time the Emperor instructed his agents to offer Barbarossa what he had balked at before; he would abandon Muley Hassan and give up Tunis; he might even consent to the dismantling of Tripoli and La Goletta. At first Barbarossa professed himself satisfied, and everything seemed to indicate that the Emperor's hopes would be realized, when suddenly at a moment's notice the whole affair was dropped. One story is that the French representative at the Porte, the Argus-eyed Rinçon, got wind of the negotiations and reported them to the Sultan; but it seems more probable that Khaireddin had been duping the Emperor from the first, that he never had had any intention of deserting his master, and that his sole object in listening to Charles's proposal was to learn his designs and report them to headquarters.[42] Suleiman continued to command the allegiance of his admiral-in-chief, together with such measure of control of his North African possessions as he brought with him.[43]

The failure of his plots left the Emperor no alternative save to fight, and he determined to get in a hard blow before his attention should be distracted by the renewal of his struggle with France. This was rendered inevitable by the murder, in July, 1541, of the French King's agents Rinçon and Fregoso, as they were descending the Po on their way to Constantinople. Whether the imperial repre-

[42] R. B. M., III, 333–334.
[43] See below, pp. 230–233.

sentative in Milan was actually responsible for the deed is doubtful, though there can be little doubt that Charles approved of it.[44] But serious hostilities did not begin till the spring of 1542, and in the meantime a golden opportunity was offered to attack Barbarossa, and thus prevent him from coöperating with his French ally in the forthcoming campaign in the West. There was no question where that attack could be most effectively delivered. The desires of Spain, her ambitions in North Africa, and the safety of navigation in the western basin of the Mediterranean, all dictated an assault on the town of Algiers. It had been the chief headquarters of corsair fleets since its capture by Aruj Barbarossa in 1516, and the principal starting point of their raids. It stood out unsubdued in a region most of the rest of which acknowledged Spain's overlordship; it was a bar to the development of her Mauretanian empire. As usual, an attempt was first made to induce Hassan Aga, the lieutenant of Barbarossa who commanded it, to surrender the place without a fight. At the outset it promised well, but it ultimately ended in failure; and Charles, despite the lateness of the season, and the warnings of his councillors, resolved to risk everything on a grand expedition to take Algiers by force.[45]

The rendezvous for the different contingents was fixed in the Balearics. In the first weeks of October, 1541, Spanish, Italian and German levies were concentrated there. All told, the Christian forces numbered sixty-five galleys and 400 other ships, carrying 12,000 sailors and twice as many troops. Almost all the greatest of Charles's soldiers were there, among them Hernando Cortés, the conqueror of Mexico, who had returned from the Indies in the previous year. On October 23, the troops were successfully landed in the bay to the east of the town, and on the morrow they established their batteries on the heights above, so that

[44] R. B. M., III, 269, 334.   [45] R. B. M., III, 334-335.

they could rake Algiers with a devastating fire. The inhabitants were terrified, and sought means of escape, but Hassan Aga scornfully refused Charles's demand that he surrender. The Emperor, however, on the evening of the twenty-fourth, was convinced that he had the game in his hands.

But the weather was to come to the rescue of the Turks. At midnight a gale blew up and the rain began to fall in torrents. The besiegers could not keep their powder dry; their cannon and muskets were rendered useless. The defenders were quick to perceive the situation and to profit by it. A sortie in force was attempted; though ultimately repulsed, it spread havoc among the assailants, who, according to Hājjī Halifā, "fell upon each other . . . in the confusion which ensued," so that three thousand of them were killed." [46] The Turks used their bows and the Moors their crossbows with deadly effect. The Christians had no means of replying, and their discouragement reached the point of demoralization when daylight dawned and showed them that the gale had driven some 140 of their ships, utterly helpless, onto the shore. Large bodies of troops had to be detached to protect their crews from Moslem attack. A little later Andrea Doria sent a swimmer ashore to advise the Emperor to abandon the enterprise, and inform him that he would await him, with such ships as he had been able to save, in the more sheltered waters off Cape Matifou. Bitter as it must have been to him, Charles was obliged to retreat. On November 1 his army began to reëmbark, and when the scattered remnants of his great expedition got home, it was found that he had lost some 150 ships and 12,000 men, not to speak of large quantities of munitions and supplies. The moral effects of his defeat were of course immense. It was his first great reverse; it weakened his confidence in his

[46] Hājjī Halifā, pp. 67–68.

own good fortune and correspondingly encouraged the Turks.[47] Old Barbarossa had longed to participate in the conflict, but was detained in Constantinople by palace intrigues; he arrived on the scene just too late to catch the Emperor on his return to Spain. But he made himself heard from in the course of the next two years. The Franco-Turkish alliance, which Charles, when he attacked Algiers, had hoped to break, was now at its height. Barbarossa aided the Duc d'Enghien to besiege Nice, which held out for the Emperor's vassal, the duke of Savoy. During the year 1543 Francis handed over the port of Toulon to the Turks. Most of the inhabitants were commanded to leave the town in order to make room for their Moslem guests; and when, in the spring of 1544, the French king decided that "good policy" demanded that he should disavow his ally, he was obliged to pay Barbarossa a generous bribe in order to induce him to depart.[48] —The Turks had now extended their control over waters hitherto dominated by Spain; they were also, without question, the preponderant power in North Africa.

So discouraged was Charles by his failure before Algiers that he took no further active part in the war in the Mediterranean. In 1545 he made one final effort to approach Barbarossa, which revealed the full measure of his impotence. He was in mortal terror at the time lest the triumphant mariner should attack Tunis, and he sent him word that if he would refrain, he would promise, on his part, to make no further effort to oust Barbarossa from Algiers. This singularly one-sided proposal was naturally refused, but the Emperor was relieved of the worst of his anxieties in that quarter by the death of the old sea-dog on July 4, 1546, at the age of at least eighty.[49]—Barbarossa

[47] R. B. M., III, 336–339.
[48] Ursu, pp. 144–152.
[49] R. B. M., III, 340–341.

was certainly one of the most notable figures in the annals of naval warfare. With the powerful and incessant support of the Sultan, he had made the Ottoman navy the master of the Mediterranean. He was a statesman as well as an admiral. His death marks the end of an epoch; and though the Turkish fleet was to win further notable victories in the succeeding years, it will be more convenient to postpone the account of them to a later chapter.

A few words remain to be added in regard to the government of North Africa in Suleiman's day; for after Selim the Terrible had granted the title of beylerbey to Khaireddin Barbarossa in 1518, it remained officially an integral part of the Ottoman Empire down to the great revolt of the Janissaries in the early years of the eighteenth century.[50] The centre of it was of course the town of Algiers, and the most interesting thing about it is the extent to which, *mutatis mutandis*, its administration, on a smaller scale, resembled that of the great empire to which it owed allegiance.

Since it was so remote from Constantinople, it was evident that the Sultan must give its beylerbey an unusually large measure of autonomy. Khaireddin and his successors were granted absolute authority, under the Ottoman government, over the regions committed to their charge. But it was no easy task to make that authority effective. In the first place, the shores of Algeria were dotted at the time of his death with Spanish outposts which were a constant menace. Most of these were recaptured, as we shall later see, in the following decade; but Oran, the most important of them all, remained a thorn in the side of Barbarossa's successors till the end of the Turkish domination. An even more difficult problem was presented by the Berber tribes of the interior. Traditionally independent and unsub-

[50] Mercier, *Histoire de l'Afrique Septentrionale*, III, 336–338.

missive, they resented all efforts of the beylerbey to extend his sway over them. Barbarossa was too shrewd to interfere with their local rites and customs, but he did insist that they recognize his supremacy. To accomplish this, he had at his disposal some 15,000 Janissaries (in Algeria they were known as Yoldachs), who were largely recruited, as were those of his master, from men of foreign origin, and were organized and paid in similar fashion; but of these a scant one-third was available for the purpose; the rest were stationed at Algiers and other coastal towns or held available for participation in pirate raids. The beylerbeys had to supplement their services by efforts to break up the ancient tribal organization through smaller groups, such as the zmul, who were primarily loyal to the authority of a religious chief, or the maghzen, who followed the lead of a noted warrior. By dint of well-timed concessions, these groups were induced—probably without their realizing it—to render the central government inestimable service.

Yet the administration of the interior was, after all, but a subsidiary affair. Algiers was first and foremost a seaport; and the people to whom its greatness was primarily due were the corsairs whom it bred and protected—the pupils of its terrible ruler and the foremost mariners of the Mediterranean. Their galleys, which were stripped of everything not essential for combat, were incredibly swift. Their rowers were Christian captives; their soldiers and gunners were subjected to the strictest discipline. They seldom left port without bringing back large rewards in merchandise and men. The latter were stripped and sold at auction in the market-place; the former also was quickly disposed of, for the return of a pirate fleet meant a holiday in Algiers, and everybody was on hand to pick up what he could. The government took pains to assure itself of its share. Twelve per cent of the profits went to the bey-

lerbey or his representative, one per cent to the upkeep
of the fortifications, and another to that of the mosques;
the rest was divided among the commanders (reis), soldiers, sailors, and outfitters of the successful fleet. The
reis had the "ville basse"—or seaside portions of the town
to themselves. There they spent their leisure in palaces of
Oriental luxury, surrounded by the bagnios in which their
captives were imprisoned. They formed, in fact, a sort of
maritime aristocracy, whose piratical achievements were
the principal source of the wealth and prosperity of Algiers. They were by no means all of them Moors or
Turks. A list of the thirty-five reis at Algiers in the year
1588 makes twenty-three of them of European origin,
including two Spaniards, one Corsican, one Sicilian, one
Neapolitan, one Calabrian, and six Genoese. The attrac-
tions of a life of adventure in the sixteenth century were
wellnigh irresistible to all those who were capable of
living it.

Algiers reached the heyday of its power and prosperity
in Suleiman's time. The city, which probably at that time
had a population of nearly 100,000 souls, and had already
begun to resemble the Algiers of today, comprised an
amphitheatre of white, cubical houses, rising tier on tier
above a semicircle of blue sea. It was strongly governed by
able representatives of its distant overlord, who were amply
competent to keep the discordant and potentially dangerous elements of its cosmopolitan population under
control, and render it a standing menace to Christendom.
The splendid "Fort of Victory," built on the spot where
Charles V had pitched his tent in the campaign of 1541,
served as a constant reminder to its inhabitants of one of
the most glorious of the triumphs of the Crescent over the
Cross. But the greatness of Algiers, like that of the Ottoman Empire of which it formed a part, was almost wholly
dependent on the character and ability of its ruler. Under

the unworthy successors of Barbarossa and of Suleiman, revolts against the government became increasingly frequent and difficult to put down. The tie with Constantinople became weaker and weaker and was finally broken. The piracy on which Algiers had chiefly depended in the sixteenth century was no longer tolerated in the nineteenth; and with its disappearance the picture gradually changed, until opportunity and excuse were given for the French occupation of 1830.[51]

[51] Lavisse and Rambaud, IV, 816–821.

❧ X ❧

Persia, India, and Abyssinia

We have several times noticed that Suleiman's attention was diverted from his European campaigns by the necessity of waging war on Persia, and we shall later see other instances of the same thing. The Sultan led three great expeditions against Persia during the forty-six years of his reign—in 1534, in 1548, and in 1553—and each one kept him absent from Constantinople for a year and a half or more. They were all more or less directly connected with the affairs of the West, for as Francis I had begged and received the aid of Suleiman against the Emperor in order to catch their common enemy between two fires, so the Hapsburgs strove to enlist the sympathies of the Persians against the Sultan. These efforts began with the despatch from Hungary of a Maronite of Lebanon, called Brother Peter, to the court of the Shah in 1518; and it would seem that the Shah responded cordially.[1] The Emperor at first was not anxious to follow the matter up. Not till 1529, when he first began to appreciate the possibilities inherent in the Franco-Turkish alliance, did he send a certain Jean de Balby to the Shah to ask for an anti-Turkish diversion in Asia Minor. Nothing came of it at the time, for the Shah had just obtained a friendly understanding with Suleiman in order to enable himself to attack the Usbegs of Khorasan, and when the project was revived eight years later, it was found that the Emperor in turn had lost all interest in it, and the whole affair van-

[1] R. B. M., III, 301–302.

ished in smoke.[2] Yet the fact that Charles had been willing even to entertain the idea is significant of the trend of the times.[3] It is a pretty illustration of the fact that ever since the emergence of strong national states, the usual policy of each one of them has been to seek an ally on the other side of his immediate neighbor, who has generally been his rival and foe. France and Scotland made common cause for many centuries against England. So did England and Portugal (and sometimes Spain) against France. France has always sought an ally on the other side of Germany; first it was Turkey, then Poland, then Sweden, and finally Russia; and there are other examples innumerable. The Asiatic powers were being gradually drawn into the orbit of intercontinental politics.

The hatred between the Turks and the Persians was both national and religious, and stretched back for centuries. The former were supposed to be descendants of the second son of the legendary King Faridun, who was named Tur, and who had murdered his younger brother Iraj; and the latter was believed to be the ancestor of the Persians. This tradition of hostility was passed on from generation to generation, until it developed on both sides into an article of national faith; the Turks, moreover, were orthodox Sunnites, and the Persians heretical Shiites. Nevertheless there had been almost no recent clashes between the two powers until Selim the Terrible's great expedition against Shah Ismaïl, which ended with his victory at Chaldiran. For the next few years Ismaïl made no attempt to avenge himself. The revolt of Ghazali in Syria (1521) seemed to offer him a chance, and he gathered his troops at the frontier in order to profit by it in the

[2] R. B. M., III, 302–303.
[3] Cf. also K. G. Jayne, *Vasco da Gama and His Successors* (London, 1910), pp. 108–110, for some account of early diplomatic relations between Portugal and Persia.

event of success. But Ghazali was defeated, and in the following year the Turks captured Rhodes; and the Shah decided that discretion was the better part of valor. In the early months of 1523 he deemed it prudent to send an ambassador with an escort of five hundred cavalry to express, though somewhat tardily, his regret at the death of Selim, and to offer his congratulations to his successor. The size of the escort was greater than Suleiman liked. He ordered that only twenty of its members should be allowed to accompany the envoy on his entry into Constantinople; and the ambassador and his suite were later put to death by Ibrahim, at the Sultan's command, when he learned of the decease of Shah Ismaïl and the succession of his ten-year old son Tahmasp.[4] Suleiman also sent to the new Shah a letter, not of congratulations, but of abusive menace, in which he announced his intention of attacking him at once.[5] He appears only to have considered whether the extensive military preparations which were then under way should be directed against Persia or against Hungary. Whatever the reasons which caused him to choose the latter alternative, the threatened expedition against Persia was postponed till 1534. But meantime the hatred between the two Eastern sovereigns and their peoples increased apace. Fresh provocation was continually given by the semi-independent chiefs and governors along the frontiers, who transferred their allegiance from one master to another whenever it seemed to be their interest to do so. They could always count on a favorable reception from the one whose cause they had espoused, and the relations between the Shah and the Sultan went consequently from bad to worse.

While absent on the Austrian campaign of 1532, the

---

[4] It is apparently impossible accurately to determine the date of Ismaïl's death, but it seems probable that it was in 1524. Cf. *Encyclopedia of Islam*, s. v. Ismaïl; also *Encyclopedia Britannica*, eleventh edition, p. 230, n. 5.

[5] Hammer, V, 63–65.

Sultan received word that his forces had been repulsed in an attempt to retake the town of Bitlis south of Lake Van, whose Khan had deserted to the service of Tahmasp. More bad news arrived a little later from Baghdad. Its governor had recently promised Suleiman his allegiance and sent him the keys of the city, but now word came that the governor had been murdered and the place restored to the control of the Shah. Ibrahim had been advising a campaign against Persia for years past, and the news of these two reverses determined the Sultan to undertake it at once. He made peace with Ferdinand in the early summer of 1533. In the autumn of that year he sent on the Grand Vizir in advance into Asia Minor. It was to be his first duty to recapture Bitlis; but that task was accomplished for him by the Turkish forces on the spot, before his own army had proceeded far. Ibrahim accordingly turned southwest to Aleppo, where he spent the winter in preparations for the ensuing campaign. Among the most effective of these were his negotiations with several of the commanders of the Persian frontier fortresses, who were induced to surrender without resistance. The Shah himself, warned by the experience of his father, did not venture to risk a pitched battle, and evacuated his capital Tabriz, which Ibrahim entered in triumph on the first day of the nine hundred and forty-first year of the Hegira (July 13, 1534). In spite of the fact that the ulema had advised that its heretical inhabitants be plundered and slaughtered, the Grand Vizir protected them from injury of any kind. One of Ibrahim's most attractive characteristics was his tolerance.[6]

Meantime on June 10 the Sultan himself had left Constantinople.[7] His march across the mountains of Asia Minor was long and very difficult. Even in August snow fell.[8]

[6] Hammer, V, 202–210.
[7] Suleiman's *Journal*, quoted in Hammer, V, 495.
[8] Suleiman's *Journal*, quoted in Hammer, V, 495–497.

Most of the news received from Ibrahim was good, but on September 20 there came word that a large body of Ottoman troops had been waylaid by their enemies and cut to pieces. It was a really serious disaster, for even the Turkish historians admit the loss of 10,000 men.[9] The Grand Vizir now begged his master to hurry forward and unite with him, and a week later Suleiman rejoined him outside Tabriz.[10] Thence their combined forces toiled painfully southward towards Baghdad. They met with no serious annoyance from their foes, but the hardships of their march were very great. The country they had to traverse was exceedingly difficult, the roads were often impassable, and the weather was unusually bad. Provisions ran short, pack animals died, and wagons and cannon had to be abandoned, but finally on November 30 the Sultan made his entry into the ancient capital of the Abbasside caliphs and the scene of the *Arabian Nights*.[11]

Baghdad had by this time lost much of the splendor for which it had been famous in the days of Harun-al-Rashid. It had been sacked by the Mongols in 1258 and by Tamerlane in 1393; yet it still remained one of the most renowned of the cities of Asia. To Suleiman, who regarded himself as the successor of the Abbassides, the conquest of the place that had so long been the Rome of the Mohammedan world must have meant much, the more so because he had rescued it from the heretic. Yet he took pains to see to it, as Ibrahim had done at Tabriz, that the inhabitants were not molested in any way. He spent the next four months in the city, busying himself with affairs of state and the administration of his newly conquered territory. But his religious duties and responsibilities as Commander of the Faithful and Lieutenant of the Envoy of God

[9] Hammer, V, 210 and note 2.
[10] Hammer, V, 499.
[11] Hammer, V, 499–504.

were never absent from his mind. It was essential that his capture of this stronghold of heresy be signalized by some pious wonder which would impress his orthodox followers, and Suleiman seems to have arranged that they be provided with one by the discovery of the bones of Abu-Hanifa (700–770), the first of the four great imams of Sunnite Islam, and the founder of the sect that bears his name. When the heretic Persians had captured Baghdad in the time of Shah Ismaïl, they were believed to have destroyed the remains of this holy man together with his tomb; but now its former guardian came forward to announce that he had been warned in a dream of the intended sacrilege by the imam himself, and at his command had removed the body and put that of an unbeliever in its place. Investigation revealed the real remains in the spot where they had been concealed; it would appear that they made their presence known by emitting an odor of musk. On the news of this infallible sign, the Grand Vizir hurried to the place and removed with his own hands the stone that covered the entrance to it. The Sultan then proceeded thither and descended into the grave. He afterwards gave orders for the erection of a new tomb for Abu-Hanifa, which has remained a favorite resort of orthodox pilgrims ever since.[12] This fortunate affair could not fail to remind all good Moslems of the similarly wonderful discovery, on the eve of the taking of Constantinople, of the remains of Ayub, the standard-bearer of the Prophet.[13] The capture of the traditional strongholds both of the infidel and of the heretic had thus been marked by outward and visible signs of the pleasure and approval of God.

On April 1, 1535, Suleiman left Baghdad.[14] An un-

[12] Hammer, V, 220–223.
[13] Hammer, II, 393–394.
[14] Hammer, V, 505.

eventful journey of ninety-two days brought him back to Tabriz, where a Persian envoy was permitted to kiss his hand. The Sultan remained in the vicinity till August 27, and did everything in his power to impress the inhabitants with the irresistible might of the Ottoman arms. Knowing that he would be unable to retain control of a region so remote, he sacked the town and burned the palace before his departure. His return to Constantinople was constantly harassed by the attacks of his Persian foes. The rearguard, becoming too widely separated from the main body, was badly mauled by the enemy, on October 13, in the mountains west of Bitlis.[15] On November 24 the Sultan reached Aleppo, on December 5 Antioch, and on January 8, 1536, Constantinople.[16]

Ten years passed and produced little change in the situation in Western Asia. In 1547 the Turks were once more at peace in Europe, this time not only with Ferdinand but also with Charles V. As in 1533, the conclusion of these treaties with his Christian foes was in large measure due to the fact that the Sultan had already begun to meditate another Persian campaign, and before they were signed he had commenced his preparations. The immediate occasion for this new expedition was the arrival of a certain Prince Elkass Mirza, a brother of Shah Tahmasp, in Constantinople, where he was received with a distinction which produced murmurs among the people, who protested against the welcome accorded to an accursed heretic who, after all, might be only a traitor in disguise. When news of these complaints reached his ears, Suleiman answered, "We have done what the honor and dignity of the empire demanded; should there be treachery in the affair, we leave its punishment in the hands of God, our Lord!" [17] Nevertheless the

---

[15] Oman, *Art of War*, p. 683.
[16] Hammer, V, 505–512.
[17] Hammer, VI, 9.

Sultan's conduct was not solely dictated by motives of generosity. The aid of Elkass Mirza might prove to be of immense service in obtaining for him a lasting triumph over an enemy with whom he found it so hard to come to close quarters.

On April 28, 1548, the Sultan left Constantinople on his second Persian expedition. In the summer he recaptured Tabriz and then took Van and other fortresses; on November 26 he was back at Aleppo, where he spent the winter and spring.[18] In June, 1549, he took the field again, and led his army across the Euphrates. Once more he captured a number of fortified places, and his generals fought with varying success against the armies of the enemy; but it was as impossible as ever to induce the Shah to join in a decisive battle. In the meantime Elkass Mirza fell into the hands of the foe and was delivered over to his brother, who kept him a prisoner for the rest of his life; and therewith ended all Suleiman's hopes of supplanting the Shah. On December 21 the Sultan was again in his capital. His second Persian campaign had been a grievous disappointment.[19]

Fresh troubles in Europe occupied his attention for the next three years, till in 1552 Tahmasp, profiting by the concentration of Ottoman energy in Hungary, took the offensive once more. He won a number of battles, the most important of which was the victory of his son Abbas Mirza over the pasha of Erzerum. Suleiman sent a comforting letter to the pasha, who had deserved well of him on many previous occasions; but there was no doubt of the necessity for another campaign. At first the Sultan was not inclined to lead it in person. He was now nearly sixty years old, and the hardships of another long arduous expedition, where there was so little prospect of gaining permanent advantage, determined him at first to intrust it to one of

[18] Suleiman's *Diary*, quoted in Hammer, VI, 462–465.
[19] Hammer, VI, 14–15.

his vizirs. We have already seen the reasons that led him to alter his decision. In August, 1553, he left Constantinople; on October 6 came the tragic execution of Mustafa, which terrified the troops and the people. The winter was spent in Aleppo. In the summer the army passed through Erzerum, crossed the upper Euphrates, and laid waste the territory far beyond it with a savagery not permitted on the earlier campaigns. The Shah, however, as usual kept out of the way, and as his forces won numerous successes over isolated Turkish divisions, there was nothing for the main army to do but to retreat. Before turning his face homewards Suleiman wrote a violent and abusive letter to his adversary, and Tahmasp replied in the same tone.[20] The correspondence was continued by the ministers on both sides; but, curiously enough, it served as a prelude to an end of hostilities. The last victories in the field were won by the Turks, and on September 26, 1554, a Persian ambassador appeared at Erzerum to ask the Sultan for a truce, which was granted. Both sides were heartily tired of a war which had lasted for so many years with such meagre results. The Persians dared not meet the Turks in the open field, and the latter found the task of retaining distant conquests against a foe who was always able to attack, and yet could never be brought to bay, as difficult as it was unprofitable. By a treaty of peace signed at Amasia on May 29, 1555, the one hundred and second anniversary of the capture of Constantinople, Suleiman ended his Asiatic campaigns: they had resulted in a considerable extension and consolidation of his empire. He abandoned all claim to the region of Tabriz, but he kept Lower Mesopotamia with Baghdad, the mouths of the Tigris and Euphrates, and a footing on the Persian Gulf.[21] These territories, in spite

[20] Hammer, VI, 60–65. This type of literature seems akin to the "flytings" of the Scottish poets of the sixteenth century, as *The Flyting of Dunbar and Kennedie*, *The Flyting betwixt Montgomery and Polwart*, etc.

[21] Hammer, VI, 65–70, 478; Iorga, III, 125.

of many rebellions and occasional temporary loss, were still in the hands of his successors until the first World War.

Turning to the relations of Suleiman with more distant Asiatic peoples, we note an interchange of embassies and suggestions of alliance with the successive rulers of the Usbegs of Khorasan. Their Turkish blood, their orthodox Sunnite faith, and their inveterate hostility to the Persians marked them out as the natural friends of the Ottomans. It was the same old story; the Sultan wanted the help of the power to the east of the Persians, just as Charles V wanted the friendship of the Persians against him. The practical nature of his policy is demonstrated by the fact that the ambassador he sent to their Khan took with him three hundred Janissaries and cannon to show the Usbegs, whose armies consisted solely of cavalry, the new military methods of the West. The rising power of the Mogul emperors in Northern India, on the other hand, was too distant to be of the same interest to the Turks that it was to the Persians. Thus, whereas Tahmasp not only cordially received the fugitive Mogul sovereign Humayun (1543), but also aided him to recover his throne, Suleiman merely granted a trifling pension to the son of a claimant to the throne of Delhi, one Burhan Beg, whom Humayun had driven from his dominions.

The Moslem princes of the Malabar coast were another matter; and the story of Suleiman's relations with them is an interesting evidence of the way in which the horizons of the sixteenth century expanded. In the waters of the Indian Ocean the Turks once more came into contact with the forces of Europe, and the struggle there was regarded by both sides as a part of the great contest between the Mohammedan and the Christian worlds. From Suleiman's point of view it was not primarily a war of aggression. The Sultan felt himself in honor bound to listen to the prayers of his coreligionists, asking aid against the rapacity of an oppressor who had suddenly appeared from beyond the seas.

Scarcely had the Portuguese made their way around the Cape of Good Hope (1486) before they conceived the grandiose idea of diverting the trade of the East from its old channels through the Red Sea and the Persian Gulf to the new route which now was in their hands. Lisbon was to be the eastern mart for all Europe. Competition from those who would suffer by the change was to be put down with ruthless severity. The petty princes of the Malabar coast were able to offer little resistance. The heavily armed Portuguese galleons could easily defeat the immensely superior numbers of their lighter vessels. Two greater powers—Persia and Egypt—were also directly affected. The Persians were not a maritime nation, and made little trouble. Their hold on the regions near the Gulf was but recent. The Portuguese exerted themselves to keep on good terms with them. A clash was averted, and the two parties even talked of an alliance. The Egypt of the Mamelukes, however, was much more seriously threatened by the Portuguese attempts to block the Red Sea; the Venetians, also, were deeply concerned, and kept pointing out to the Soldan the necessity for vigorous action. The latter finally bestirred himself, and, after threatening the Portuguese with the destruction of the Holy Sepulchre and the slaughter of all the Christians in Palestine, he fitted out a considerable squadron, and sent it to the aid of the hard-pressed Malabar princes. This combined Egyptian and Indian fleet was, however, defeated in February, 1509, by Francisco de Almeida with fearful loss off the island of Diu in a battle which has been said to have "turned the Indian Ocean for the next century into a Portuguese sea." [22]

[22] Sir William Wilson Hunter, *A History of British India* (London, 1899), I, 116–118.

The next few years saw everything develop favorably for the Portuguese. Their most dangerous enemies, the Egyptians, were obliged to leave the Indian Ocean and devote all their energies to efforts, which proved vain, to repel the attacks of Selim the Terrible; by the end of the year 1517, as we have already seen, their kingdom was in the hands of the Turks. Meantime Affonso de Albuquerque, the greatest of all the Portuguese viceroys in the Orient, had disposed of his rival Almeida, and had begun to carry into effect the magnificent program of imperial expansion which had been the dream of his youth. In 1507 he had seized the island of Socotra, off the mouth of the Gulf of Aden, and constructed a fort there. In the same year he took Ormuz; for the time being he was unable to hold it, but in 1515 he returned, and definitely established it in the control of the Portuguese, who remained for over a century the guardians of the entrance to the Persian Gulf. In the meantime he seized the island of Goa, and converted it into the chief centre of Portuguese power in the East; he also penetrated to the Strait of Malacca, where he installed a Portuguese government which dominated the Malay Peninsula and commanded the trade with China, Japan, and the Spice Islands—"the most lucrative source of Moslem commerce in the Far East." In only one place did he suffer defeat. He was full of great plans for striking at the vitals of Moslem power in the Red Sea, but to get into the Red Sea it was necessary to conquer Aden, and Aden defied him. An attack on it, which he delivered in 1513, was repulsed with heavy loss, and though the local ruler, in the course of the next two decades, agreed from time to time to pay tribute, the Portuguese never obtained effective possession of the place.[23]

We may well believe that Suleiman was deeply disturbed by this meteoric rise of the Portuguese power in the Indian

[23] Hunter, I, 118–128, 131; K. G. Jayne, pp. 93–96.

Ocean. He had inherited Egypt from his father, and
therewith the task of repelling the Christians which the
Egyptians had so courageously begun, but he was so much
occupied during the early years of his reign with his campaigns in the Mediterranean and on the Danube that he
could not afford to divert his attention to other things.
His first effort in behalf of his Indian coreligionists was
apparently made in 1525, when, according to the historian
Hājjī Halifā, "the Sultan Suleiman appointed the corsair
Salman Reis a capudan and commander, and sent him with
twenty galleys to that quarter. He proceeded along the
coasts of Aden and Yemen, and plundered the habitations
of the rebellious and such as were not well affected to the
Porte; in consequence of which, the sheiks and Arabs of
those districts came out to him with numerous presents,
offered their services, and bound themselves to transmit
their taxes." [24] This expedition, however, was no very
serious affair. In fact, though it was ordered from Constantinople, it should properly be regarded as a part of the
pacification and reorganization of Egypt, on which the
Grand Vizir was at that time engaged. The submission of
the Arab chieftains was only nominal, and very temporary.

Seven years later the Sultan sent orders to the pasha of
Egypt to construct a fleet of eighty ships of different sizes
at Suez. Obviously it was intended to operate in the
Indian Ocean, but Suleiman the Eunuch, who was to
command it, was called off to serve in the Persian campaigns
before the work could be completed, and the project ended
in nothing.[25] In 1536, however, Suleiman's interest in the
affairs of the Malabar coast was once again aroused in such
fashion as to lead to more definite results. In that year, an
ambassador from Bahadur Shah, the ruler of Gujarat, arrived in Constantinople to beg for his aid. It would appear

[24] Hājjī Halifā, *Maritime Wars of the Turks*, pp. 26–27.
[25] Hammer, V, 299–300.

that under pressure of an invasion of his dominions by the Mogul Emperor Humayun, Bahadur had permitted the Portuguese to establish themselves on the island of Diu, where they had built a fortress and made themselves intolerable. There was every reason why Suleiman should listen sympathetically to Bahadur's appeal. Over and above his desire as "Commander of the Faithful" to help his coreligionists against the enemy who had so suddenly descended on them out of the West, he had his own private grudges against the Portuguese. Their recent conquests had struck a heavy blow against the commerce of the Ottoman Empire. Their tenure of Ormuz prevented him from reaping due advantage from the footing that he had recently won on the Persian Gulf. They had sent a powerful contingent to aid Charles V to capture Tunis. Obviously, despite all his manifold activities and responsibilities in other quarters, Suleiman was in honor bound to take vigorous action in the Indian Ocean. On June 13, 1538, a fleet of seventy ships, commanded by Suleiman the Eunuch, and carrying 1500 Janissaries and 5000 other soldiers, set sail from Suez to seek revenge.[26] Among the men at the oar were a large number of Venetians, who had been seized in Egypt when the republic declared war on the Porte. Heavy cannon, some of which threw projectiles of ninety pounds, and other supplies had been sent on from Constantinople, and were dragged across the isthmus of Suez by hand.[27]

Sailing down the Red Sea, Suleiman Pasha reached Aden on August 3. There he enticed the sheik to come aboard his flag-ship and promptly hanged him from the yardarm.[28] The town was then sacked and a Turkish governor installed; the rest of the expedition crossed the Indian Ocean

[26] R. S. Whiteway, *The Rise of Portuguese Power in India, 1497–1550* (Westminster, 1899), p. 256.

[27] Hammer, V, 300–303.

[28] Hunter, I, 147.

with favorable winds, and on September 4 arrived off Diu. The Sultan's orders had been to seek out the Portuguese fleet and destroy it, which the Turks, with their formidable artillery, could probably have done. Nevertheless Suleiman the Eunuch elected instead to land his troops, capture two fortresses which guarded the approach to Diu, and finally, in early October, to lay siege to Diu itself. But the small Portuguese garrison defended the place with the utmost heroism, and in November the Turks withdrew. The memory of the great Moslem disaster there in 1509 was still fresh in their minds; provisions were running ominously short; worst of all there was no effective coöperation between them and their Indian allies. Shah Bahadur, at whose invitation they had come, was now dead; and matters were probably not helped by the fact that the Turkish leader gave orders that Bahadur's treasures, which he had sent on to Mecca for safekeeping, should be despatched to Constantinople as a present to the Sultan. Bahadur's successor began to wonder if, after all, the Portuguese were not less to be feared than the Turks. He failed to deliver the supplies that had been promised, and, mindful of the fate of the sheik of Aden, took care to keep himself out of his ally's way. Rumors also reached the Turks that the Portuguese were gathering together a great fleet at Goa to be despatched to the rescue of Diu. Under all the circumstances it is no wonder that they elected to retire.[29] On their return they avenged themselves for their failure before Diu by various deeds of violence on the coasts of Yemen, where they slew the local ruler, and set up a Turkish governor in his place. At Jiddah Suleiman the Eunuch left the fleet in order to make his pilgrimage to Mecca; evidently he wanted to convince both his master and his followers that the expedition he had commanded had gone forth on a Holy War. The Sultan was properly impressed, and when

[29] Whiteway, pp. 256–265.

the Turkish leader returned overland to Constantinople, he was given a seat in the Divan, and two years later was made Grand Vizir.[30]

The Turks did not venture to penetrate to the Malabar coast again. Diu sustained another and even more terrible siege in 1546, but the assailants on this occasion were Indian Moslems; the Ottomans took no part in it save in so far as stray renegades were enrolled in the forces of the new prince of Gujarat.[31] The Sultan's efforts to extend his authority over the West Coast of India had failed. But in the Persian Gulf he continued for many years more to struggle against the Portuguese. Their hold on Ormuz blocked his access by that route to the Indian Ocean; it rendered nugatory, from the point of view of maritime expansion, his conquest of Baghdad and of Basra, farther down the river, where he had established an arsenal and base of operations. In 1551 he commanded Piri Reis, the capudan of Egypt, and the author of a work on the geography and navigation of the Mediterranean which has been highly esteemed by the Moslems, to sail down the Red Sea with a fleet of thirty ships, and oust the Portuguese from Ormuz. Piri Reis began well by capturing Muscat, some three hundred miles to the southeast, on the southern shore of the Gulf of Oman.[32] Thence he proceeded to the neighborhood of Ormuz, and laid waste the country round about, but failed to take the fortress; thereafter he went on up the gulf and the river to Basra. On his arrival there he learned that "the fleet of the vile infidels was advancing towards him," so as to prevent the possibility of his escaping; he therefore hurried away with three galleys which were his private property and were laden with his own treasures, and got out of the Strait of Ormuz before the

---

[30] Hammer, V, 202–203.
[31] This despite Hunter, I, 131, to the contrary. See Whiteway, pp. 305 ff.
[32] Hājjī Halīfā, pp. 71–72.

Portuguese could prevent him. The mass of his fleet, which he had left at Basra, was abandoned and ultimately destroyed. One of the three ships with which Piri had escaped was lost on the way home. With the other two he got safely back to Egypt, only to be seized and imprisoned by the Turkish authorities on the spot. Information of his disgraceful conduct was forthwith despatched to the Porte, whence orders were at once received to put him to death, and he "was beheaded accordingly in the Divan of Cairo." [33] Suleiman had no use for behavior such as his.

His successor, one Murad Bey, who had had much experience in the waters of the Indian Ocean, was no more fortunate than Piri Pasha. Defeated by the Portuguese near Ormuz while attempting to escape, he succeeded in fleeing into Basra with the remnant of his fleet, but the question still remained, how could it be got out again? The task was intrusted to Sidi Ali Reis, better known by his *nom-de-plume* of Katibi Rumi, and distinguished as a writer on theology, mathematics, navigation, and astronomy, both in prose and in verse. He was the son and grandson of governors of the imperial naval arsenal at Constantinople, and an experienced sailor who had seen service under many commanders.[34] Crossing by land from Aleppo, he finally reached Basra, and after taking several months to refit his ships, sallied boldly forth, in July, 1554, to meet the foe. Outside of Ormuz he encountered a larger Portuguese fleet, with which he had two fierce encounters; of the second he tells us that "even in the war between Khaireddin Pasha and Andrea Doria no such naval action as this has ever taken place." [35] After losing six of his ships,

---

[33] Hājjī Halifā, pp. 71–72.

[34] Hājjī Halifā, pp. 72–73; Hammer, VI, 186–187. See his autobiographic *Travels and Adventures*, translated from the Turkish, with notes, by Armin Vámbéry (London, 1899). This work is otherwise known as *The Mirror of Countries*.

[35] Vámbéry, *Travels and Adventures*, p. 14.

Sidi Ali broke through with the nine that remained to him into the Indian Ocean, where he encountered a hurricane "compared" to which "a storm in the Mediterranean is as insignificant as a grain of sand; day could not be distinguished from night, and the waves rose like huge mountains." [36] Here he was tossed about for a long time, and finally stranded off Gujarat, where, as he was in no condition to proceed further or to defend himself against the Portuguese, he surrendered his fleet to the ruler of the place, after receiving his promise "that the value of the arms and other effects which were left with him should be sent to the Sublime Porte." [37] Most of his followers had already enlisted in "the service of King of Gujarat," [38] but Sidi Ali himself, with fifty of his companions, wandered about through India and Persia for many months, and finally got back to Constantinople in May, 1556. "Shortly afterwards he was admitted to the royal presence at Adrianople, and had an addition of eighty aspers made to his salary; whilst all his companions were promoted in Egypt; and the royal order was issued that they should be paid their four years' salary which was in arrear. The capudan then wrote an account of his voyages and travels, which he called 'The Adventures of Sidi Ali.' " [39]

Such was the rather sorry ending of Suleiman's attempts to wrest the control of the Indian Ocean from the Portuguese. We need not wonder that he was not more successful. The parallel to Charles V's failure to hold the western basin of the Mediterranean is very close. In both cases the cause was the same; each sovereign had too many other irons in the fire. Suleiman had been forced to give up all hope of dominating the Malabar coast. On the Persian Gulf he had been unable to take Ormuz, and his enemies

[36] Hājjī Halifā, p. 75.
[37] Hājjī Halifā, p. 77.
[38] Hājjī Halifā, p. 77.
[39] Hājjī Halifā, p. 77.

kept him bottled up at Basra. On the other hand, the presence of his sailors and soldiers on the Tigris and Euphrates compelled the Portuguese to maintain a powerful garrison at the narrows. Moreover the Sultan had succeeded in retaining his hold on Aden, and therewith the control of the Red Sea. Neither Albuquerque nor any of his successors were able to take it away from him; one is reminded of the way in which the Spaniards in North Africa held on to Oran. And finally the fact that the Sultan had striven to oust his Christian rivals from the Indian Ocean is an interesting evidence of the grandeur of his conception of the task which he believed that God had called on him to perform. As Commander of the Faithful he felt it his duty to extend his protection over all the Moslem peoples in the world, and support the Crescent wherever it clashed with the Cross. Like others of his predecessors, contemporaries, and successors who have held similar creeds, he was destined to fail, but so far as we can judge, the motives that inspired him were less selfish than those of the great majority of them.

One curious episode of the struggle between the Turks and the Portuguese in the Indian Ocean remains to be noticed. "Encompassed on all sides by the enemies of their religion," the Christian inhabitants of the kingdom of Abyssinia had "slept near a thousand years, forgetful of the world, by whom they were forgotten." [40] But the advance of the Ottoman power since the capture of Constantinople was a far more serious threat to their independence than any that they had ever encountered before. When the Turks conquered Egypt under Selim the Terrible their peril was more manifest than ever, and their sovereign, or Negus, was consequently delighted when the Portuguese began to show an interest in him and in his

[40] Gibbon, *Decline and Fall*, ch. xlvii (V, 165, in J. B. Bury's edition).

country. The westerners apparently believed that he was none other than the famous Prester John, the mythical Christian monarch who was popularly believed, ever since the twelfth century, to have made extensive conquests from the Moslems, and whose domains had been alternately located in Asia and in Africa. Embassies and messages began to be exchanged during the first two decades of the sixteenth century, and in 1522 the Turkish danger became so imminent that the Negus sent a monk named Saga za Ab to Lisbon to ask for a definite alliance with the Portuguese in order to expel the Turks from the Red Sea. Apparently the ambassador also carried a letter to the Pope, in which the Abyssinian ruler professed himself willing to abandon the Coptic and accept the Latin form of worship, and recognize the Bishop of Rome as the vicar of Christ.[41]

Nothing came of these proposals for the time being, but the news of them naturally alarmed the Turks. The Moslem inhabitants of the region of Adal, which intervenes between Abyssinia and the mouth of the Red Sea, were supported by their Turkish neighbors at Zeila to the southeast of them in a vigorous offensive. They had firearms, with which the Abyssinians were apparently totally unfamiliar, and they were ably led by the famous "Achmet the Left-Handed," the emir of Harrar, further southward. They gained one victory after another in the succeeding years. Every triumph that Achmet won was followed by increasing Turkish reënforcements. He speedily conquered all the eastern part of Abyssinia; the Negus was forced to flee into the interior. The only remaining hope for the latter was to make a final desperate appeal to

---

[41] W. E. Conzelman, tr. and ed., *Chronique de Galâwdêwos, roi d'Éthiopie* (Paris, 1895), pp. xiv–xv; Francisco Alvarez, *Narrative of the Portuguese Embassy to Abyssinia, 1520–1527*, tr. and ed. Henry E. J. Stanley, 3d Baron Stanley of Alderley (London: Hakluyt Society, 1881), p. x. It seems probable that the letter was a pious fraud.

Christian Europe to help him.[42] A certain John Bermudez, who had remained in Abyssinia after the last Portuguese embassy had departed, was accordingly despatched to Rome and to Portugal. As a proof of the sincerity of his desire to become a vassal of Rome, the Negus persuaded the aged Abuna of Ethiopia, or head of the Abyssinian church, who was about to die, to designate Bermudez as his successor and the next religious representative of the land. This of course the Abuna had no right to do, for the appointment to his office was in the hands of the Patriarch of Alexandria, but the urgency of Bermudez won the day. On his arrival at Rome he was warmly welcomed and, according to his own statement, probably false, was confirmed by Paul III in his new dignity as "Patriarch of Abyssinia." [43] At Lisbon the king of Portugal gave him an order commanding his Indian viceroy to despatch a force of 450 men to his rescue with the firearms which he so desperately needed. But the Negus did not live to see the arrival of the forces that had been promised him. He died on September 2, 1540, and the Portuguese, who were commanded by a son of Vasco da Gama, did not reach Abyssinia till the following year.[44]

Galâwdêwos (Gradeus, or Claudius), who succeeded to the Abyssinian throne, was only eighteen years old at the time; but he was a man of indomitable energy, and had been carefully trained as a soldier. Even before the arrival of the Portuguese reënforcements, he had seized the offensive. He was not invariably successful, but at least he let the Turks know that he was alive.[45] When da Gama and his followers appeared, he naturally redoubled his

---

[42] Conzelman, pp. xvi–xvii.

[43] Miguel de Castanhoso, *The Portuguese Expedition to Abyssinia in 1541–1543,* tr. and ed. R. S. Whiteway (London: Hakluyt Society, 1902), pp. lxxxi–ci.

[44] De Castanhoso, pp. xxxviii–xl; Conzelman, pp. xvi–xix.

[45] Conzelman, pp. xvii–xviii.

efforts; in April, 1542, the Ottoman commander was badly defeated in an attempt to prevent the union of the two detachments of his enemies. From that time onward fortune wavered between the two sides. The Turks got the aid of the pasha of Zebid, on the other side of the Red Sea, who sent them 1000 troops and ten cannon. They caught a small detachment of the Portuguese who had got separated from the main army, slew most of them, and captured their leader, who was brought before Achmet, tortured, and beheaded.[46] But a little later Galâwdêwos resumed the offensive. For the next fifteen years, he was almost invariably successful. His arch-enemy Achmet was killed in 1543, and the neighboring tribes, who had supported the Turks when victory seemed within their grasp, now reversed their policy, and rallied to the standard of Galâwdêwos. It is worth noting that the latter, now that the tide had turned in his favor, refused to fulfil his promise to become a Roman Catholic; even an urgent appeal from Pope Julius III failed to move him. His famous *Confession of Faith* was a splendid justification of the Abyssinian form of Christianity.[47]

Until the latter part of the life of Galâwdêwos, there is little evidence that Suleiman took any active interest in the affairs of Abyssinia. The whole affair doubtless seemed to him too remote. He had many more important responsibilities in other lands, and he trusted the local Turkish officials to see to it that the Abyssinian king was kept in bounds. But the latter's recent victories convinced him that it would not do to delay too long, and a Circassian, Ugdunin Pasha, obtained his consent and support in undertaking the conquest of Nubia, thereby threatening Abyssinia on the north. In 1557 Ugdunin captured Massawa on the western shore of the Red Sea, and thus possessed

---

[40] De Castanhoso, pp. 150–167; Conzelman, pp. xviii–xx.
[47] Conzelman, pp. xxvii–xxx.

himself of what had been the sole base of the operations of the Portuguese in the interior.[48] The latter had by this time departed and Galâwdêwos was left alone. The valiant ruler defeated his assailants in several encounters in the course of the next two years, but was himself killed in battle in March, 1559.[49] With his death hostilities soon dwindled away. Abyssinia was no longer a threat to the power of the Ottoman Empire, and the Turks were too busy in other directions to try to extend their victories at its expense. Since then the country has often been exposed to the peril of Moslem conquest, but down to its annexation by the Italians in 1936 it was never in such danger of losing its independence as it was in Suleiman's day. It is poetic justice that the period of its captivity has lasted less than five years.

[48] Conzelman, pp. xxviii, 164–167.
[49] Conzelman, p. xxx.

⚮ XI ⚮

Hungary Again: 1533-1564

The tale of Suleiman's doings in the Danube valley during the thirty years which followed the peace of 1533 is one of the most difficult and complicated in the history of Europe, and can be dealt with but briefly here. It contains plenty of fighting, but the Sultan's failure to take Vienna in 1529, and his voluntary retirement, three years later, after the capture of Güns, had convinced him that there was a point beyond which land campaigns in Central Europe could not profitably be pursued. His attention, moreover, was continually distracted, and at the most critical moments, by the necessity of waging war on Persia. The main interest of the story is really diplomatic, and there is much treachery and deceit in it—most of which was on the Christian side. Suleiman constantly strove to play off the Hapsburg Ferdinand on the northwest against John Zápolya and his son on the northeast, and thereby to insure his own hold on the much richer south-central portion of the realm. The measure of his success in this effort is attested by the fact that the tripartite division of Hungary which had been established at the close of his reign remained practically unaltered down to the Peace of Carlowitz in 1699.

The central figure of the early years of the story is that of the Venetian Ludovico Gritti.[1] Even before the peace

---

[1] See Heinrich Kretschmayr, "Ludovico Gritti," in *Archiv für österreichische Geschichte*, vol. LXXXIII, 1 (1896), pp. 1–106, an article to which I have already referred.

of 1533 was actually signed, he was in Buda, the trusted representative of the Sultan, empowered to arrange all differences between Ferdinand and Zápolya and to superintend the drawing of their respective boundaries. But the instructions which Gritti had received from the Sultan, and the verbal orders that he had been given by Ibrahim, varied widely. The former spoke of the whole of Hungary as belonging to his protégé Zápolya, whereas the latter had assured the representatives of Ferdinand that settlement would be made on the basis of *uti possidetis*, and had ordered Gritti to proceed on that principle. It was but another instance of the Grand Vizir's arrogance, and the ultimate results of it were to be fatal for Gritti. He listened to Ibrahim and not to Suleiman, and when ambassadors from Ferdinand arrived in Constantinople to present their side of the case as Gritti had pictured it to them, the Sultan was furious.[2] "Hungary," he declared, "is mine, and in it I have put my slave Janus Kral (Zápolya) who can do nothing without me. I have given that kingdom to him, and I can take it away when I wish. . . . Therefore do not let Ferdinand meddle in these things, because I will not give that kingdom to him. . . . If Ferdinand does nothing against it, so much the better for him. . . . What Janus Kral does, he does from me, for he does not dare to do anything unless I order him to."[3]

How far the Sultan suspected that Gritti had disobeyed him, we can only guess; in any case the Venetian was not removed from his post. His position, however, was exceedingly precarious. Ibrahim, his chief friend and patron, had already gone off to Asia Minor to prepare for the Persian campaign,[4] and Gritti had many enemies in Constantinople. In his extremity, he confided in Cornelius

[2] Kretschmayr, pp. 47–53.
[3] Gévay, vol. II, pt. 2, pp. 57–58.
[4] Gévay, vol. II, pt. 2, p. 104.

Hans Guldenmund.

Suleiman the Magnificent
Engraving by Michael Ostendorfer, dated 1548,
broadsheeted by Hans Guldenmund
(cf. p. 299)

Schepper, the envoy of Ferdinand. He declared that he had always been at heart a Christian; and he offered to betray important fortresses if a Christian league was formed against the Turk. He made no mystery of the line that he intended to take with the Hungarians; he spoke of them with contempt and declared, with some truth, that "they had always been, all of them, on both sides." "He who wishes to rule," he avowed, "must not shudder at the shedding of blood." [5] But he was quite unable to make good his word. He began by summoning all the great nobles and representatives of the cities in Transylvania to assemble and listen to his orders. There was much hesitation about obeying, and Emerich Czybak, one of the greatest of the magnates, refused to appear. Gritti thereupon sent a body of horsemen to seize him, and as he defended himself desperately, he was murdered. At this the whole region rose in fury. Within a few days 40,000 men had assembled, secretly encouraged by Zápolya. Gritti, after barricading himself for a time in a castle, was caught as he was attempting to escape, and immediately beheaded (September, 1534). [6]

Both Ferdinand and Zápolya tried to make capital for themselves at the Porte out of Gritti's fate. The former pointed out that the voivode was really responsible for the death of the Sultan's representative; the voivode took the ground that Gritti's dealings with the Hapsburgs had been so treacherous as to make his removal a blessing to his master. But Suleiman refused to take any definite line. Under the circumstances it suited him far better to continue to play the double game in Hungary, and he doubtless secretly rejoiced at the repeated failures of Ferdinand and Zápolya to reach any agreement. Meantime in Croatia, in spite of the existing peace, desultory fighting con-

[5] Kretschmayr, pp. 66–70; Gévay, vol. II, pt. 2, pp. 104–118.
[6] Kretschmayr, pp. 73–82; Gévay, vol. II, pt. 3, pp. 2–7.

tinued between the Hapsburgs and the Turks. The latter
made constant raiding expeditions into Austrian territory,
until Ferdinand, in 1537, resolved to put a stop to them
by besieging the town of Esseg on the Drave, whence
most of them emanated. But the effort was a lamentable
failure. The Hapsburg force, of some 8,000 cavalry and
16,000 infantry, was a motley horde of Austrians, Bohemians, Hungarians, and Italians, and Hans Katzianer,
their commander-in-chief, was an officer of small merit.
The pasha of Semendria, who opposed him, refused to be
lured into a combat in the open field, but harried his advance with clouds of light cavalry, who cut off his supplies and finally forced him to retreat. The Turks pursued
and cut to pieces most of the Christian infantry, while
the greater part of the cavalry escaped. Katzianer fled
with them, abandoning his artillery and baggage; on his
return to Vienna he was cast into prison for his cow-
ardice. The tale of the remaining months of his life is an
interesting comment on the instability of Hungarian affairs. He bribed his jailers in Vienna, and got away to
one of his own castles in Croatia, where he promptly
opened negotiations with the Turks, until Count Nicholas
Zriny, whom he had invited to participate in his treason,
stabbed him in the back. His body was flung from a
window into the castle moat, and his head was sent off
to Vienna.[7]

The failure of his attempt to repel the Turks made
Ferdinand more willing to come to terms with Zápolya,
and the latter also was more than weary of the existing
situation. Under the mediation of Charles V they accordingly concluded a treaty of peace on February 28, 1538,
at Nagy-Várad or Grosswardein. Both were to have the
title of king. Each was to retain such parts of Hungary
as he then possessed. After the death of Zápolya, who was

[7] Hammer, V, 277–278; Busbecq, II, 271.

then unmarried and childless, his portion was to pass to the House of Hapsburg, though provision was made for the endowment of his offspring, should he ever have any. The Emperor and Ferdinand were to help Zápolya reconquer Belgrade from the Turks, and defend him against all Ottoman attacks.[8]

The news of this treaty soon reached Constantinople. Its exact provisions were probably not known, for Zápolya had done his utmost to keep them secret; but the fact that his two Christian vassals had dared to conclude an agreement without consulting him was enough to arouse the wrath of the Sultan, who regarded the whole of Hungary as belonging to himself by right of conquest. Yet for the time being he was in no condition to take vengeance. The war in the Mediterranean against the Spaniards and Venetians was occupying most of his attention; he was also intent on punishing his insubordinate vassal the prince of Moldavia. This last proved an easy task. The prince did not venture to await the Turkish onslaught, but hid himself in Transylvania. The Moldavian lands along the Black Sea, between the Pruth and the Dniester, were taken away and directly incorporated as a new sanjak in the Ottoman Empire.[9]

It is probable that this new demonstration of Turkish power made Zápolya wonder whether, after all, the Sultan was not a safer vessel to trust his fortunes to than was Ferdinand. In any case he now made haste to wed Isabella, the daughter of Suleiman's loyal friend, the king of Poland. There is every reason to believe that Zápolya took this step at the advice of a shrewd, ambitious, and determined monk named Martinuzzi, who had been his chief mentor for some time past, and was at that time bitterly

---

[8] *Österreichische Staatsverträge, Fürstentum Siebenbürgen, 1526–90* (Vienna, 1911), pp. 65–85.

[9] Hammer, V, 288–292; Iörga, II, 424–426.

opposed to the House of Austria; he cherished hopes that if Zápolya should have issue, the treaty of Grosswardein might be broken.[10] He also persuaded his master to send an embassy to the Porte to soften the wrath of the Sultan and regain his favor by a money gift. Ferdinand heard of the mission and resolved if possible to anticipate it. We need not be surprised that the envoy whom he despatched for the purpose was none other than that same Hieronymus Laski who ten years before had been so successful in Constantinople on behalf of Zápolya. Laski had quarrelled with his former master, been imprisoned, and then, after regaining his liberty, had changed sides; he now lusted for revenge on his Hungarian patron. The whole proceeding was entirely characteristic of the times. He was instructed to point out how much more advantageous for the Sultan it would be to have Ferdinand rather than Zápolya on the Hungarian throne; he also revealed to Suleiman the provisions of the treaty of Grosswardein. On this the Sultan turned to his Grand Vizir and burst out, "These two kings are unworthy to wear crowns; they are faithless; neither the fear of God nor of man has been able to prevent them from breaking the treaty which they have sworn to observe."[11]

Meantime the sudden death of Zápolya, on July 21, 1540, brought matters to a crisis. On his sickbed, he had received the news of the birth of a son, and he besought his adherents not to give up their country to a foreign ruler, but to elect the child and to appeal to the Sultan for aid. Led by Martinuzzi, they proclaimed the infant king, under the name of Stephen. It was a flat violation of the treaty of Grosswardein, and Ferdinand could not

[10] On the remarkable career of Martinuzzi, or Utiešenović, also known as "Brother George," consult Antoine Bechet, *Histoire du ministère du Cardinal Martinusius* (Paris, 1715), and O. M. Utiešenović, *Lebensgeschichte des Cardinals Georg Utiešenović, genannt Martinusius* (Vienna, 181).

[11] Hammer, V, 321–322.

be expected to submit to it. If he had been ready with a powerful army, he might perhaps have been able to conquer Hungary before it could receive aid, for some of Zápolya's old followers had by this time joined his side; but as usual he was short of funds. Nevertheless, after an embassy to the widowed queen had received unsatisfactory replies, he attempted to use force. With the aid of 50,000 ducats from the Emperor and sundry loans, he collected a small army, which, after capturing several towns, laid siege to Buda. But the affair was halfheartedly undertaken and quickly abandoned. The besiegers retired, leaving behind them a garrison across the river in Pesth. Henceforward the pivot of the situation, as both sides were quick to recognize, was in Constantinople. The ambassadors of the infant king were received there with marked favor. Their gifts were graciously accepted, and they had the influential support of the representative of France. Their request that the Sultan confer Hungary on Stephen was granted on condition of an annual payment of 30,000 ducats; [12] but Suleiman was determined not to be tricked, and as enemies had spread the report that Isabella had not really borne a child, he sent a chaush on a special mission to ascertain the truth. In order to convince him, the queen gave her breast to the baby in his presence; and the chaush, falling on his knees, kissed the infant's feet and swore in his master's name that it should rule Hungary. [13]

Ferdinand was naturally worried by the news of the *rapprochement* between the Sultan and the adherents of his late rival, and sent Laski back to Constantinople in the autumn of 1540, to see if he could not arrange a fresh truce. But the envoy was received with wrath and contempt; in fact the best of his friends among the Ottoman

[12] Hammer, V, 324.
[13] Hammer, V, 323-324.

officials told him frankly that he would have done far better to stay away. At an audience granted him on November 7, the Sultan burst into such a furious rage that the frightened vizirs, standing with bowed heads before the imperial throne, motioned Laski to retire at once. On the following day, according to the established Turkish custom with ambassadors of hostile powers, he was arrested and placed in confinement; it would appear, however, that the nature of his detention was not so severe as to prevent him from making fresh efforts to get the truce that he had been sent to obtain, and to secure his own release.[14] He was taken along in the train of the Turkish expedition into Hungary in the following year, and was finally set free in pity, when his captors recognized that the state of his health was so precarious that his death could not long be postponed. In the meantime, the Sultan decided that war on Ferdinand should be begun as soon as possible. The winter was spent in preparations, and on June 23, 1541, Suleiman left Constantinople to begin a new series of Hungarian campaigns.[15]

The Turkish march on Buda, which was the Sultan's objective, was far easier than it had ever been before, and Suleiman reached the old Hungarian capital in less than two months. Ferdinand was the nearer the scene of action, and ought to have been ready to receive him. But Ferdinand found it very difficult to collect the necessary forces. His brother was intent, for the moment, on the capture of Algiers, and could send him no help. In the Empire and in Bohemia, men's minds were chiefly concentrated on the religious question; Lutheranism was in the ascendant, and there was general reluctance to contribute to the cause of the Hapsburg. With all his efforts Ferdinand was able to muster only a bare 20,000 troops. Their aged

[14] Gévay, vol. III, pt. 3, pp. 1–65.
[15] Hammer, V, 328.

commander, William of Rogendorf, had Pesth in his hands, and should have attacked Buda vigorously before the Turks could arrive; but instead he tried to terrify it into submission by a feeble bombardment. Its garrison was but 2,400 strong, and many of the inhabitants, among whom was Queen Isabella, were inclined to treat with the besiegers; but Martinuzzi donned a cuirass over his priestly robes, and directed the defence with splendid energy and skill.[16] He foiled the plots of the friends of the queen at the same time that he repulsed all attacks from without. There was much secret negotiation between the assailants and the besieged, but it ultimately came to naught, and in the meantime the first detachments of the Turkish army had arrived. Rogendorf dared not risk a battle, nor would he consent to retreat; instead he remained inactive for an entire fortnight, waiting for reënforcements which never came. But when the Sultan reached the scene with the mass of the Turkish army, it was impossible to hesitate any longer, and he started to transport his forces to the other side of the river. The Turks, learning of his intentions, waited till his cavalry and artillery had got across; then, falling on the infantry, they nearly exterminated it. The Ottomans in their turn then crossed over to Pesth, and dealt with such portions of the Christian cavalry and artillery as had remained there; old Rogendorf himself died of his wounds. Seldom has a campaign been worse mismanaged, and seldom has a foe been more alert to profit by it.[17]

On August 26 Suleiman entered Pesth and ordered that several hundred captives be executed. On the following day he crossed the river, and on the twenty-eighth he received Martinuzzi and other Hungarian delegates. After thanking them for their brave defence and after sending

[16] Bechet, pp. 140–158; Utiešenović, pp. 53–54.
[17] Utiešenović, pp. 54–55.

presents to the queen and to the infant king, he demanded that, as the law of Mohammed forbade his visiting them, the child should be brought for him to see, and also that the city councillors should present themselves to deliberate with him on further measures. These words produced profound consternation; people realized that the Sultan was resolved to install a Turkish government at Buda; but as resistance was out of the question, his orders were obeyed. When the baby, accompanied by three nurses and the chief magnates, was brought into Suleiman's tent, he gazed at it, then told his son Bayezid to pick it up in his arms and kiss it. The child was sent back to his mother in the evening; but under cover of the festivities the Turkish troops, entering Buda in the guise of sight-seers, treacherously seized the city. After some days of pretended deliberation, Suleiman finally announced that, as Buda was too important to be intrusted to a woman, he should take care of it himself until the young king came of age. (Incidentally, the latter soon changed his given name of Stephen to that of John Sigismund, in honor of his father and of his maternal grandfather.) He and his mother were presently sent off to Transylvania, and before their departure were presented with a document, written in letters of blue and gold, in which Suleiman swore by the Prophet, by his ancestors, and by his own sword that he would only continue to hold Buda during the minority of the baby prince.[18] Whether he intended to abide by his promise at the time that he made it may well be doubted, though the situation was to change so rapidly in the next ten or fifteen years that he certainly had some excuse for failing to observe it when the moment came. In any case there can be no question that for the time being he was determined to make the Ottoman occupation of Buda and the adjacent lands a reality. All the territory between the

[18] Bechet, pp. 172–189; Hammer, V, 333–337, 539–540.

Danube and the Theiss was placed under the control of Turkish officers,[19] and other measures were taken, farther south and west, to widen, at the expense of his Christian neighbors, the comparatively narrow strip which he had hitherto held, and which up to the present had not extended far to either side of the Turkish line of march. One sanjak bey after another was set up, as the process went on, until their number finally reached twenty-five; but a considerable amount of local autonomy was left, in accordance with Turkish custom, to the Magyars. The two races and the two religions kept for the most part to themselves, and we are told that if a Christian ventured, even in jest, to don a turban, he was forced to go over to Islam.[20] Such were the foundations of the Turkish Hungary of the next century and a half.

The obvious intention of the Ottomans to establish themselves at Buda caused the Austrians to tremble for the safety of Vienna, and, as usual, ambassadors were despatched to try to stay the progress of the invader. Their gifts included a great clock, which, besides telling the hours, the days, and the months, also showed the movements of the sun, moon, and planets. It was carried in by twelve men, accompanied by a clockmaker to show how to wind it, while a book gave a full explanation of its mechanism.[21] Suleiman, who was versed in astronomy and cosmography, received it with evident pleasure. All this, however, had no influence on the result of the negotiations. The envoys had come with the same old demand: the whole of Hungary for their master, who would be willing in return to make an annual payment of 100,000 ducats. When they had kissed the Sultan's hand and begun their speech, he interrupted it with the exclamation,

[19] Bucholtz, V, 160.
[20] Lavisse and Rambaud, IV, 624.
[21] Hammer, V, 341; Bechet, p. 191.

"What do they say? What do they want?" and then, turning to his vizirs, "If they have nothing more to say, let them go." "Do you think," said Rustem Pasha, who was charged with the negotiations on the Turkish side, "that the Padishah is out of his mind, that he should give away what he has won for the third time with his sword?" Between the proposals of the ambassadors and the demands of the vizir, who insisted that Ferdinand should yield all the places in Hungary he had taken, no agreement was possible, and after a few days, during which Rustem took care that they should be suitably impressed with the irresistible power of the Turkish arms, the envoys were permitted to return to Vienna. In view of the Ottoman tradition in regard to the treatment of representatives of hostile powers, they were fortunate to have escaped imprisonment.[22]

The failure of these negotiations made Ferdinand think of a fresh appeal to arms, the more so as his military prospects seemed brighter than ever before. The Empire was much alarmed by the establishment of the Turks at Buda, and in 1542 the Diet of Spires voted him twice the usual contingent. Some of the Hungarian nobles also, who had hitherto adhered to the House of Zápolya, now rallied to his standard. Even Martinuzzi began negotiations for a treaty with him, according to which John Sigismund, in return for a money indemnity, was to abandon all claim to the Hungarian throne; he was careful, however, not to sign it till he should see what Ferdinand's forces could do. But Ferdinand was as unfortunate as ever on the battlefield. In August, 1542, his motley army of 50,000 men laid siege to Pesth, but six weeks later it was obliged to retreat ingloriously, and in the ensuing winter his forces

---

[22] Bucholtz, V, 160–161; Hammer, V, 343–344; cf. autobiography of the ambassador Sigmund, Freiherr von Herberstein, in *Fontes Rerum Austriacarum Scriptores*, I (1855), 331–336.

melted away.[23] His futile aggression, moreover, had the effect of bringing Suleiman into the field once more. In 1543 the Sultan reappeared with a great army and took and garrisoned Gran, Stuhlweissenburg, and other fortresses, thereby considerably enlarging his own dominions, while Ferdinand remained immobile at Presburg with a force of 40,000 men. When Suleiman retired, Ferdinand's troops refused to pursue. In the following year the war was continued by the pashas on the frontier, with the Turks almost invariably victorious.[24]

Obviously the only way for Ferdinand to preserve the scant portion of Western Hungary that still remained to him was once more to sue for peace. His hopes of military support were now far less bright than in 1542. The Hungarian nobles were disgusted by his failures; his brother was now intent on defeating the Lutherans in the Empire, and wrote that he could send him no aid. The result was the despatch of a new embassy to Constantinople in the end of the year 1544. Its most permanently important member was to be a Bolognese named Giovanni Maria Malvezzi, who had originally accompanied it in the character of secretary. In 1545 it was joined at the Porte by Gerard Veltwyck, the ambassador of Charles V; for the moment, at least, the heads of both branches of the House of Hapsburg were convinced that it was essential to come to terms with the Turk.[25] The ensuing negotiations lasted for over two years, but as the months rolled by the attitude of the Sultan became steadily less and less intransigent, because of the increasing imminence of his second campaign against Persia. On the Mediterranean, as we have already seen, Suleiman would yield nothing; he preferred to leave everything there in

[23] Utiešenović, pp. 59–61.
[24] Utiešenović, pp. 61–62.
[25] R. B. M., III, 340, with note 2.

the hands of Barbarossa and Dragut, who could not possibly be of any use to him in his campaign against the Shah. But his Janissaries on the Danube were another matter, and on June 19, 1547, he granted Ferdinand a peace, or rather a truce for five years, on the basis of *uti possidetis*. The Emperor, the Pope, the republic of Venice, and France were also included in the arrangement. Save for the corsairs, there was apparently to be a general suspension of hostilities between the Cross and the Crescent. In return for it Ferdinand agreed to pay the Sultan the sum of 30,000 ducats a year, part of which was the equivalent of the estates of certain Hungarian nobles who had recently deserted the Turks and gone over to the House of Hapsburg, while the rest of it was termed "a pension" by the Austrians, but was more justifiably regarded by the Turks as a tribute.[26] There could be no doubt that the Sultan had come out on top. In a very real sense the peace of 1547 marks the climax of his victories on the Danube.

The truce of 1547 was not suffered to run its full five-years' course, for the machinations of Martinuzzi obliged the Turks to intervene in Hungary again before its term had expired. This wily prelate now professed to be convinced that it was essential, at all costs, to get the Ottomans out of the land, and that the only hope of doing so was to bring about a permanent union of Christian Austrians and Hungarians. On the other hand, he continued to cherish personal ambitions of his own, and he was far too practical a politician to embark on any line of conduct which did not promise assured success. Isabella was very jealous of the power he wielded in her dominions, and constantly complained of him to Suleiman, who is said to have demanded in 1550 that either the traitor himself

[26] Hammer, V, 394–398, 554–555.

or his head be sent to Constantinople.[27] But Martinuzzi was more than a match for all his foes. By force, by threats, and by cajolery, he persuaded Isabella to exchange the portion of Hungary that still remained to her for certain territories in Silesia, and to install Ferdinand in her place; it was a masterpiece of statecraft, and was formally confirmed in August, 1551, by the Diet of Kolosvár.[28] Ferdinand, for the moment, was of course delighted, and rewarded Martinuzzi by getting him a cardinal's hat; [29] Suleiman, equally of course, was furious when he heard the news, and vented his rage on the Austrian ambassador Malvezzi, who was imprisoned in the Black Tower of the Castle of Anatolia.[30] This measure, and the mustering of fresh Turkish troops for a new invasion in the following year, convinced Martinuzzi that he could not possibly hope to carry through the program which he had laid out; he was also deeply discouraged by the dilatoriness of Ferdinand, who in turn began to suspect him of designs to secure Hungary for himself. Martinuzzi was now persuaded that at all costs Suleiman must be placated, at least for the time being. When the imperialist generals found him privately endeavoring to mediate between their master and the Turks, they represented him to Ferdinand as a traitor, and asked permission to kill him. He was murdered on December 18, 1551.[31] After a searching examination of the facts of the case, which lasted till February, 1555, Pope Julius III finally pronounced Ferdinand guiltless of all blame.[32] The whole episode is typical of the

[27] Hammer, VI, 18, Andrew Báthori to Thomas Nádasdy, September 30, 1550, in György Pray, *Epistolae Procerum Regni Hungariae*, 3 vols. (Posonii, 1806), II, 208.

[28] Utiešenović, pp. 69-97, and its Urkundenbuch, pp. 36-39; *Österreichische Staatsverträge. Fürstentum Siebenbürgen (1526-1590)*, pp. 114-136.

[29] Utiešenović, pp. 100-101, and Urkundenbuch, pp. 41-42.

[30] Hammer, VI, 21-22.   [31] Utiešenović, pp. 64-137.

[32] Pastor, *History of the Popes*, XIII, 172, note 3.

kaleidoscopic shifts of the political scene which are the dominant feature of tripartite Hungary.

In the following year the Turks came on again. This time the Sultan was not with them, but under the leadership of the second vizir, Achmet Pasha, they were at first uniformly successful. In February they won a great victory at Szegedin; in April Weissprim fell, and in July Temesvár. The rest of the Banat soon followed, and the territories in Ottoman control were thereby greatly increased. In the autumn, however, the Turks were repulsed at Erlau to the northeast of Buda. The heroism of its defenders was beyond all praise, and after a siege of thirty-eight days the Ottomans withdrew.[33] This check, and still more the necessities of the impending campaign against Persia, made the Sultan willing to grant a six-months' truce, which the Christian envoys to the Porte endeavored to have converted into a five-years' peace; but the representatives of Ferdinand and of Queen Isabella did their best to thwart each other's efforts, and little was accomplished.[34] Meantime the war of raids continued with unabated fury in Hungary. Success was more nearly evenly divided than before; particularly was the Sultan mortified by the failure of his forces in 1556 to take Sziget, between the Danube and the Drave—a minor fortress, though difficult of access because of the then adjacent swamps.[35] Suleiman never forgot this reverse, and vowed that when the moment came he would avenge it.

From that time onward there is little of importance to record about Hungarian affairs down to the great Sultan's final invasion and death. A peace, on the usual terms, was arranged by Busbecq between Austria and the Porte in 1561, but as important differences were found to exist

---

[33] Hammer, VI, 33–52.
[34] Iorga, III, 44–49.
[35] Hammer, VI, 105–115.

between its Latin and Turkish versions, it availed nothing
to check the incessant border warfare.[36] The diplomatic
thrust and parry between the Hapsburgs and the House
of Zápolya continued unabated, though the *dramatis per-
sonae* had changed. Queen Isabella died in September,
1559, leaving John Sigismund in full control; in 1564
Ferdinand was succeeded by his son Maximilian II.—It is
interesting, incidentally, to note how much the existing
political confusion was increased by the rapid advance of
the Reformed faith in the Hungary of this period. Maximilian was the least intolerant of all the Hapsburg Emperors, and John Sigismund was the patron and protector
of Lutherans, Calvinists, and even of Socinians, all of
whose numbers increased apace. Not only did the Ottomans exercise a powerful influence on the course of the
Protestant Reformation. They also derived great profit
from it.

[36] Busbecq, II, appendix, 279–281.

❧ XII ❧

Malta and Sziget

We have already observed that the death of Khaireddin Barbarossa in 1546 marks the end of an epoch in Suleiman's Mediterranean wars. None of his successors combined all his qualities. There were plenty of efficient corsairs left, but none of them seemed to the Sultan to be quite the man to be safely intrusted with the task of representing him in North Africa. That office was finally conferred on an Egyptian named Salah Reis, who remained for the most part at Algiers and effectively upheld the Ottoman power in the interior and on the adjacent coasts.[1] But in the meantime the campaign against the Christians on the sea was vigorously continued by independent corsairs.

Of these the most active was Dragut, whose four years as a galley-slave in the service of Doria made him burn for revenge on his Christian captors.[2] After being ransomed by Barbarossa in 1544, he devoted all his energies to the collection of a fleet which should enable him to attain his end. He carried neither the banner of the Sultan nor of any of the North African states, but flew a red and white flag with a blue crescent on it, emblematic of his resolve to fight for his own hand.[3] At first he was not very successful. With the idea of gaining a base from which he could ravage the coasts of Sicily and Naples, he

[1] Mercier, *Histoire de l'Afrique Septentrionale*, III, 73.
[2] R. B. M., III, 329–330.
[3] R. B. M., III, 341.

274

managed to possess himself of Monastir and El Mehedia, on the North African coast to the southeast of Tunis; but Doria soon ousted him from them, and early in 1551 he sought refuge in the island of Gerba. Thither Doria pursued him, and blockaded the mouth of the narrow inlet in which his fleet had taken refuge; the Christians were convinced that they had their enemy bottled up. But Dragut was more than equal to the occasion. Distracting Doria's attention by a heavy fire from the shore, he had all his ships dragged overland on greased ways—like Mohammed II before Constantinople in 1453—to the other side of the island, whence he got away without his opponents being any the wiser. Suleiman took note of the performance; the next time that Dragut appeared, he bore an official title as commander of the Sultan's galleys, and was supported by another strong fleet under "Sinan the Jew." This time his objective was the strongholds of the Knights of St. John of Jerusalem. At Malta he was repulsed, but he defeated his foes on the neighboring island of Gozzo; then, turning back to the North African coast, he took Tripoli (August 16, 1551) where the Order had maintained a subsidiary establishment since 1528. El Mehedia would doubtless have shared the same fate, had not its garrison been permitted, three years later, to abandon and dismantle it.[4]

In the meantime the Turks had won other victories further westward. The Spaniards were disastrously defeated in an effort to reëstablish their authority in Tlemcen. In 1555 they were forced to surrender Bugia, which had been uninterruptedly in their hands for the past forty-five years; in 1558 they were routed in an attempt to capture Mostaganem. The Emperor, with whom Suleiman had so often longed to measure swords, died in September of the same year. There could be no question that the Turks

[4] R. B. M., III, 343.

had got the better of him on the sea. The Sultan could reflect with pride on the story of their long rivalry.[5]

Christian Europe looked eagerly forward to Charles's son and successor, Philip II, as the champion of the Cross against the Crescent. The new king had got back to Spain in September, 1559. The Franco-Spanish wars had been ended in the previous April by the Peace of Cateau-Cambrésis. Philip was known to be a most devout Catholic; there was a general hope that he would try to revive the crusades. But, as usual, when the time for action came, the Spanish king held back. His attention for the time being was chiefly occupied with internal affairs; and the initiation and leadership of the expedition by which the Christians hoped to reëstablish their prestige in the Mediterranean were consequently the work of others. Jean de La Valette, the new Grand Master at Malta, was determined to recover Tripoli for his Order, and persuaded the viceroy of Sicily to help him. After long delays a fleet of some ninety vessels, carrying 10,000 to 12,000 soldiers, was collected and sailed for North Africa on February 10, 1560.

Ill fortune dogged the expedition from the first. Its commanders were ignorant of the geography of the region about Tripoli, while Dragut knew every inch of the ground. A landing was attempted on the coast, some seventy-five miles west of their ultimate objective, but the place proved unhealthy and the water bad, so that the Christians retired to the island of Gerba to refit. At first they were warmly welcomed by the inhabitants, who hated Dragut, and hoped the newcomers would rid them of him; but when the latter showed signs of intending to establish a permanent base there, they changed their minds, and began to make plans to expel them. All of these de-

[5] R. B. M., III, 343–346.

lays gave Dragut an admirable opportunity not only to repair the defences of Tripoli but also to send for aid to Constantinople. On May 10, a galley from Malta reached the Christians with the stunning news that a Turkish fleet of 85 sail, under the terrible Piali Pasha,[6] had been sighted off Gozzo, and was making straight for Gerba. A panic seized the defenders. There was a mad rush for the ships, but the Turks bore down on them with a favorable wind, capturing twenty-seven galleys, and killing or taking prisoners some 5000 men. The remainder shut themselves up in the castle of Gerba, where they remained, without adequate food or supplies, to await the joint assaults of Piali Pasha and Dragut. The Turks had the game in their own hands, and they knew it. Instead of attempting to storm the fortress, they occupied themselves with cutting off its water supply, and after two sorties had failed, the place surrendered on July 31. All of its 6000 defenders who were not already dead were taken prisoners. The fortifications were razed to the ground.[7] The victors returned triumphant to Tripoli, which was to be Dragut's principal headquarters in the immediately ensuing years, and was to remain in Turkish possession, theoretically at least, till 1912. Piali Pasha got back to Constantinople in September with a magnificent train of captives and booty. It was by far the most significant victory of the Turks in the Mediterranean since the repulse of Charles V at Algiers, but "those who saw Suleiman's face in this hour of triumph failed to detect in it the slightest trace of undue elation. . . . The expression of his countenance was unchanged; his stern features had lost nothing of their habitual gloom; . . . So self-contained was the heart of that grand old man, so schooled to meet each change of For-

---

[6] On this man see Hammer, VI, 188–189, 193–196; Henry Seddall, *Malta* (London, 1870), p. 58.

[7] Hammer, VI, 189–193.

tune however great, that all the applause and triumphs of
that day wrung from him no sign of satisfaction." [8]

The Turks had not failed to note the slackness of the
Spanish king in supporting the expedition against Tripoli.
The moral was obvious; they must carry the war into
enemy waters. In the spring of 1561 a Turkish fleet appeared out of the blue before Soller in Majorca and attacked it. The inhabitants were brave and resourceful, and
the onslaught was ultimately repulsed, but the assailants
were not discouraged. [9] In 1562, if not before, they had
passed through the Strait of Gibraltar, and ventured out
into the broad Atlantic to prey upon the treasure-laden
galleons returning from the New World. On June 24 of
that year, Sir Thomas Chaloner, the English ambassador
to Spain, wrote home to Queen Elizabeth that "the Moors
have spoilt many merchant ships about Seville and Cadiz,
and amongst them three English ships, with a booty of
more than 100,000 ducats." [10] Taken literally, the words
of the English envoy would mean that the damage had
been done by the Berbers, but the British of that day
were not too accurate in their designations of remote
states, and as the Turks were now in control of nearly all
of the Mauretanian coast, there can be little doubt that
they played a prominent part in the affair. There was, in
fact, but one important point on the North African shore
between Tunis and Morocco that still defied them, namely,
the fortress of Oran and its strategically indispensable
satellite at Mers-el-Kebir. Ever since the Turkish victory
at Gerba, the Sultan had been maturing his plans for an
attack on it. In the early months of 1563 he intrusted the
execution of the project to Hassan, the son of Khaireddin

[8] Busbecq, I, 322.

[9] R. B. M., IV, 108.

[10] *Calendar of State Papers, Foreign*, 1562, no. 248, p. 127; cf. letter of
June 27, no. 262, p. 136. A report to Chaloner from Seville, July 4, says
"twenty sails of Turks and Moors are before the haven" (no. 279, p. 145).

Barbarossa, who now represented him at Algiers. Hassan was given a small fleet to carry his cannon and supplies, and he had an army of 25,000 men. In April he arrived before Oran, and at once made his preparations for a vigorous attack. Crucial events were about to take place there, as they were to do again in July, 1940.

It was just at this point that the tide turned. Now that the war had been carried into Spanish waters, Philip shook off his lethargy, and began vigorous measures of defence. The combined Spanish garrisons at Oran and Mers-el-Kebir probably numbered little more than 1000 men. During late April and early May they were able to delay the besiegers before the subsidiary outside forts, but it was obvious that they could not maintain themselves indefinitely without aid from Spain. Meantime, Philip had succeeded in collecting thirty-four galleys, and despatched them to the relief of his hard-pressed subjects. They reached Oran just as Hassan, who had been apprised of their coming, was about to launch a decisive blow which should forestall them; in fact they arrived at the very moment that the attack was beginning, and threw the assailants into confusion. Twenty of the Turkish ships escaped, but five others were captured. Taken with these were four large French vessels, a significant evidence of the fact that though the Franco-Turkish alliance had long since passed its prime, it was not yet extinct. The Turkish land forces made haste to raise the siege and take flight, leaving behind them sixteen pieces of artillery and large quantities of munitions and supplies. Altogether it was the most serious reverse that the Ottomans had sustained in North Africa since their loss of Tunis in 1535.[11]

Obviously the Christians would follow it up with a counter thrust, and as Algiers was much too strong, they elected to deliver it at Vélez de la Gomera (popularly

[11] R. B. M., IV, 109–111.

known as the Peñon de Vélez) far to the westward, in Morocco, two-thirds of the way from Oran to Tangiers. The Spaniards had taken it in 1508, but lost it fourteen years later; Philip was now eager to recover it, more especially because it lay so close to his own beloved shores. The first attack, which was launched in July, 1563, had hoped to effect its object by a surprise; but the defenders were keenly on the watch, and the Christians withdrew defeated. The Turks were of course correspondingly encouraged, and showed it by venturing out again into the Atlantic. This time it would appear that their depredations reached as far as the Canaries.[12] The Christians saw that the sole way to rehabilitate their prestige was to capture the Peñon de Vélez at all costs, and in August, 1564, Don García de Toledo, a cousin of the Duke of Alva and the son of the viceroy of Naples, was despatched for the purpose with a force over three times as large as that of the preceding year. He was given the title of Captain General of the Mediterranean—previously held by Andrea Doria, who had died in 1560. So imposing was his armament that the mere sight of it was enough to cause the defenders of Vélez to flee into the interior. The Peñon itself promised to give more trouble, but Toledo entered it without serious difficulty on September 8. He had captured with the loss of only thirty men one of the most dangerous of pirates' nests, which had generally been regarded as impregnable.[13] He was rewarded for his success with the viceroyalty of Sicily, while Suleiman at Constantinople laid his plans for revenge. There was to be one more great clash between the Cross and the Crescent in the Mediterranean before the curtain fell.

There could be little doubt where the Sultan would elect to launch his last attack. He had captured Rhodes

[12] Cesáreo Fernández Duro, *Armada Española* (Madrid, 1895–1903), II, 59.

[13] R. B. M., IV, 111–114.

from the Knights of St. John of Jerusalem in 1522. His fleets had expelled them from Tripoli in 1551. But they still held Malta, and Malta, even more than Tunis and Oran, was the chief barrier to his control of the Mediterranean. Tradition and expediency both dictated a grand assault on the last remaining stronghold of the Knights, and Mihrmah, the daughter of Roxelana and the widow of Rustem, who exercised much influence over Suleiman in the later years of his life, never ceased to represent it to him as a sacred duty to the Faith.[14] Yet the Sultan had many difficulties to contend with. There were plenty of ships and men to man them, but there was trouble about the high command. Suleiman had never accompanied his naval expeditions, and did not propose to do so now. He intrusted the fleet to Piali Pasha, and the land forces to Mustafa Pasha, who was no less than sixty-five years old, and had commanded his master's armies with distinction in Europe and in Asia. Both were typically successful military leaders according to the standards of the Porte.[15] Yet the Sultan wondered whether, after all, they would know how to conduct a Mediterranean campaign anywhere nearly as well as the officially less well accredited but far more experienced Dragut. Another star, moreover, had recently risen in the piratical firmament in the person of Aluch Ali, a renegade Calabrian fisherman who had become a fanatical convert to Islam; he was to be a thorn in the side of the Christians for many years after Suleiman's death, and ultimately recaptured Tunis and La Goletta.[16] For the present he was at Tripoli with Dragut, and both of them advised against an attempt to attack Malta. In their opinion it was essential to clear the Christians out of Mauretania first.[17] They failed to persuade the Sultan to abandon the enterprise on which he had set his

[14] Hammer, VI, 198, 214.
[15] Hammer, VI, 198–199; Seddall, *Malta*, pp. 57–58.
[16] On his career see R. B. M., IV, 126, 138, 143–144, 147, 150–152.
[17] Mercier, III, 103.

heart; on the other hand, he had so much respect for their ability and knowledge that he charged Mustafa and Piali to take them into their confidence and attempt nothing without their approval and support.[18]

On April 1, 1565, the Turkish fleet left Constantinople. It numbered nearly two hundred ships, of which at least one hundred and thirty were fit for combat, and it carried land forces of about 30,000 men. The Grand Master Jean de La Valette had realized for months the peril of his position, and had been making every possible effort to avert it. He strengthened his defences. He called in his absent Knights from the different commanderies in Europe, and begged for outside aid. He mustered his auxiliaries and armed the inhabitants of the island; but he was unable in all to raise more than 8,500 men. When the Turkish fleet arrived on May 18—a full month earlier than it had been expected—his situation seemed desperate. There was a difference of opinion among the Turkish commanders as to whether to begin operations immediately or await the coming of Dragut, who had not yet appeared; but Mustafa insisted on taking the offensive at once before Christian reënforcements could arrive, and on the nineteenth he began to land his troops.[19] His immediate objective was the strong fort of St. Elmo, on the outer tip of the promontory of Mount Sceberras, which juts out to the northeast between the Great Harbor and that of Marsa Muscetto, and serves as a protection to them both.[20] La Valette had taken infinite pains to render it as nearly as possible impregnable, though it could hold but a bare

[18] Seddall, *Malta*, p. 57.

[19] Hammer, VI, 200; Seddall, *Malta*, p. 61.

[20] There is an excellent map of Mount Sceberras, St. Elmo, the two harbors, and adjacent fortifications in Major Whitworth Porter's *History of the Knights of Malta*, 2 vols. (London, 1858, in vol. II, facing p. 1); it also shows where the Turkish batteries were emplaced. It has since been reproduced in Seddall's *Malta* (facing page 68); but, unfortunately, in both cases it is printed upside down. Cf. also map inside the covers of this volume.

thousand men; its site is that of the city which bears his
name today. The Turks at once installed batteries on the
adjacent shores and bombarded it furiously from the fleet;
trenches were opened and preparations made for a grand
assault. Dragut, who arrived with twenty-three ships on
June 2, bluntly declared that the operation should never
have been undertaken; but as it had been already begun,
he insisted that it should be carried through, and did his
utmost to make it a success. The story of the heroism of
St. Elmo's defenders is one of the most thrilling in the annals
of Christian warfare. The Turks were so much more numerous that they seemed ultimately certain to capture it;
the object of the besieged was to slay as many of their
enemies as possible, and above all to delay them before its
walls, in the hope that reënforcements would arrive. Over
6,000 Moslems were killed—among them Dragut[21]—before
the place was entered on June 23; and it is said that the
Turks found only nine of the defenders alive.[22]

So disheartened were the Ottoman leaders by the losses
they had sustained that they made a vain effort to induce
La Valette to surrender his two chief remaining fortresses
—St. Angelo and Il Burgo, on the other side of the Great
Harbor—without a fight; after its failure they started to
besiege them both. At this juncture Hassan Barbarossa
arrived from Algiers with twenty-seven more ships and
2,500 men. As he was not only the son of his father but
also the son-in-law of Dragut, he demanded, in deference
to the names of these distinguished sailors, that he be
given some voice in the conduct of the siege, and the differences between the Ottoman commanders were thus
perpetuated.[23] Open conflict between them was avoided
by giving each one of them an independent operation to

[21] The point opposite St. Elmo on the west, across the Marsa Muscetto,
appropriately bears the old corsair's name today.
[22] R. B. M., IV, 116–117.
[23] Hammer, VI, 203.

carry out, but meantime the Turks were getting more and more discouraged. The defenders of St. Angelo and Il Burgo fought as furiously as had their comrades at St. Elmo, and the assailants lost four times as many men as the besieged. In the end of August, the first detachment of the long awaited Christian reënforcements was at last despatched from Sicily. The story of the reason for their long delay is very interesting, but it can only be briefly summarized here. Don García de Toledo in Sicily did his utmost to hurry their departure. His recent experiences in North Africa had filled him with the ardor of the true crusader, and he longed to rescue the Knights. He got ready all the ships and men at his disposal; he perfected all his plans. One thing alone was lacking, namely, the approval of his master Philip II. But the "Prudent King" held back. In the first place Malta was too remote to appeal to one whose horizons were as narrow as his. He had been enthusiastic for the defence of Oran, and for the capture of the Peñon de Vélez, because they were close to Spain, but he had not forgotten Gerba. Moreover La Valette was a Frenchman, and most of the Order were French, and though the Franco-Spanish wars were over, the memory of them was still vivid. Not till August 20 did Philip give his reluctant consent to the landing of troops at Malta. Storms delayed their departure; not till September 7 was the viceroy able to report to his master that 9,600 Christian soldiers had been put ashore, without loss, on the western end of the island. Their arrival was the signal for the retreat of the Turks. For almost four months they had been stood off by a force of only a quarter the size of their own, and they dreaded combat with the Spanish infantry which was the terror of Europe. They had lost at least 20,000 men, and the differences between their leaders must have added to their despondency. One last attack was tried and failed. On September 11 they broke camp and began to retire. The next day the last of their sails disappeared over the horizon, Hassan toward Algiers, Piali Pasha and the rest to the eastward.[24] It was significant that the Sultan gave orders that his fleet should not enter the harbor of Constantinople till nightfall.[25]

Such was the sorry ending of the great Mediterranean adventure which the Sultan had so gloriously begun at Rhodes, and which he had had such high hopes of continuing and expanding when in March, 1534, he had made Khaireddin Barbarossa admiral in chief of the Ottoman navy. Worse was yet to come, for six years after their failure at Malta the Turks were routed at Lepanto. Yet, curiously enough, these events had but little effect on the actual situation in the Mediterranean. Aluch Ali's recapture of Tunis in 1574 was a telling answer to the Christian victory of three years before, and Philip II was as reluctant to force the fighting as was Suleiman's unworthy successor, Selim the Sot. The result was that the Turks and the Christians made a truce in 1580, which soon after lapsed into a permanent peace.[26] The Turks kept all the North African coast, east of Oran, and also Tlemcen, for over a hundred years; the Christians have held Malta until this day. All this, however, the old Sultan could not foresee. All that he knew was that his last great maritime venture had failed. It roused the lion in his heart, and strengthened his resolve in the final year of his life to revenge himself on the land.

Ever since the death of Roxelana Suleiman had become more and "more scrupulous in religious matters, or in other words," so Busbecq tells us, "more superstitious.

[24] R. B. M., IV, 117–121.
[25] Hammer, VI, 211.
[26] R. B. M., IV, p. 154.

He used to enjoy hearing a choir of boys, who sang to the accompaniment of stringed instruments. But all this has been done away with by the interposition of some old hag, renowned for her profession of sanctity, who threatened him with heavy punishments hereafter if he did not give up this amusement. Alarmed by her denunciations, he broke up all his musical instruments and threw them into the fire, though they were of excellent workmanship, and adorned with gold and jewels. Some one found such fault with him for eating off silver plate, that he has used nothing but earthenware ever since." [27] But the Sultan found little real happiness in renunciations. The one thing that could satisfy him was a final victory on the field of battle. The Turks had attained their greatness by their military achievements. Their empire was personified by their army. Everything demanded, after the failure at Malta, that Suleiman should himself lead his forces on one last grand campaign. There could be no doubt about its objective. Maximilian II, the successor of Ferdinand, had not paid the tribute prescribed by the treaty of 1561; he had attacked Turkish towns, and had demanded the cession of others; the local Ottoman commanders called loudly for support. The repulse of the Sultan's forces before Erlau, and still more before Sziget, could not be suffered to remain unavenged. Clearly Suleiman must launch a new attack on Hungary.

On May 1, 1566, Suleiman left Constantinople for the last time at the head of one of the largest armies he had ever commanded—probably not less than 200,000 men. It was the thirteenth campaign which he had conducted in person, and the seventh which he had led into Hungary.[28] But there were many tragic contrasts to the earlier days. The old Sultan could no longer sit a horse, save on special

[27] Busbecq, I, 331.
[28] Hammer, VI, 216, note 2.

state occasions.[29] He rode in a carriage, for which the way was smoothed by troops sent on in advance; when he wished to confer with his viziers, they were summoned to meet him there. On June 29, at Semlin, he received John Sigismund Zápolya with splendid ceremony. The occasion was marked by the utmost friendliness. Magnificent presents were exchanged. Young Zápolya realized that Suleiman was still his master, and thrice bent his knee before the great Padishah, but the Sultan graciously raised him, and renewed the solemn promise which he had made twenty-five years before at Buda, that he would ultimately place him on the Hungarian throne. John Sigismund's territorial demands were so modest that Suleiman unhesitatingly accepted them. It was evident that the enemies whom he had gone forth to seek were the representatives of the House of Hapsburg.[30]

From Semlin the Sultan was about to move northward to avenge his repulse at Erlau in 1552, but he had scarcely started when word came that at Siklós, Mohammed of Trikala, one of his greatest favorites and a prominent sanjak bey, had been attacked, robbed, and murdered by Count Nicholas Zrinyi. The latter had been the constant enemy of the Turks ever since the siege of Vienna in 1529; he believed that at all costs the Ottomans must be driven back, and was willing to adopt any means to that end. Croatian by origin, he had been of such service to Hungary that he had been accepted by the Magyar nobles as one of themselves, and he strengthened his position by successive marriages with two rich heiresses who put their vast estates at his disposal.[31] He was at present at Sziget,

[29] Hammer, VI, 219.

[30] Hammer, VI, 219–222.

[31] See biographical sketch in *Allgemeine Deutsche Biographie*, XIV (1900), 441–443, with references. A letter of Zrinyi of April 19, 1566, in regard to his preparations against the Turk, is printed in György Pray's *Epistolae Procerum Regni Hungariae* (Posonii, 1806), III, 177–180.

where Suleiman had another memory of a defeat to erase, and this, together with his fury at the killing of his favorite, determined the Sultan to turn all his forces against Zrinyi. He was out for blood, and was as ready to sacrifice that of the incompetents among his own officers as he was eager to shed that of his foes. On his way to Sziget he ordered the execution of his representative at Buda, Mohammed "the Lion," for slackness and inefficiency in his warfare with the Christians round about him.[32]

The fortress of Sziget was then almost wholly surrounded by marshes and lakes. The only access to it was over a causeway, which was defended at both ends by advanced outworks which were known, respectively, as "the old and the new towns." Zrinyi had plenty of provisions and supplies and fifty-four cannon, but no more than 2500 soldiers. The disparity between the forces of the besieged and the besiegers was even greater than at Malta, and Zrinyi's name deserves to be coupled with that of La Valette. The Sultan did his utmost to inspire his men with the idea that they were fighting a holy war. Appropriate passages of the Koran were read to them, and chants of victory and conquest were sung as they passed along. On July 31 their advance guards reached the city, and Suleiman arrived on August 5. When he showed himself on the top of a hill above the marshes, Zrinyi bade him a formal welcome by discharging a heavy cannon.[33]

Fierce fighting ensued during the next two weeks. Dry weather favored the besiegers and facilitated their approach across the marshes. By the nineteenth of August both "the old and the new towns" were in their hands. Batteries, protected by bags of sand, were set up, and the bombardment of the citadel began. Suleiman had been so much impressed by the heroism of the defence, that he offered

[32] Hammer, VI, 225–227.
[33] Hammer, VI, 228–229.

generous terms to Zrinyi if he would surrender, and when they were refused he tried to sow sedition among the garrison by shooting blunted arrows into the town, bearing letters in Hungarian and German.[34] The failure of these efforts made him more furious than ever. Three successive assaults were launched against the walls, in which the Sultan urged on his men to conquer or die. The first was easily repulsed, but Suleiman was confident that the second would be victorious, for it was delivered on August 29, the anniversary of his triumphs at Belgrade, at Mohács, and at Buda. Nevertheless it was beaten back, and the third, on September 1, was so half-heartedly conducted that it effected nothing at all. What the old Sultan was doing and thinking during these last dreadful days we can only surmise. He had given orders for the laying of a tremendous mine under the principal bastion of Sziget. His sappers had been at work at it for two weeks past, and he had high hopes of the results of its explosion. On September 5 it was fired with terrible effect. The walls were shattered, and a fierce wind carried the flames into the citadel. From that moment the fall of Sziget was inevitable. But it is doubtful if Suleiman was on hand to witness the ensuing conflagration; in a very true sense it was his funeral pyre. On the night of September 5–6 he died in his tent, at the age of about seventy-two, probably of a heart attack brought on by his superhuman exertions. The satisfaction of being present at the culmination of the last of his triumphs was denied him. He did not live to see the bloody repulse of the desperate sortie of Zrinyi and the gallant six hundred who accompanied him, the slaughter of its heroic leader and all save a few of his companions-in-arms.[35] But Suleiman himself had also died

---

[34] Zrinyi, it is said, had refused to accept any German soldiers among his garrison; Vámbéry, *Hungary*, p. 313.

[35] Hammer, VI, 228–234.

standing, as Vespasian had declared that an Emperor should.[36]

Mohammed Sokolli, the Grand Vizir, kept the death of the great Sultan a secret for no less than three weeks; it is said that he had Suleiman's doctor strangled to make assurance doubly sure. The interval was none too long, for the heir apparent was at Kutahia in Asia Minor, and it was essential that he should have time to reach Constantinople, 125 miles away, before the news was generally known. But Mohammed Sokolli did far more than that. For thirteen long years, down to his death in 1579, that is, throughout the whole of the miserable reign of Selim the Sot and the first five years of that of his successor Murad III, he kept the reins of government firmly in his own hands, and did his utmost to conceal from the eyes of Western Europe the tragic fact that the long and glorious rise of the Turks, from a petty principality to one of the foremost powers of the world, was now to be succeeded by an appallingly rapid decline.

For the tide had turned with a vengeance and with dramatic suddenness—far more suddenly than was the case with the contemporaneous Spanish Empire of the West. Suleiman's reign marked the culmination of a national advance of nearly three centuries, to which there are few parallels in human history. With the possible exception of his ancestor Mohammed II, he was the greatest of the long line of illustrious rulers who had brought it about. The vicious Selim who followed him was a nonentity as a soldier and a statesman, and few of his successors were much better. Such triumphs as the Ottomans were to win in the next three hundred and fifty years were chiefly due to the energy of their Grand Vizirs—notably to the Kiuprilis in the second half of the seventeenth cen-

[36] Suetonius, *Vespasian*, 24.

tury. The Turks, in fact, did not come into their own again till the days of the republic and Mustafa Kemal. When we seek to estimate the causes of this great reversal, we are confronted with one of those mysteries which are the truest fascination of the study of history. There can be no definite answer; the subject is too complex.[37] Many writers have laid the fault at the door of Suleiman himself. Some have blamed him for his failure regularly to preside at the Divan, thus setting a bad precedent for his successors. Others, with more justice, have pointed out the disastrous consequences of his occasionally delegating to others the supreme command of the army; for the heart of the Ottoman Empire was its army, and all men expected the Sultan to lead it in person.[38] Suleiman himself fully appreciated the danger here: witness his personal conduct of the campaign against Sziget. But what could ultimately be done about it? So rapidly had the Turks expanded that they had constantly to be fighting on two or more fronts at the same time, and the Sultan could not be everywhere at once. Had not Suleiman's dominions become so vast that, under the existing regime, it was impossible to defend them?

If the great Sultan is to be reproached at all for the disasters which ensued after his death, it is because of his dealings with the members of his own family. The Ottoman Empire was first and foremost a despotism, and no despotism can be successful unless its despot is able and energetic. It is incredible that as shrewd a judge of men as Suleiman should have failed to realize that Mustafa and Bayezid were better stuff than Selim; and in so far as the latter's succession was due to the influence of Roxe-

---

[37] Leopold von Ranke's *Die Osmanen und die Spanische Monarchie*, though written more than a hundred years ago, is still well worth consulting on this point.

[38] Lybyer, pp. 110–113; Halil Ganem, *Les Sultans ottomans*, 2 vols. (Paris, 1901–02), I, 195–206.

lana, "Khurrem" was doubtless responsible for much. But the Sultan could not foresee the full consequences of yielding to her blandishments. His faith in the blood of Osman was unshaken. He at least had bequeathed to his successor the ablest of Grand Vizirs, and we must judge him by what he brought to pass in the age in which he lived, rather than by the events of the future, which he could not hope to control. Like all the rest of us, he had his triumphs and his failures, but he won far more often than he lost. Of the grandeur of the work he accomplished, and of the extent of his influence on the destinies of three continents, there can be no doubt, and his character will bear comparison with those of the best of his contemporaries. Since he was the official champion of the Crescent against the Cross, it was impossible that the Christian writers of his own day and generation should do him justice, but the modern verdicts have been far more fair. The longer one studies him, the greater he seems to be.

A Note on Some of the Portraits of Suleiman the Magnificent

Like his great grandfather Mohammed II, Suleiman the Magnificent does not seem to have felt it necessary literally to observe the precept of the imams to avoid pictures and images "as abominations invented by the Devil." Yet I can find evidence of only two Western European artists who unquestionably made pictures of the great Sultan from life, and the work of the earlier of these can scarcely be called a portrait. It is a drawing by Peter Coeck van Aelst (or Alost) made in Constantinople in 1533, and shows Suleiman on horseback, preceded by twelve "hacquebutiers ou archiers" and followed by two of his "plus nobles Chambrelains," at the end of a procession about the streets of the Turkish capital. This picture is reproduced between pages 174 and 175 of this volume. (Cf. also Th. Wiegand "Der Hippodrom von Konstantinopel zur Zeit Suleiman's d. Gr." in *Jahrbuch des Kaiserlich Deutschen Archäologischen Instituts*, XXIII, for 1908, 4–5. The "plus nobles Chambrelains" are here described as "Janitscharenoffiziere.") This drawing and six others of different scenes on the way to Constantinople were published, from woodblocks, by Coeck's widow, at Antwerp in 1553, and there is one perfect copy of them in the print room of the British Museum. They were reproduced by Sir William Stirling-Maxwell in 1873 in a privately printed portfolio volume entitled *The Turks in MDXXXIII*, of which only one hundred copies were put forth. Stirling-Maxwell's work contains many precious facts about Coeck van Aelst, and a wealth of other information besides.

The other western artist who portrayed Suleiman from life was a Dane, Melchior Lorichs, Lorch, or Lorck, born at Flensborg in Schleswig about 1527, who managed to attach himself to the embassy of Ogier de Busbecq, reached Constantinople early in 1556, and remained there "vierthalb Jahr." (Cf. Hans Harbeck, *Melchior Lorichs*, Hamburg, 1911.) He did two engravings of Suleiman, both apparently in 1559. The more famous is the full-length portrait, which forms the frontispiece to the present volume, and of which there are excellent impressions in the National Bibliothek and in the Albertina in Vienna; the other is a head and shoulders, of which there is an impression in the Metropolitan Art Museum of New York; it is also reproduced on page 195 of C. F. A. von Lützow, *Geschichte des deutschen Kupferstiches und Holzschnittes* (Berlin, 1891), and also on page 4 of *Konstantinopel unter Suleiman dem Grossen, aufgenommen im Jahre 1559 durch Melchior Lorichs aus Flensburg*, herausgegeben und erläutert von Eugen Oberhummer (Munich, 1902). This last book is principally a collection of reproductions of twenty-two drawings, made by Lorichs between 1556 and 1560. The originals are in the library of the University of Leyden. Cf. also F. Kenner, "Die Porträtsammlungen des Erzherzog's Ferdinand von Tirol," in *Jahrbuch der Kunsthistorischen Sammlungen des Allerhöchsten (Oesterreichischen) Kaiserhauses* (hereinafter referred to as *Sammlungen*), XIX (Vienna, 1898), 129; also G. Ladner, "Zur Porträtsammlung des Erzherzog Ferdinand von Tirol," in *Mitteilungen des Oesterreichischen Instituts für Geschichtsforschung*, Band XLVII, pp. 470–482 (Innsbruck, 1933); Elfried Bock, *Die Deutsche Graphik* (1922), p. 223; and Adam Bartsch, *Le Peintre Graveur* (Leipzig, 1866), IX, 508, no. 4.

We next come to several portraits made by western artists who never saw their subject. What their work was based on it is impossible definitely to say. Many descriptions of Suleiman, as we have already pointed out, had reached Venice, and not improbably further west, and the portraits follow them very closely; it is also perfectly possible that some drawing, miniature, or medal of the Sultan may have somehow got to Europe. Leo Planiscig, *Die Estensische Kunstsammlung, Katalog* (Vienna, 1919), I, 185, no. 385, and Tafel 16, describes and gives a reproduction of a medal with a profile of the Sultan on it and the inscription *Solyman Imp. Tur.* which he ascribes to Alfonso Citadella, commonly called Lombardi. He is of the opinion that the profile of the Sultan was made shortly after his accession, or at the time of his expedition against Belgrade in 1521. Cf. here A. Armand, *Les Medailleurs Italiens*, second edition (Paris, 1883), I, 180–181. There were, besides, the portraits by Gentile Bellini of Suleiman's great-grandfather, Mohammed II (cf. *ante* p. 16), whom Suleiman was known to resemble; and one of them, or at least a copy of it, had certainly reached Venice by the time of Suleiman's accession. (Bayezid II, who was far more scrupulous in his obedience to the imams than was his father, sold all the latter's pictures and other *objets d'art* in the bazaars of Constantinople. Cf. L. Thuasne, *Gentile Bellini et Sultan Mohammed II*, p. 32.) Of these portraits of Suleiman, by artists who had never seen him, the earliest and most famous is the profile by Albrecht Dürer. It is a silver-point drawing, dated 1526 (the year of the battle of Mohács), and the original is in the Musée Bonnat at Bayonne (cf. Panofsky, *Dürer* (1943), II, 107, No. 1039); it is reproduced opposite page 76 of this book. It is not without interest that Dürer should have been the artist. He had paid two long visits to Venice, in 1494–95 and in 1505–07, and had made friends and established connections there. Venice was the gateway to the Levant; is it not likely that some kind of a representation of the Sultan found its way into the hands of the great artist of Nuremberg? We can only surmise, with the data at present available, but the general resemblance of the profile to that drawn by Coeck van Aelst in 1533 suggests that Dürer had more than the many descriptions of the aspect of the Sultan by the bailos at Constantinople to guide him. In any case it would seem clear that Dürer's silver-point was copied by the Augsburg engraver Hieronymus Hopfer—probably soon after Suleiman laid siege to Vienna; the two portraits are almost exactly alike, though the face is turned in opposite directions; moreover Hopfer's older and more distinguished brother Daniel also did an equestrian portrait of the Sultan, in which the face is essentially the same. These two Hopfer portraits are reproduced on pp. 47–50 of Stirling-Maxwell's *The Turks in MDXXXIII*; the head and shoulders, by Hieronymus, may also be seen opposite page 166 of Stanley Lane-Poole's *Turkey* (1891). Thieme-Becker's *Künstler-Lexicon* gives much valuable information about the Hopfers. The "Verkleinertes Facsimile eines anonym Holzschnittes aus dem ersten Drittel des 16 Jahrhunderts" on p. 675 of G. F. Hertzberg's *Geschichte der Byzantiner und des Osmanischen Reiches* (Berlin, 1883) is obviously copied either from Dürer or Hopfer. Another "anonymous" profile of Suleiman is reproduced on page 566 of Richard Knolles's *Generall Historie of the Turkes* (1603), and the same portrait (in reverse) forms the frontispiece of J. Chesneau's *Le Voyage de Monsieur d'Aramon*, ed. Ch. Scheffer (Paris, 1887). The Introduction to Chesneau's book (p. lx) tells us that the picture was taken from a "Recueil" entitled *Vita et Icones Sultanorum Turcicorum*, published at Frankfort in 1596, and reëdited there by Johann Ammon in 1648; but this book I have been unable to find.

Agostino de' Musi (often known as Agostino Veneziano)
also did an engraving of the Sultan in 1535, now in the
National Gallery at Budapest: it is reproduced opposite
p. 294 of E. Sayous, *Histoire Générale des Hongrois*
(1900).

There is a story that Suleiman sent the historian Jovius
a portrait of himself (probably a miniature) together with
an inkwell and a golden pen shortly after Jovius' retirement to his villa on Lake Como in 1535, and that the historian proudly exhibited it as one of the gems of his collection there. (Cf. A. L. Millin, *Voyage dans le Milanais*
(Paris, 1817), I, 335, n. 1; *Sammlungen*, XIX, 128, note 1;
E. Müntz, "La Musée des Portraits de Paul Jove," in *Mémoires de l'Institut Nationale de France (Académie des Inscriptions et Belles Lettres)*, hereinafter cited as *Mémoires*,
XXXVI (1901), 307.) The tale may well be true. Jovius
had dedicated his *Turcicarum Rerum Commentarius* to
Charles V at Rome in January 1531, and it was frequently
reprinted in Latin and Italian in the next ten years (the
Latin edition at Paris in 1538, and the Italian one at Venice
in 1540 are the most important). It was also translated into
English by Peter Ashton, and was published in London
in 1546, under the title of "A shorte treatise upon the
Turkes Chronicles." The book in fact had served to make
Western Europe cognizant of the power of the Ottoman
Empire and of its ruler as it had never been before; and
though Suleiman was the most loyal of Moslems, he was
by no means averse to having his name and fame spread
abroad among Christians. He was doubtless gratified by
the appearance of Jovius' book, and may well have taken
this method of showing it. There is also an interesting tale
of an "exchange" by which Khaireddin Barbarossa, while
wintering in southern France in 1543, gave Virginio Orsini
a box containing the portraits of eleven Sultans, and of
Jovius' borrowing it from Orsini, "um sie in einem grös-

seren Formate kopieren zu lassen." (Cf. E. Müntz, in *Zeitschrift für Bücherfreunde*, Achter Jahrgang (1904–05), p. 123. Müntz, in *Mémoires*, XXXI, 307, also declares that there is an engraving of Jovius' picture of the Sultan in the Uffizi, but the catalogues I have been able to consult do not bear him out.) In any case, we have a reproduction of a woodcut of Suleiman, in profile, by the German engraver Tobias Stimmer, on page 372 of the Basel (1575) edition of Jovius' *Elogia virorum bellica virtute illustrium*, which was unquestionably copied from the portrait of Suleiman in the historian's collection. (Cf. Max Bendel, *Tobias Stimmer* (1940), pp. 18, 89; and C. F. Kossman, "Giovio's Porträtsammlung und Tobias Stimmer," in *Anzeiger für Schweizerische Altertumskunde*, Neue Folge, XXIV (for 1922), 49–53.) Stimmer's woodcut is quite recognizable as that of the same man who is depicted in the portraits previously enumerated.

A word should be added here about the portraits of Suleiman by Titian. On August 23, 1538, Benedetto Agnello wrote to Duke Federigo Gonzaga that since the Duke desired to possess a portrait of the Sultan, Titian "ha fatto uno, cavato (se non me inganno) da una medaglia e da un altro retratto," and had done it so well that many who had been in Constantinople declared that it was absolutely true to life (cf. Crowe and Cavalcaselle, *Titian, His Life and Times*, II, 498). This picture is lost. It is said that a "Kupferstich" of it by Boldrini is preserved (cf. *Sammlungen*, XIX, 128), but I have been unable to find any evidence of it. Nor can I discover any trace of the equestrian portrait of Suleiman which Titian is said to have painted in 1561–62 for Cardinal Ercole de Gonzaga "da una carta fatta far in Constantinopoli" (cf. *Sammlungen*, XIX, 128). But there seems little doubt that the model drawing, miniature, or medal from which this picture, and possibly that of 1538, was made was the same as that used for the figure of "a Turk, the counterfeit of Sultan Soliman, in a white turban" which brings up the rear of the procession in the great "Ecce Homo" now in Vienna, which Titian painted in 1543. "It was natural that Soliman, whose likeness Titian had so often taken from medals, should be numbered amongst those who asked for the blood of Christ" (Crowe and Cavalcaselle, II, 94–95).

Sixteenth-century Europe was probably less familiar with any of these portraits of Suleiman than with another which was issued in broadsheet form by the Nuremburg publisher Hans Guldenmund (1490?–1560), and was consequently more easily accessible to the general public. It is a full length engraving of Suleiman, in profile and standing up, by Michael Ostendorfer (1490?–1559) of Ratisbon; it is dated 1548, and the original is now in Gotha. There is a good reproduction of it in *Deutsche Einblatt-Holzschnitt in der ersten Hälfte des XVI Jahrhunderts*, no. 978; and no. 979 is a genealogical tree of the sovereigns of the House of Osman, with their busts, also by Ostendorfer, who was evidently much interested in the Turks (cf. *Bilder-Katalog zu Max Geisberg*, p. 172). There is no evidence as to where Ostendorfer got his information about Suleiman's looks, although his picture bears a general resemblance to the others already enumerated, but he makes the Sultan appear particularly ferocious; in fact, it is quite likely that he had it issued by Guldenmund in broadsheet form in order to warn his countrymen of the imminence of the "Turkish peril." This picture is reproduced on the jacket of this book and also opposite page 257 of the text. Guldenmund himself also did an equestrian engraving of Suleiman, which seems much more true to life, at the time of the siege of Vienna in 1529, but it does not seem probable that it was ever given wide publicity. A reproduction of it may be found opposite page 116 of vol. XV of *Mittheilungen des Alterthums Vereins zu Wien* (1875), together with a brief article (pp. 106–116) by Albert Ritter von Camesina, telling all about it and its present whereabouts (in the Sammlung von S. Exc. Ritter von Hauslab) and also containing two little-known ballads by Hans Sachs (in 1529 and 1539) about the siege of Vienna.

All these pictures, save that of Lorichs, represent the Sultan in profile, and they are all recognizable as portraits of the same man. The figure by Veronese in the "Marriage of Cana" (1562–63), to which reference has already been made, is purely imaginary. It is seated, next to Vittoria Colònna and in close proximity to Francis I and Charles V, near the left-hand rear corner of the table; but the face bears little resemblance to the other portraits of the Sultan, and the artist did not even take the trouble to clothe his subject aright.

There is an article by A. Welcker in *Die Graphischen Künste*, Neue Folge, vol. I (for 1936), Heft 3, pp. 103–05, entitled "A wedding gift by Jan van der Straet (also called Johannes Stradanus) to Christina of Lorraine in the year 1589: the retreat of the Turks from Vienna after the siege in the year 1529"; and there are four interesting illustrations. The original turned up at an auction at Amsterdam in 1932; but a sketch of it, which was apparently made by van der Straet (1523–1605) to be engraved by A. Collaert (1545–1618), is now in the Albertina in Vienna (inventory, no. 23437). There is no evidence that the portraits of Suleiman in these pictures are authentic.

There are at least two portraits of the Sultan by Turkish artists (probably miniatures) in London today, and many more in Constantinople. I regret that the war has made it impossible for me to obtain further information about them.

Bibliographical Note

Bibliographies, generally speaking, are unpleasant things, save for the specialist, and mere lists of titles are even worse; "most of us," it has been well said, "they merely snow under." On the other hand, those who may wish to investigate in detail any phase of the great Sultan's reign have the right to know the sources on which this book is based, and to be given "leads" for further research. It is in the hope of being of service to them that I venture to append the following abbreviated bibliographical note.

The names and authors of most of the principal works on the Turkish history of the period are to be found on pages 782–785 of the third volume of the *Cambridge Modern History*, on pages 303–330 of A. H. Lybyer's *Government of the Ottoman Empire under Suleiman the Magnificent*, and on pages 108–125 of G. W. F. Stripling's "The Ottoman Turks and the Arabs" in *Illinois Studies in the Social Sciences*, vol. XXVI, no. 4 (1942); and these bibliographies dispense me from the necessity of enumerating the standard authorities. Of the three, that of Lybyer is by far the most valuable. Though officially only concerned with books on government and administration, it contains much else besides, and the scholarly analyses of the chief contemporaneous and modern works which precede the list of titles are particularly precious. It only remains for me to say a few additional words about the five authorities on whom I have principally relied, to give under each chapter heading the names of the books of a more special nature which have been used therein, and to furnish a list of abbreviations for the purpose of shortening the footnotes.

The best of all the contemporaneous descriptions of the Turkey of Suleiman's day is unquestionably to be found in the four confidential letters addressed by Ogier Ghiselin de Busbecq (cf. *ante*, pp. 176–177) to his friend Nicolas Michault, the Hapsburg ambassador from the Netherlands to Hungary in the time of Charles V. They were written in simple, concise Latin, between the years 1555 and 1562; the first three from Constantinople, the last from Frankfort. As they were intended for private consumption, they contain much that is not to be found in the official reports of the Venetian *bailos* in Alberi's *Relazioni*, and shed a flood of light on what, without them, would have remained unknown (cf. G. Sarton, "Brave Busbecq," in the Third Preface to volume XXXIII of *Isis* (March, 1942), pp. 557–575). Because of the notes and additional information which it contains, I have used the two-volume English edition and translation entitled *The Life and Letters of Ogier Ghiselin de Busbecq*, by Charles Thornton Forster and F. H. Blackburne Daniell (London, 1881), rather than the more convenient single volume *Turkish Letters of Ogier Ghiselin de Busbecq*, ed. E. S. Forster (Oxford, 1927).

The *Urkunden und Actenstücke zur Geschichte der Verhältnisse zwischen Österreich, Ungern und der Pforte im XVI. und XVII. Jahrhunderte* (Vienna, 1840–1842), ed. Anton von Gévay, is fundamental for the relations between the Hapsburgs and the Porte between the years 1527 and 1541. The original work was most inconveniently divided into eleven unnumbered parts, each with a title-page of its own and a separate pagination; but it has usually, though not always (cf. the catalogues of the Bibliothèque Nationale and of the British Museum), been published in three volumes, of which the first contains the first five parts, covering the years 1527 to 1532; the second the next three, for 1532 to 1536; and the third the last three, for 1536 to 1541. As the Harvard copy, which I have used and which seems to be the only one in this country, is one of those bound in three volumes, I have made my references to accord with it, i.e., the first figure indicating the volume, the second the number of the part *in* that volume, and the third the page. The book gives the original text of all the letters, reports, and ambassadorial instructions bearing on the Turkish advance up the Danube during the period in question. There is no introduction. The work consists of original documents and nothing else. All that I have been able to find out about von Gévay is that he was first "Scriptor an der K. K. Hofbibliothek" and later "K. K. geheimer Hof. und Haus Archivar"; clearly he was a modest scholar whose work was its own reward.

For one who, like myself, cannot read Turkish, the monumental *Geschichte des Osmanischen Reiches*, ten volumes (Pesth, 1827–35), by Joseph von Hammer-Purgstall is absolutely indispensable. The author has been somewhat roughly treated by a number of his contemporaries and successors (cf. F. C. Diez, *Umfug und Betrug*), and there is no doubt that his work does not always measure up to the highest standards of the critical historical scholarship of today; yet when all is said and done, our knowledge of Ottoman history would be vastly less than it is if his great book were not there to blaze the trail; the German word "bahnbrechend" is the aptest of all to describe it. He knew and used his Turkish authorities as no other European historian has ever done. He gives a mass of material which is available nowhere else, and precious indications where to find more; particularly valuable are the numerous excerpts from Suleiman's diary while on campaigns. J. W. Zinkeisen's *Geschichte des Osmanischen Reiches in Europa* (7 volumes, Hamburg and Gotha, 1840–63) will be found a useful supplement to him, particularly on matters of diplomacy and the Mediterranean campaigns. All my references to Hammer-Purgstall are to the eighteen-volume French edition "traduit . . . sur les notes et sous la direction de l'auteur," by J. J. Hellert (Paris, 1835–43). It contains everything that is to be found in the original, and corrects some minor errors; it is better indexed, vastly more convenient to read, and also more easily obtainable. The two shorter second editions (in German, at Pesth, in four volumes, 1834–36, and in French (tr. Dochez) at Paris, 1840–42) are much less satisfactory.

Of collaborate histories as of the curate's egg, it may be truthfully said that parts are very good. Chapter xvi in vol. III and chapters xix and xx in vol. IV of Lavisse and Rambaud's *Histoire générale* were written by A. Rambaud and E. Masqueray, both recognized masters of the fields with which they deal, and every page of them is typical of the most perfect French historical scholarship. Necessarily brief, they will be found to contain much that is available nowhere else.

The *Geschichte des Osmanischen Reiches* in five volumes (Gotha 1908–13), by my old friend and fellow-pupil, the late Nicholae Iorga, is the most recent history of the Ottoman Empire, and the largest and most important of the works of the great Rumanian statesman and historian whose assassination in November 1940 was one of the many tragedies of the present war. The book was written too hurriedly to be as accurate as one could wish, particularly in the narrative portions, and the footnotes are so abbreviated that it is often well-nigh impossible to find the references that they were intended to give. On the other hand Iorga's work has a magnificent sweep to it, clearly indicating the hand of a great master. It brings the whole picture up to date, and its portrayal of manners, customs, and social and economic conditions—a side which his predecessors had for the most part neglected—is beyond all praise.

Bibliographical Notes on the Separate Chapters

Chapter I

For the early history of the Ottoman Turks, Edward Gibbon's *Decline and Fall of the Roman Empire* is still fundamental. I have used Bury's edition. Teodoro Spandugino's *Commentari dell' origine de Principi Turchi* (Florence, 1551, and in French, ed. C. Schefer, Paris, 1896) is one of the best of the earlier accounts. Recent monographs, which deal with controversial points, are H. A. Gibbons, *The Foundation of the Ottoman Empire, 1305–1403* (Oxford, 1916); J. Marquart, *Uber das Volkstum der Komanen* (cf. note 3 above); and W. L. Langer and R. P. Blake, "The Rise of the Ottoman Turks and its Historical Background" in the *American Historical Review*, vol. XXXVII, no. 3 (for April, 1932), pp. 468–505. L. Thuasne's *Gentile Bellini et Sultan Mohammed II* (Paris, 1888) and his *Djem Sultan* (Paris, 1892) are the latest authorities on the subjects with which they deal. G. W. F. Stripling, *The Ottoman Turks and the Arabs* (cf. *ante* p. 301), is valuable on the conquests of Selim.

Chapter II

Paolo Giovio's *Turcicarum Rerum Commentarius* (cf. *ante*, p. 297) was the first book to make Western Europe realize the power and ambitions of the Turk. Marino Sanuto's *Dairii, MCCCCXCVI–MDXXXIII*, 58 volumes in 59 (Venice, 1879–93), and E. Alberi's *Relazione degli ambasciatori veneti al Senato*, 15 vols. (Florence, 1839–63), are fundamental for this chapter and the immediately succeeding ones; and the *Calendars of State Papers Venetian* (ed. E. Rawdon Brown, vols. III–VII, 1869–1890) almost equally so. The *Deutsche Reichstagsakten (Jüngere Reihe) unter Karl V*, vols. II and III (Gotha, 1896–1901), are the principal source for the attitude of the Empire towards the Turk.

Chapter III

Cf. bibliographical notes on Chapter II, and, in addition:

Suleiman's diary, which may be found (in French) in the appendices to vols. V and VI of Hammer, is our best source of information on the siege of Belgrade, and on all Suleiman's subsequent campaigns. A. Vámbéry's *The Story of Hungary* (New York, 1886) gives a good brief account of conditions within that realm.

The first two volumes of E. Charrière, *Négociations de la France dans le Levant*, 4 vols. (Paris, 1848–60), are a mine of information for the period 1515 to 1565, and contain all the important documents on Franco-Turkish relations at the time; it is indispensable for the siege of Rhodes. *La grande et merveilleuse et très cruelle oppugnation de la noble cité de Rhodes* (Paris, 1527), by the "Bastard" Jacques de Bourbon (son of Louis de Bourbon, Bishop of Liège), and the *De Bello Rhodio Libri Tres* (Rome, 1524) and the *Ad Adrianum Pont. M. Epistola missa e Rhodo* (Tübingen, 1523), by Jacobus Fontanus, are precious accounts of the siege by eye-witnesses. As Bourbon was a member of the Order, and Fontanus a *Judex Appellationum*, they describe the event from different standpoints. The two best modern accounts of the topography and fortifications of the island are *Rhodes of the Knights*, by Fradin, Baron de Belabre (Oxford, 1908), and *La Cité de*

Rhodes, MCCCX–MDXXII, by Albert Gabriel (Paris, 1921). Much useful information may also be found in C. W. C. Oman, *The Art of War in the Sixteenth Century* (New York, 1937).

CHAPTER IV

The most important contemporaneous Turkish account of the Mohács campaign is that by the learned Kemal Pasha Zadeh, who was Sheik-ul-Islam from 1525 to his death in 1533. It has been beautifully translated into French, and edited, with valuable notes, by M. Pavet de Courteille (Paris, 1869) under the title of *Histoire de la Campagne de Mohács*. On the Christian side the *Clades in Campo Mohacs* by István Brodarics, which appears on pp. 1185–86 of vol. II of Simon Schard's *Historicum Opus* (Basel, 1574), and the *Oratio Protreptica* by John Cuspinianus (Vienna, n.d.) are the most valuable. Brodarics was a Hungarian statesman and prelate who had been sent to Rome to get aid against the Turks, was present at the battle, and survived it. Cuspinianus had been doctor and diplomatic agent to the Emperor Maximilian, and was also the author of a work published at Leyden in 1654 entitled *De Turcarum Origine, Religione ac immanissima eorum in Christianos tyrannide, etc., etc.*

CHAPTER V

Suleiman's diary on the Vienna campaign was carefully translated into German and edited, with notes, by W. F. A. Behrnauer at Vienna in 1856. There are many accounts of the siege: among the best are those of M. Smetz, *Wien in und aus der Türken-Bedrängniss (1529–1683)* (Vienna, 1883), and the Earl of Ellesmere's translation of K. A. Schimmer's *Wien's Belagerungen* (Vienna, 1845) under the title of *The Siege of Vienna by the Turks* (London, 1879); the latter has an excellent map. Martin Rosnak's *Die Belagerung der Königl. Freystadt Güns* (Vienna, 1789) is practically the only book on the subject. F. B. Bucholtz, *Geschichte der Regierung Ferdinand's des Ersten*, 9 vols. (Vienna, 1831–38), still contains much that is to be found nowhere else. H. Kretschmayr's "Ludovico Gritti," in the first half of vol. LXXXIII of the *Archiv für österreichische Geschichte* (1896), and also separately printed, is a model of thoroughness and accuracy, and typical of the very best historical monographs that were produced in the days when German scholarship was still respected.

Chapter VI

Charrière's *Négociations* and von Gévay's *Urkunden* (cf. *ante*, pp. 302–303) are the principal sources for this chapter. J[on] Ursu, *La Politique orientale de François I*, is one of the best of historical monographs, and contains a full bibliography.

Chapter VII

It would be superfluous for me to point out how much I have depended for the material contained in this chapter on A. H. Lybyer's *The Government of the Ottoman Empire in the Time of Suleiman the Magnificent*, and his bibliography is so complete that there is no point in enlarging upon the sources on which he has relied. I can only add that many of the contemporaneous Italian accounts have been admirably translated in Sir William Stirling-Maxwell's *The Turks in MDXXXIII*. Joseph von Hammer-Purgstall's *Des Osmanischen Reichs Staatsverfassung und Staatsverwaltung* (Vienna, 1815) may still be consulted with profit, while the *Encyclopedia of Islam*, 4 vols. and supplement (Leiden and London, 1913–38), is a mine of accurate information, brought abreast of the most modern historical scholarship by leading Orientalists.

CHAPTER VIII

Cf. notes on the preceding chapter and add N. Iorga's *Geschichte des Osmanischen Reiches* (vol. II). E. J. W. Gibb, *A History of Ottoman Poetry*, 6 vols. (London, 1900–09), is the standard authority on the subject with which it deals. Dr. Barnette Miller's *The Palace School of Muhammad the Conqueror* (Cambridge: Harvard University Press, 1941) is a scholarly monograph which contains much that is useful for Suleiman's time; her *Beyond the Sublime Porte* (New Haven, 1931) and N. M. Penzer's *The Harem* (London, 1936) are perhaps chiefly valuable for the excellent maps, plans, and illustrations which they contain. Edmondo de Amicis, *Constantinople*, tr. Maria H. Lansdale, 2 vols. (Philadelphia, 1896), is pleasant and profitable reading.

CHAPTER IX

Cf. notes on Chapter VI and add Hājjī Halifā (the name is often spelled Haji Khalfah), *The History of the Maritime Wars of the Turks*, tr. James Mitchell (London, 1831)—a precious seventeenth-century authority. Volume I (Madrid, 1895) of C. Fernández Duro, *Armada Española*, and volume III (Paris, 1891) of E. Mercier, *Histoire de l'Afrique Septentrionale*, are the standard works on the subjects with which they deal. Further information may be found in the footnotes to chapter xxv (vol. III) of my *Rise of the Spanish Empire*.

CHAPTER X

The principal sources for this chapter are Sidi Ali Reis, *Travels and Adventures* (otherwise known as *The Mirror of Countries*), tr., with notes, by A. Vámbéry (London, 1899); *The Chronique de Galâwdêwos, roi d'Ethiopie*, tr. and ed. W. F. Conzelman (Paris, 1895); Francisco Alvarez, *Narrative of the Portuguese Embassy to Abyssinia* (*1520–1527*), tr. and ed. H. E. J. Stanley (London: Hakluyt Society, 1881); and Miguel de Castanhoso, *The Portuguese Expedition to Abyssinia in 1541–1543*, tr. and ed. R. S. Whiteway (London: Hakluyt Society, 1901).—Sir William W. Hunter, *A History of British India*, 2 vols. (London, 1899), is a standard authority, and K. G. Jayne, *Vasco da Gama and His Successors* (London, 1910), and R. S. Whiteway, *The Rise of Portuguese Power in India, 1497–1550* (Westminster, 1899), are useful monographs.

CHAPTER XI

György Pray, *Epistolae Procerum Regni Hungariae*, 3 vols. (Posonii, 1806); *Fontes Rerum Austriacarum Scriptores*, 69 vols. (1855–1931), especially vol. I; and *Osterreichische Staatsverträge*, vol. IX (*Fürstentum Siebenbürgen, 1526–1590*, Vienna, 1911), are the principal sources for this chapter, and the list may be indefinitely extended by consulting K. M. Kertbeny's *Ungarn betreffende deutsche Erstlings-Drucke, 1454–1600* (Budapest, 1880), and Graf Alexander Apponyi's *Hungarica*, vols. I and III (Munich, 1903 and 1925). The only lives of Martinuzzi are those of A. Bechet, *Histoire du ministère du Cardinal Martinusius* (Paris, 1715), and O. M. Utiešenović, *Lebensgeschichte des Cardinals Georg Utiešenović, genannt Martinusius* (Vienna, 1881).

CHAPTER XII

Cf. notes to Chapters IX and XI, and in addition:

Halil Ganem, *Les Sultans Ottomans*, 2 vols. (Paris, 1901–02), and Henry Seddall, *Malta* (London, 1870). Further information about the siege of Malta may be found in C. Fernández Duro, *Armada Española*, vol. II, and on pp. 114–121 of volume IV of my *Rise of the Spanish Empire*.

Abbreviations of Works Frequently Cited

Alberi	*Relazioni degli ambasciatori veneti al Senato . . . edite da Eugenio Alberi,* 15 vols. (Florence, 1839–63).
Bucholtz	Franz Bernhard, Ritter von Bucholtz, *Geschichte der Regierung Ferdinand des Ersten, aus gedruckten und ungedruckten Quellen,* 9 vols. (Vienna, 1831–38).
Busbecq	Charles Thornton Forster and F. H. Blackburne Daniell, *The Life and Letters of Ogier Ghiselin de Busbecq,* 2 vols. (London, 1881).
Charrière	*Négociations de la France dans le Levant,* ed. Ernest Charrière, 4 vols. (Paris, 1848–60), in *Collection de documents inédits sur l'histoire de France.*
Gévay	Anton von Gévay, ed., *Urkunden und Actenstücke zur Geschichte der Verhältnisse zwischen Osterreich, Ungern, und der Pforte im XVI. und XVII. Jahrhunderte,* 11 pts. in 3 vols. (Vienna, 1838–42).
Hammer	Joseph, Freiherr von Hammer-Purgstall, *Histoire de l'Empire Ottoman,* 18 vols. (Paris, 1835–43), tr. de l'allemand, "sur les notes et sous la direction de l'auteur," par J. J. Hellert.
Iorga	Nicolae Iorga, *Geschichte des Osmanischen Reiches,* 5 vols. (Gotha, 1908–13).
Kretschmayr	Heinrich Kretschmayr, "Ludovico Gritti," in *Archiv für österreichische Geschichte,* vol. lxxxiii, 1 (1896), pp. 1–106.
Lavisse and Rambaud	Ernest Lavisse and Alfred Rambaud, editors, *Histoire générale du IVe siècle à nos jours,* 12 vols. (Paris, 1893–1901). My ref-

erences are to vol. III, chapter xvi, and vol.
IV, chapter xix, by Alfred Rambaud, and
to vol. IV, chapter xx, by Émile Masqueray.

Lybyer Albert Howe Lybyer, *The Government
of the Ottoman Empire in the Time of
Suleiman the Magnificent*, Harvard Historical Studies, 18 (Cambridge, Mass.,
1913).

R. B. M. Roger Bigelow Merriman, *The Rise of the
Spanish Empire*, 4 vols. (New York, 1918–
34).

Ursu J[on] Ursu, *La Politique orientale de
François Ier, 1515–1547* (Paris, 1908).

Index

315